To the Field of S

TO THE FIELD OF STARS

A Pilgrim's Journey
to Santiago de Compostela

Kevin A. Codd

WILLIAM B. EERDMANS PUBLISHING COMPANY

GRAND RAPIDS, MICHIGAN / CAMBRIDGE, U.K.

Published 2008 by

Wm. B. Eerdmans Publishing Co.

2140 Oak Industrial Drive N.E., Grand Rapids, Michigan 49505 /

P.O. Box 163, Cambridge CB3 9PU U.K.

Printed in the United States of America

17 16 15 14 13 12   10 9 8 7 6

Library of Congress Cataloging-in-Publication Data

Codd, Kevin A.

To the field of stars: a pilgrim's journey to Santiago de Compostela / Kevin A. Codd.

p.   cm.

ISBN 978-0-8028-2592-6 (pbk.: alk. paper)

1. Christian pilgrims and pilgrimages — Spain — Santiago de Compostela.

2. Codd, Kevin A. — Travel — Spain — Santiago de Compostela.

3. Santiago de Compostela (Spain) — Description and travel.   I. Title.

BX2321.S3C63   2008

263'.0424611 — dc22

2007046615

www.eerdmans.com

To my Mother and Father
who taught me to walk

Contents

INTRODUCTION
The Field of Stars

It may well come to pass at a certain point in the course of a life that a person hears of stars dancing in a field at night. It is possible that such a story would be immediately dismissed as the stuff of childish fantasy or a piece of old wives' tale, not to be taken seriously in these modern times. At best, the story might be taken as simply another happy ending to a fable created by the likes of the Grimm brothers or perhaps J. R. R. Tolkien. It could also be that the image of stars coming low to earth and performing a joyful circle dance in the dead of night might nevertheless capture a person's imagination *even if* such an image would seem not to belong to the world of facts and history and our modern understanding of what transpires in the course of real life.

I am about to share here a story about stars at dance. May I advise you to exercise a modicum of caution in attending to what follows, for the story of stars dancing over a field in a faraway land may so draw you away from the ordinary business of daily life that you find yourself, quite to your surprise, in a new world of unexpected adventures and remarkable people and some very profound mysteries. If this should happen to you, if the story of stars playing above the dusty bones of an old saint should capture you in its strange field of gravity, it may well draw you out of your house, down the street, and out of town. And if you leave home to see these stars cavort for yourself it will surely change you. You will come to see that which was previously unseen. You will witness miracles. You will, in the end, find yourself coming to know what is most true about these brief lives we have been given to live out on this tender earth.

So, if you are satisfied being a very contemporary person living in a world formed by the likes of Descartes, Freud, and Henry Ford, if you have no interest in adventures of the spirit, or if you have no desire to ramble on foot across a fair piece of this earth's lovely skin, then the story I am about to tell will not matter to you. If, on the other hand, the very thought of seeing stars dance piques your curiosity at some deep level of your soul, then pay attention to what follows, for the walk to the Field of Stars, to Santiago de Compostela, is a journey that has the power to change lives forever.

Stars dancing over a barren field at night: *Compostela*. Somewhere and somehow I heard of this old place, I don't know where or when, but like millions of others over the past millennium, once I did hear of it, the notion of it captivated me. Those stars and bones tugged at my imagination and pulled at my soul until, quite out of character for me, I threw my usual caution to the wind and succumbed to the age-old attraction of those beautiful words, *Camino de Santiago de Compostela*, and became for thirty-five days a pilgrim.

A *pilgrim*? A pilgrim is a believer who travels to a holy place, a place where God seems especially close, to ask for pardon, to beg a favor, or to give thanks for blessings received.

It may seem ridiculous to us altogether modern, practical, well-educated people of the third millennium, but there was a time, not so long ago, especially in Europe, when popular religious belief often included an unshakeable sense that the space between God and us in certain places on the face of this earth was especially thin; such holy places were made so by their relationship to extraordinarily holy people, saints if you will, even if they were long dead. These were places where such saints might have been born, where they worked or where they died and were buried. These were places where these saints' living presence seemed to perdure and where access to their on-going ministrations seemed especially available. These saints could, if asked, intercede on behalf of those still living in this earth's "vale of tears" and get things moving with the Lord. Some saints had excellent reputations in this regard, and word of which saint produced the goods with God spread rapidly from one town and village to another, until it reached the far frontiers of Europe and beyond.

Of course, a believer could always make his or her request to the saint in the privacy of his or her own home, as many did, but it was better to do it in a church where an image of the saint could be found and candles could be lit to symbolize the intention, as still more did. Even better, and this is where the notion of the pilgrim begins to take shape, one could go to the place where that saint lived, or better still, where that saint died, and best of all, where he died and left behind his bones as a physical memento of his status as an intermediary between a gracious God and a needy humanity. Such bones or other parts of the saints' bodies were called *relics* and were highly regarded as a contact point, a sort of physical bridge, between heaven and earth. They were placed in magnificent boxes made of silver or gold and encrusted with precious jewels and set on display in the proud churches that possessed them. People in need of a favor from above would go in droves to those churches so as to make their petition to the saint as much "in person" as humanly possible. In many cases, there was only one way to get there: on foot. It didn't matter if the church was down the street or a couple thousand kilometers[1] across the continent; on foot they traveled to plead their good cause with the saint and ask for his or her great help on the other side of the heavenly divide. Those who walked to such holy places were pilgrims.

It might seem all very superstitious to the scientifically sophisticated populations of our modern western world, but for centuries much of life in the Christian world revolved around relics, prayers, and pilgrimages. Our predecessors in the faith held firmly to three simple beliefs. One: God cares infinitely about us. Two: the saints know what we are up against and direct God's kind attention our way. And three: miracles happen.

Some saints and their relics had more fame and authority than others. After Jesus and Mary, apostles were top-level intermediaries; martyrs, virgins, and doctors of the Church followed in importance. Jerusalem was the top pilgrim destination because it was the earthly place most

---

1. Since most everything in Europe is measured metrically and since this story takes place in the world of modern Europeans, I use here their manner of measuring size, weight, distance, and temperature. A kilometer is a little more than a half a mile (.62 actually), a liter is about a quart, a kilogram is a little more than two pounds (2.2 to be exact). The conversion to Celsius is often the most difficult for those accustomed to the Fahrenheit scale: 20°C is a comfy 68°F, while 30°C is a warm 86°F, and 40°C is a blistering 104°F.

closely connected to Jesus. There were only two places within medieval Europe where believers could discuss their needs with a sainted apostle: Rome, where they could pray at the tombs of Saints Peter and Paul, and an improbable town in Galicia in what is now the northwestern corner of Spain where tradition had it that the relics of the apostle James resided: Santiago de Compostela. A very few had the time and money to walk all the way to Jerusalem; a few more had the time and money to walk to Rome; others not quite so blessed with time and material wealth could only afford to walk to Santiago de Compostela. It might have been the closest of the three, but it still required hoofing it for up to several thousand kilometers, depending on the pilgrim's starting point. Of course, the pilgrim, if he survived, also had to walk back.

A pilgrim's lot was not easy. He had to endure all manner of obstacles and problems, not least of which were surely such mundane difficulties as blisters, tendonitis, heat stroke, frostbite, gastroenteritis, wolves, thieves, murderers, and very high mountains. Many didn't make it to their destination; even fewer made it back home. They all too often got sick and died, or fell into the hands of brigands and died, or froze and died. What would make them take these risks? Faith. Faith that God and his friends would truly assist them in dealing with life's many tribulations.

Now the story of Santiago de Compostela is worth the telling, even if to the modern ear it may seem really rather ridiculous in an old-fashioned sort of way. Anyone who has read the Christian New Testament knows that there were twelve apostles, two of whom were named "James," or in Latin, *Jacobus*. One was known as "the Lesser." Our James was "the Greater" and was one of two brothers who were nicknamed by the Jesus "the Sons of Thunder."[2] That is about all the real history anybody knows. But the unofficial word that spread into Europe in later centuries had it that, in responding to Jesus' commission to take the gospel to all corners of the world, James took the Lord at his word and traveled to the actual end of the known world of the time: the Atlantic Coast of Iberia, Finisterre. There he was a miserable failure as an apostle and made few converts among the pagans. So he trudged back to Palestine, where he was martyred by King Herod, who had the poor apostle's head lopped

2. Mark 3:17.

off in A.D. 44. Then the story goes that a couple of his faithful followers smuggled his body to the Mediterranean coast, where a mysterious boat made of stone awaited them. The body of James was put out to sea in the stone boat with no oars, no sails, and no sailors. Nevertheless, within a week it miraculously made its way through the Mediterranean and up the Atlantic coast until it came ashore in Galicia, where it was met by other disciples, who then placed James's body in an unmarked cave, where it was lost to view for the next eight hundred years or so.

All those centuries later, when Spain was more Muslim than it was Christian, and the Christians were desperately trying to reclaim the peninsula with remarkably little success, something wondrous happened. One night some persevering Christian monks saw beautiful lights playing across the sky over a field not far from Finisterre. When they went to investigate what seemed to them to be dancing stars, lo and behold, they found the bones of the long-lost apostle James, and this just in time to inspire them and the rest of the Christians of Iberia to push back the Muslims once and for all. The story was later told that James even appeared on horseback as a great soldier and routed a Moorish army single-handedly with his mighty sword, lopping off heathen heads right and left. (You would have thought he might have chosen some other manner to dispatch the Moors, having suffered the same fate himself a millennium earlier.) Thereafter, he was known not only as James the apostle, but also as James the Moor Killer, *Matamoros*, in Spanish.[3] Well, that is a grisly end to an otherwise wonderful tale. Nowadays, almost no one takes much of it as historical fact, not even dedicated church people. The important thing is that back then everybody did.

On another note, if you know just a little bit of Latin, you can see where the name *Compostela* comes from: *campo* being "field" and *stella* meaning "star": The Field of Stars. Or it could just be a corruption of *compostum*, the Latin word for cemetery. You may take your pick, but I myself prefer the less morbid and more celestial *campo stella* version. The name *Santiago* is a linguistic development from the Latin *Jacobus*, which

3. Though the populations of Latin America call their language *Español* or "Spanish," many in Spain refer to it as *Castellano*. Having learned the language in the Americas, I will for the most part use my "native" Latin American vocabulary in this text, including the preference for *Español* or "Spanish" for the name of this beautiful and diverse language common to both continents.

with time transmogrified into *Iago*, which, when the *San* for "Saint" was added, became *San-Iago* and then with more time became simply *Santiago*.

So what to make of the legend of Santiago? It is easy to dismiss it as medieval nonsense, and in a sense, it is. But on the other hand, legends speak truths for those who have the patience to listen, and this one is no exception. Even the most secular of anthropologists understand that myths are like dreams; they capture our joys and fears in startling images and feed them back to us as a way of making sense of our world. If we didn't have them, we'd go crazy. A good legend keeps on revealing at ever deeper levels; the more you pay attention, often not looking at it directly but only from the side of your interior eye, the more likely you will see something new just beneath the surface of what you already have seen. The more you will come to know yourself. The more you will understand the mysteries out of which life and death are woven.

There is one important difference between the legends associated with Santiago and other more fanciful tales, like those of the Grimm brothers or Tolkien's hobbits: there is an historical person at the bottom of this story; even after setting aside the myth and storytelling, there was a real James and this James actually lived, loved, served, cared, failed, hurt, and died. Even in these modern times, Christians still believe in life after death, and so the sentiments that our beloved dead are still part of the family, that it is good to chat with them from time to time, and even to bring our daily concerns to them for their assistance, do not seem so ridiculous. To the contrary, it makes a lot of sense to many of us, at least those who have grown up as Catholic Christians. Even the notion of relics isn't so odd to us; I often hold in my hand before going to bed a small wooden box with a sliding cover that has a cutting of my deceased father's hair and another of my more recently deceased mother. It feels good to hold it so; I feel connected to them, and it is a *physical* connection. It's better than a snapshot. And so you see, for us, it is easy to believe that the historical Santiago is not "dead dead," but alive and present in spirit and therefore not so far away. Is it all that crazy? Well, I yet look forward to visiting my folks' graves when I head home to Spokane; why not visit that of James in Compostela? "Visit those bones; there may be life in them yet!"

By the way, the bones held in Santiago's tomb go back to some time between the first century B.C. and sixth century A.D. They've been around for a very long time; the millions of pilgrims who have suffered and died to venerate them since at least the ninth century make them Santiago's in spirit and truth even if they were not the actual skeleton upon which he hung his physical skin. At least that's the way I look at it.

Getting back now to my own story, the vague tug at my heart to walk to Santiago de Compostela sometime before I died became much more possible when quite unexpectedly my work as a Catholic priest took me to Belgium, where I would be living for a number of years. I knew then that one of my goals before I returned home to the States for good would be to walk to Santiago de Compostela. I wanted to be a real pilgrim.

The word *real* has a certain tone of bravura about it because even now I know that I could never be a *real* pilgrim, not like those hundreds of thousands who walked their way to Santiago de Compostela in times past. At best, I now realize, most of us in these times can only be approximate pilgrims, for few of us can actually do what they did: step over the threshold of our kitchen door with almost nothing to sustain us and begin walking to a place we have never seen and which is hundreds if not thousands of kilometers away, endure no end of tribulations along the way, arrive, say our prayers, then walk all the way home again. Some still do that, but very few. I met two or three of them along my way, and the very memory of them yet humbles me.

Why be a pilgrim whether approximate or real, in this day and age? Why be so medieval a pilgrim in today's smart and sassy world? Why walk to Santiago de Compostela if there is probably no physical Santiago there? Why suffer the agonies of blisters and tendonitis and physical exhaustion and the risk of heatstroke and all of that when you could be spending your vacation on a beach sipping gin and tonics and getting a tan and eating all the lobster your stomach can hold? None of us who do it really know the answer to that question, at least an answer that we can put into a few simple sentences. I asked many pilgrims along the way exactly that and most of the time the answer would be a shrug, a smile, a peaceful silence. Telling the story in long form is the only real way to sift the mountain of smaller stories for the answer. That's what I know now, after the fact. What I thought were my reasons before I took even one step towards Compostela were these:

First, over the years, I have not failed to notice that Jesus spent a lot of time on the road. He was a walker and surely he was a pilgrim often enough. I wanted to know what it was like to live as he lived, depending on his feet to keep him bound to the earth and moving him forward towards his destiny. Know his feet, know him.

Second, I was head of a small American seminary established in Leuven,[4] Belgium, in 1857; I believed in the place and the good that it does, but it had been a difficult job. There were days in my first couple of years as rector when our future looked pretty grim. I was in need of some help. Pilgrims have been going to Santiago for centuries with requests much bigger than mine, and enough of them got good enough answers to encourage others to make enormous sacrifices to go as well. Why not give it a shot? "Santiago, I've got this seminary here that needs more than I can give it. I've got some work for you to do on my behalf, so here I come!"

Third, I had recently turned fifty years old and was about to start my twenty-fifth year in ministry. What better juncture to take stock of my life, get to know myself a little more deeply and re-appreciate my small place in this world? What better way to do all that than by walking eight hundred kilometers by myself, or *almost* by myself?

Fourth, I wanted to drop five kilos.

But when all is said and done, what I really wanted was to see those stars of Compostela dance for myself.

4. Leuven is a small town located about twenty kilometers from Brussels. It is home to one of Europe's most important Catholic universities, founded there in 1425. In the English-speaking world, both the town and the university are usually referred to as "Louvain."

TO THE FIELD OF STARS

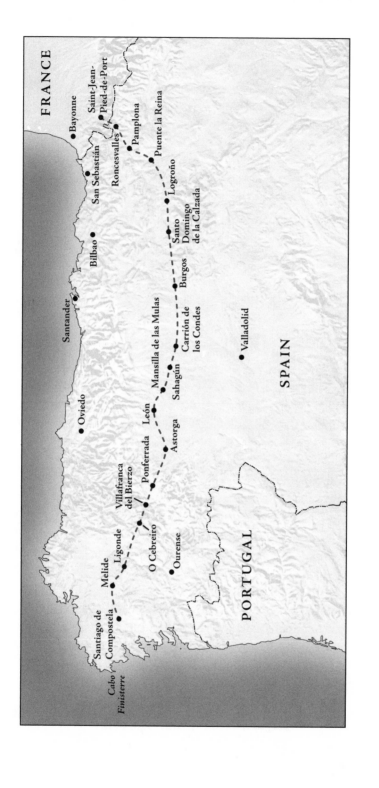

Saint-Jean-Pied-de-Port

July 8: Saint-Jean-Pied-de-Port

It is a gray morning in the French Pyrenees. With my backpack making everything awkward I carefully step down from the aging train that has carried me to Saint-Jean-Pied-de-Port, a French village set high in the Pyrenees and one of the usual jumping-off points for the *camino*. I set my feet firmly on the platform of this small train station and then glance down at my black Casio watch: ten o'clock. I gaze up at the leaden sky and wonder if it is really July. I find myself in a new world. It is a very odd feeling to be somewhere you have never been before and have not even had imaginings about. There is no sense of direction, no sense of history, really no sense of anything. You just look, scan the scene from left to right, taking it all in for a moment, then begin to take possession of it bit by bit. In this case, there is the small station, a street, the outside hem of a village and not much more. A few signs in the station window in French indicate, as best I can decipher them, that I and the gaggle of other would-be pilgrims who have landed on this platform, should march ourselves out to the street, up a hill, and following a few winding streets work our way into the heart of the town where we would find the information center for the *Chemin de Saint Jacques*. The skimpy map in the window and the scene beyond the station hardly seem to coordinate, so being still unsure of my directions I follow behind a couple of other new arrivals presuming for some reason that they know more than I, and so our mostly silent group, if it is even a group, straggles its way towards the town center. With the hill, insignificant as it is, I can feel the pull of the backpack on my shoulders for the first time and the hint of a muscle straining against it: uncomfortable, yes, but no big deal.

We wander a bit through some picturesque streets made mostly of stone until we find our way to the *Saint Jacques* information center. It is a small, old-fashioned storefront with posters and maps posted to the walls and a number of tables spread around with piles of papers and cards scattered about. Several very nice people belonging to the local branch of the *Amis du Chemin de Saint-Jacques*, "Friends of the Way of Saint James," are here to greet us and help us get started. One asks me my preferred tongue and I inform her that I can do well in either English or Spanish, so she hooks me up with an Australian gentleman who begins to attend to my needs by handing me the forms I need to complete so that I might become an officially recognized and bona fide *pèlerin* or pilgrim. Unfortunately for me, two very pretty young girls from some other English-speaking country show up right after me and so my *ami* swings his attentions completely to them, leaving me quite alone at his table as he takes them on a guided tour of the office explaining the wall maps and other interesting sights in great detail. I dutifully sit at the table, fill in my forms and wait for his return. He does not return. Finally, a more thoughtful lady comes along and asks if I am being attended to; I respond, "Well, the gentleman there *was* taking care of me, but somebody prettier came along." The lady glances back at the old codger, laughs, and then kindly takes me under her wing as we complete the registration process. I am given my *credencial*, number 3344, a simple white document made of light cardboard that unfolds like an accordion to reveal almost nothing inside except flaps and flaps of white space. It is explained to me that in each place where I am to spend the night, I will have to get a stamp, just like a passport, to prove to the authorities in Santiago that I have actually walked the road as claimed. It will also be required to gain entry to the *camino's* pilgrim hostels or *refugios*,[1] as they are called in Spanish. There is

---

1. Along the *camino*, the hostels developed for the pilgrims are interchangeably called in Spanish, *refugios, albergues*, or in some cases, *hospitales*. For simplicity's sake I will use the word *refugio* throughout the telling of this story.

one lone green *sello,* or rubberstamp seal, already proudly occupying the first space within my brand new *camino* passport: Saint-Jean-Pied-de-Port. I tuck the credential into the nylon billfold hanging around my neck and then look at my watch: ten forty-five.

I ask my attendant if it is possible at this hour to yet make it to the first *refugio* after Saint-Jean: Roncesvalles, an ancient Pyrenean village located on the other side of the border with Spain. The *ami* informs me that it is a twenty-eight-kilometer hike, that there is nothing of civilization between here and there, but that with a medium-weight backpack, and presuming I am in reasonably good shape (she quickly examines the heft of my calves), I should make it in eight hours. If I begin now and do not tarry, I can be there by seven P.M. Adding a serious note to her helpful advice, she warns me that it is liable to be damp and quite cool up the mountain. Paying little attention to this final caution, I can see no reason not to begin. I leave a donation of five euros in the designated can, hastily select my own personal conch from a cardboard box on the floor, tie this medieval symbol of the *Camino de Santiago* to a strap on my pack, then haul the whole thing up and over my back and walk out the door of the information center. Ready or not, it is time to get this show on the road.

Saint-Jean-Pied-de-Port is a thriving little tourist stop and every store sells many cute gifts and attractive mementos but I find it easy to resist their appeal: what pilgrim needs even more stuff in his backpack than he's already got? Not this one! What I do need is some food, so I stop at a tiny sandwich shop, purchase a couple of cheese and salami subs to stash in my bag and a warm slice of quiche to eat on the run. I gobble it down, then walk a few blocks to the town's Spanish Gate and stand in perplexity as I encounter my first decision of the road. Option one: go straight up the mountain; option two: go around the mountain, which presumably is a longer route but less of a pull. A sign recommends that, in bad weather, I should choose to go around rather than up. Well, it is raining a bit but not *that* bad. There is no one else here with whom to discuss the issue. I dither a moment or two, then without really deciding, I just go up.

As I take these first confident steps towards Santiago, I am feeling quite frisky. This surprises me because I have had very little sleep last night and a very tiring day before that, made all the more stressful by the fuss involved in getting myself out the door for this little adventure. And gazing even further back in time, the past year has seen me travel to the United States at least five times, including once for my mother's death and funeral, a second time dedicated to cleaning out her house to prepare it for renters, and three other times on difficult seminary business that, all in all, has left me anxious, nervous, and exhausted. Yesterday, about midday, everything seemed to fall apart. I raced to get the last of my work done, signing thank-you letters that I just had to get out, putting together a brochure for a new program, answering e-mail, arranging cash transfers from dollar accounts in the U.S. to euro accounts in Belgium, and then, saved for the very end, packing my rucksack.

I had been warned that as an amateur hiker I should not pack on my back any more than ten kilos, maybe twelve if I were in really good shape. With that in mind I judiciously stuffed in my toiletries and pills, my socks and shorts, my pants and shirts, my beautiful Coleman stainless steel thermos, my Camelback water bag pulling its handy sucking tube through a special hole in the pack made just for this purpose. Then there was the notebook that would be my journal, several pens, my glasses, my sunglasses, a box of Kellogg's granola to get me through the first couple of days, my Swiss Army knife, my Leatherman knife (why two knives? I have no idea), two rolls of toilet paper, a small sewing kit. Everything found a place. Then I tugged at the bag, tugged again, lifted it off the floor, hauled it to my bathroom scale and read the dial in disbelief: *fifteen* kilos! Even as I worriedly pulled the pack off the scale, I came to realize that its bottom was damp. I reopened it and found my Camelback leaking water over everything I had so carefully just packed. I had not securely tightened the handy plastic screw top to the thing. Everything had to be removed, dried quickly in the hot sun then packed in again. I took the opportunity to throw out some underwear, give up on the box of Kellogg's granola, and ditch a pair of jeans. I then weighed the bag again: twelve kilos. Good enough. It was getting late and I had to get started toward the train station, a twenty-minute walk. I had about forty minutes before my train's scheduled departure from the Leuven station. I defied the rules of gravity and tipsily swung the backpack up over my left shoulder and up onto my back, inserted my arms between its nicely padded straps, straightened up, adjusted its weight evenly over my spine, then looked for my train ticket, which I had just had in my hand, or so I thought. It was nowhere to be seen. I dropped the pack, searched through the bedroom, then the living room, then downstairs in the office, then back through the bedroom and the bathroom. No ticket. John, my assistant, hadn't seen it either. "Where did it go? It didn't just walk off on its own two feet!" I was furious at John, furious at myself, furious most of all at the ticket for losing itself.

Then I remembered something: the *other* office. Maybe it's there. I raced through the hallways of our old building, fumbled with my keys, unlocked the door, turned over a pile of books and papers and, praised be Saint Anthony, patron of all lost things: there it was! I grabbed the ticket, ran back to my bedroom, tucked a few last things into the pack, lurched it up onto my back, tied up its cinches and off I double-timed it to the train station with my friend Aurelius at my side to calm me down and see me off.

The pack sat easily on my back as we walked out the front door of Naamsestraat 100, through the Sint-Donatus Park, across the Herbert Hooverplein, and past the University Central Library. We passed beneath the towering green statue of Justus Lipsius, made our way down the last stretch of Bondgenotenlaan to the train station, ambled past the monument to the local dead of the Great War and up through the doors of the pretty Leuven station. "Not too heavy after all," I cheerily thought to myself as I shifted the weight of the backpack from one shoulder to the other. As the train to Brussels rolled into the station Aurelius wished me well; we said our final goodbyes and with a youthful spring in my step to prove to myself that I was master of this situation, I boarded the train. Once I slipped out of the pack and with substantial effort loaded it onto the overhead rack I suddenly felt more than a twinge of fear: "My God, what am I doing this for? Get off this train!" But the doors had closed and the train had started moving. Aurelius waved to me from the platform as the train pulled forward. I sat down. I was committed.

The ride into Brussels was uneventful. Too uneventful. I had nothing to read, nothing to do except examine from on high my lowly boots down below. They seemed fine. I retied them anyway. Finally, I just sat back, took a deep breath and, for the first time in hours, I sat still. Twenty minutes later, I was changing trains in Brussels, leaving behind the ordinary train for the "fast train" to Paris. Running at well over two hundred kilometers an hour, European fast trains take the word "fast" very seriously, and so in just over an hour, I was in Paris. With pack

» *July 8: Saint-Jean-Pied-de-Port* «

7

firmly attached to back, I jumped into the metro, crossed town to the Austerlitz station, then waited around that mostly empty terminal until my midnight train south to Bayonne was opened for boarding.

I had reserved in advance a *couchette*, a sleeping berth, in a first-class coach with the hope that I would be able to get a good night's sleep and thus be ready to begin walking the next morning rested and refreshed. My *couchette* was waiting for me, and for a while I was the only one in the cabin. The three other pull-down beds didn't remain unoccupied for long: a pretty young French girl took one, then two older gentlemen claimed the others. As they prepared themselves for bed, I had my first encounter with a very different culture when it comes to undressing in front of others. We Americans, despite all our promotion to the contrary, I now realize, are basically prudes. Well, at least I'm a prude. It's just not an easy or common thing for me to drop my pants in front of strangers. Out of the side of my eye I watched how they did it, the girl somewhat more discreetly than the two gentlemen, but in the end it amounted to the same thing: standing in front of strangers in your skivvies. If they could do it, I guessed I could do it too, and besides, there was little choice, so I stripped down to my shorts and quickly crawled into the little flannel sheet provided by the railroad, a rather ingenious and practical thing: folded over on one side and snapped together at the bottom and open side to make a sort of trundle-bundle like small children use at bedtime. I crawled in and waited for blessed sleep to come. It never made its appearance. The rocking and rolling of the train plus the snoring of the older gentlemen, and my nerves still jangling from the hectic days just past, all conspired to keep me wide awake throughout the night. I tossed and turned through the dark hours and though I kept my eyes closed in hope, I never managed to slip into even a single dream.

At about seven in the morning we rolled into Bordeaux where my three *couchette* mates disembarked, leaving me happily alone in the cabin for the final hour or two of the ride to Bayonne. I took time to write in my new journal about the previous day and the train ride south, then put my socks and boots on, adjusted a few things in my bag and looked out the window at the passing countryside. I made an effort to ponder in a preliminary way the mysteries that were approaching. It occurred to me that this manner of transportation would soon be something very foreign to me. I looked down at my nicely polished leather boots and thought of

» *Saint-Jean-Pied-de-Port* «

my soft feet within. They would soon be my only source of forward motion. What a difference between their fleshy pads and the screechy steel wheels of this train! I sighed. I hoped those soft feet would be up to the task set before them. In my imagination I spoke to them kindly and asked them to be good to me. They responded that they would do their best but weren't making any promises. What more could I ask of them?

The train arrived at the Bayonne station at nine in the morning; I and a few others also equipped with heavy boots and overstuffed backpacks tipsily stepped down to the platform from our coach and crossed to a much more rustic train on the next track over for the final leg of our journey up to Saint-Jean-Pied-de-Port. We chugged uphill through some pleasant countryside that was becoming more and more wild-looking as we traveled along. There were perhaps ten or twelve others in the carriage with me, and though we all looked like we were up to the same thing, none of us spoke. I don't know if the quiet of that small crowd lumbering up into the Pyrenees was due to the fact that each of us in our own way was pondering the adventure we were about to begin or if we were still trapped within the fear and suspicion that is nurtured in us by the big and fast-moving world we were leaving behind. Perhaps both the unknown world we were facing and the one we all knew only too well and hoped to escape for a while were at work on us, leaving us in an in-between place where chatter was instinctively known to be a breach of the spirit of the moment. These were my first fellow walkers on this journey and we said not a word among us. Where are they now? Not a single one is out here walking with me now. I begin this adventure utterly alone. A gentle rain dampens my head. It is hardly a rain; it is more like a descending mist.

So here I am, actually walking to Santiago, being led by this ribbon of damp black pavement around a wide corner and in following it so, I leave behind all sight of Saint-Jean-Pied-de-Port.

» *July 8: Saint-Jean-Pied-de-Port* «

9

I've Been to the Mountaintop

July 9: Saint-Jean-Pied-de-Port to Roncesvalles

The misty rain turns into a shower. I am getting soaked so I throw off my backpack only five minutes into my grand journey and pull out my new canvas poncho which has been constructed to fit handily not only over my head and the trunk of my body but also over my backpack. I hoist the pack back up over my shoulders and then struggle in the rain to get the silly poncho to cover not only me but the pack as well. I try tossing it, flipping it, swirling it, but the rear flap always gets hung up on something before it covers anything. Meanwhile the shower is quickly turning into a deluge. In the frustration of the moment I utter a very bad word or two . . . or ten. I must look like a character from a Road Runner cartoon, flailing about so. Finally though, I get the thing straightened out and lumber on up the hill. In less than one kilometer of walking the road has already made a fool of me.

Now, these rain ponchos are a piece of work. Mine is particularly beautiful: bright red on the outside and shiny silver on the inside with brass grommets at the corners and silver snaps on the open sides to make sleeves out of them. In principle, it seems a poncho such as this surely would be the greatest friend a hiker could have on a rainy day. The reality is something quite different. Besides the complexity of getting the thing on over your backpack, there is the further problem of human perspiration. It really doesn't matter how much rain you keep out if on the inside you are sweating like a fat man in a sauna. You end up soaked to your drawers either way. At some point, you are so wet that you just don't care anymore and the poncho becomes little more than a noisy annoyance. I soon hate the thing but keep it on because I am not yet interested in taking the time and trouble of taking it off and re-storing it in my pack. It does serve one other purpose that I grimly appreciate: as I climb further and further away from Saint-Jean-Pied-de-Port, the heavy rain thins back into mist and then is replaced by swirling banks of fog. The cherry-red poncho does double-duty as a highway sign, warning the very occasional driver sweeping by in a sleek Citroën or Renault that there is yet another novice pilgrim on the road ahead. Who knows, maybe this poncho has already kept me from being plastered to the wet pavement I now traverse? It is one more thing to mull over as I trudge ever upward.

My breathing is already beginning to labor. A twitch in my back is a small warning that this is not going to be so easy. It only dawns on me now how unprepared I am for this. I made the decision to do this in the gray gloom of a Belgian January. It dawned on me then that with my mother's death the previous November I had no great need to go home this summer. I was free to do whatever I wanted, and like the cars of a speeding freight train, a second thought whipped past on the tail of the first: the *camino*.[1] And that was that. The decision was made. No more thought went into it. I was going. I told a few friends of my completely undeveloped plan to "do Santiago this summer" which they all agreed was a fine thing for *me* to do, but for the next four months I did nothing more about it.

Sometime in May, I decided to do something about it. I thought I had better train. So one bright Saturday morning, I pulled on these very boots, put a small backpack over my shoulder with a water bottle and a book stuffed within, and thus gently strolled out of my Belgian home-town of Leuven for a twenty-kilometer-walk toward the neighboring city of Mechelen. I walked along a paved path that follows a very passive canal

---

1. The entire experience of walking or bicycling to Santiago de Compostela is referred to by almost everyone in every language with the Spanish word for road or way: *camino*. In the common parlance of most pilgrims it has become a noun that is very personal and intimate. Pilgrims who have completed the journey often refer to "*my camino*," as in "I completed my *camino* in August 2001."

» *July 9: Saint-Jean-Pied-de-Port to Roncesvalles* «

connecting the two cities. It was pleasant, though I barely managed to work up even a light sweat. Then I took a bus back home. No problem. I was in condition. Though I promised to be tougher on myself the next Saturday by carrying more weight and walking even further, I never pulled my boots back on until yesterday. I did nothing more to prepare myself for the trip. Except buy equipment.

On the first of July, everything in Belgium goes on sale. It is the perfect time to buy anything and everything necessary for the modern pilgrim. GoSport was my favorite haunt, and I visited it often, sizing up special hiking socks, checking out the sleeping bags, and, wonder of wonders, eyeing a beautiful cobalt blue Alpine/Lowe fifty-liter rucksack with more pockets and straps and hidden features than anybody in the store that day could explain to me. Best of all, it had a microfoam sleeping pad built right into it; just pull it out, unfold it and *voilà*, you can sleep on the ground without feeling a thing! And all this for only seventy euros! I bought it.

Then there were the hiking poles. I discovered a whole rack of adjustable poles that European hikers use as they happily trek through the Black Forest or the Ardennes. They look surprisingly like ski poles; well, I suppose they *are* ski poles just re-branded for this purpose. But they have hard titanium tips and shock absorbers in the handles, the very features that make trekkers lust after them. I was sold. I bought one. Then a German friend experienced in the sport of trekking told me I should have *two*; he explained that it's much easier on the knees to walk with two poles, especially downhill. Why do things the hard way? The next day I went right back and bought another pole to keep the first one company. Then the socks had to be purchased. I bought a couple different kinds so that if one pair didn't work out, another might. My favorites were cut special for each foot and had the words "LEFT" and "RIGHT" printed on the toes. I felt like a kid again, but I had heard about bad socks and the blisters they can cause and wanted none of that on *my* pilgrimage! I bought a pair of lightweight nylon trekking pants, army green with leggings that zip off making shorts out of them in a cinch. Just the thing!

Finally, my good friends at GoSport had put out a cardboard box at the end of one of their aisles marked "50% OFF!" Inside were fully stainless steel, absolutely unbreakable Coleman thermoses, only eighteen euros each! What a bargain! I fell in love with the one I brought home and happily tucked it into a special pocket on the front of my new backpack that seemed especially made for it. Everything was working out just fine. I was ready.

I was not ready, not ready for this. My back is feeling the weight of the pack. My wet fingers can't turn the screws to adjust my trekking poles. And this road is nothing like that level path between Leuven and Mechelen. I am already huffing and puffing having only just walked a kilometer or two or three. Let me tell you about this road I have chosen. It simply ascends. And ascends. And keeps on ascending. From the Spanish Gate to the top of the pass, I traverse a road that at points has a twenty-two-percent incline. This is very steep, at least in my book. The small asphalt road upon which I tread is blessed with many curves along the way that keep me from seeing just how high I am climbing and how much higher I have yet to go. For a person who is walking without being particularly well-conditioned for this specific form of exercise, and who is carrying a backpack that is way over the weight limit for a newcomer like me, and for someone inclined to feel sorry for himself, the incessant rise becomes something akin to an oriental water torture. Each footfall in itself is not so difficult, but the cumulative effect of at first a hundred, then five hundred and before long perhaps a thousand or ten thousand footfalls results in an exhaustion of both body and spirit that leaves me squeezing every possible calorie of energy out of my sputtering organism. But the calories run dry. I reach a point where I just cannot go even one step further. Literally, I cannot go one step further. So I stop, throw off my pack and then collapse spread-eagle on the rain-soaked earth right in the middle of a patch of sheep droppings. I do not care. The rest is a gift from God as my lungs lurch for air. After about ten minutes, I take some water and a bite out of my ham and cheese sandwich and take more water and then rest for another five minutes sprawled under a sky as gray as gray can be without becoming black. And all this after perhaps just four kilometers.

When I can again breathe, I get back up, stretch a little, lift the backpack over my shoulder, then struggle again with the poncho, pick up my hiking poles, and continue . . . upwards. The second or third time I stop, or maybe it is the fourth already, I want to turn back but I also know I am too far out now for that, so then I want to just stay put, but I know I can't survive the night out here because I am fundamentally a wimp, and so I realize with dizzy resignation that there is absolutely no option but to either keep going or die. So I keep going, for who wants to die *here?*

In my case, the whole scene is made all the more strange by the weather this day. The rain eventually lets up, but as I mentioned, it is replaced by fine mists of various gradations from almost-rain to almost fog. Eventually, it becomes just fog. But a fog with a difference: this is a fog with movement and grace, a fog that dances to the mountain breezes that blow across the grassy hillocks (no trees here . . . too high). As those mists and that fog swirl about me and as I rise higher into the mountains every once in a while a hole opens above me revealing a patch of blue sky that is a wonder of color in an otherwise-white-and-gray world. Then the hole closes up and all vision is reduced to no more than five meters in any direction. I am not completely alone up here on this mountain; herds of damp woolly sheep keep me company with the off-key bells strapped around their thick necks clanging in the mostly invisible distance. I pass an old Basque shepherd sitting quietly in his small muddy pickup off the road tending to his sheep from the sanctuary of his dry cab. As I walk past, his grizzled face offers no sign of interest in me. He just stares out into another space, his black eyes and well-wrinkled face protected from above by an old wool beret. Before long I believe I come to know something of that "other space" the old man gazes into. These hours climbing forever upward with the fog wrapping itself around me like an old cat, and being completely alone except for those sheep in the gray distance, and the occasional bright apparition of a spot of blue sky above, and with a fatigue of body and mind I have never previously experienced, and yes, with all pride sucked out of my soul by it all, I believe I have walked myself into another world, a world very distinct from that which I knew down below, a world somewhere between earth and heaven that feels like nowhere and everywhere. Up here everything is close and thin and ephemeral in its blankness. I feel myself enveloped, overtaken, absorbed into something quite unnamable. It is like being with Moses on top of old Sinai or with Jesus on Mount Tabor. This may be the closest I ever get in my life to a mystical experience. I am high.

At one point I pass a rocky outcropping to my right just off the road. I look up and in the haze I notice several mountain goats peering down upon me. I stop, lean the weight of my upper body and pack against my two poles, peer through the fog back at them, then after a considerable silence, they bleat and I bleat back.

I ask them: "Do you speak Spanish or French for if you speak French we can only nod to one another and offer the simplest of greetings but if you speak Spanish, we can discuss the universe and our place in it."

They answer that either is fine with them so I ask them how they like life up here. They respond, "Enjoying life is not something we ponder; we just live. However, life here is good enough if you must have an answer. Both life's hardships and life's pleasures come to us as they will and we accept them; there is no other way for goats to live."

I ask them if in their mountain wisdom they have any advice for one who is not yet so wise. They answer that of course they do: "Remain humble on this road or the road will humble you."

I thank them and promise to do my best to be humble on this road and look forward to the road humbling me if I am not.

I ask them if they talk to many pilgrims in the way they talk with me. "Many," they say.

I salute them and end the conversation: "May Good Santiago bless you for taking time to greet me."

"We have all the time in the world. This is our life."

I shake my head as they disappear in a flash into the gray mist. I must be crazy. But then again, in the grand scheme of things, what is so crazy about talking with mountain goats? After all, the air is thin and I am so very tired and so very alone up here.

As I push onward and upward, the pack on my back becomes more and more of a problem. With each turn in the road, the weight of all that I am carrying on my back only seems to increase. Even more, the pull at my shoulders and across the back of my neck, combined with the rubbing and chafing across my damp lower back, make the burden not so much unbearable as an annoyance without end. The pretty blue backpack with orange trim that had so enchanted me at the GoSport store now seems like a vile enemy, silently and insidiously increasing the pressure upon me to give in, to break down, to collapse in a heap. No matter how often I pause to shift its heft forward or from this side to that so as to gain a bit of relief, as soon as I continue on, the ache picks up right where it left off. I curse the bag and all it contains and begin considering what I might ditch at the first available opportunity. The list takes slow shape as some

» *July 9: Saint-Jean-Pied-de-Port to Roncesvalles* «

15

things are axed then spared, then axed and spared again. Two rolls of toilet paper are an unnecessary luxury; "X" one. But they hardly weigh anything; save both. Four pairs of white Champion athletic socks are hardly needed when I already have three pairs of special hiking socks: throw them all out! But they are brand new and haven't yet even been used! Keep them; they hardly weigh anything. Ditch the stainless steel Coleman thermos — it is too heavy; but I might need it for warm coffee some cool morning or for cold orange juice some hot afternoon and it was a bargain at half-price and it's just plain cool. Keep it for now; later on we'll see. The plastic Tupperware tub filled with powdered laundry detergent: ditch half of the detergent, but not outside where it might do ecological harm; that will have to wait until I get to Roncesvalles. For hours then, I find myself wondering when this hill will peak; when, oh when, will I finally be awarded the grace of descending the other side of this mountain? I am tricked at one juncture: after perhaps twelve or more kilometers since Saint-Jean, a multitude of signs indicate that the path diverges from the paved road, thereafter winding its way across a field and past a high cross erected with its base firmly planted in a pile of stones. I think for sure this must be the long longed-for peak and so after pausing a few moments to regain my strength, I press on with a feeling of optimism in my weary heart. The thin path through the field takes another turn and before I know it, I am climbing my way up a jagged goat-path saddled on both sides with great rocks that look as if they have been lifted from the gunfight scene of a B-grade western movie. All that is missing are the bad guys and the *zing* of bullets ricocheting off the rocks and whizzing past my head. I shake my head clear of its fantasies once again and push on. After picking my way up and around and through the rocks I discover that this dirt path is decidedly more interesting and surprisingly more refreshing than the monotonous climb along the paved road of the previous hours; here I am making continual decisions about where to place my feet for best traction and where to plant my poles for optimum lift and my whole body is engaged in the challenge of bouncing from one small outcropping of rock to another. I suppose this is why mountain goats don't bother with pavement: it is just too boring.

I come to a plaque indicating that somewhere to my right there is a shelter for pilgrims exhausted by the road already walked and overwhelmed by the impossibility of the task yet ahead. I look about but all I can see is a small, dirty cave: "I'm not spending the night in that thing!" I turn back to the path and with only a few meters more, lo and behold, for the first time in four or five hours, I feel the path beneath my feet soften into a slight but very noticeable decline. I am happy and so find myself singing aloud a ditty from my childhood:

The bear went over the mountain.
The bear went over the mountain.
The bear went over the mountain to see what he could see.
But all that he could see; yes, all that he could see,
Wa-a-a-as
The other side of the mountain,
The other side of the mountain,
The other side of the mountain was all that he could see.

I don't know why but it feels absolutely right to sing a silly nursery rhyme at this moment and best of all no one is around for me to feel any shame about the matter.

Before long, beech trees and an occasional chestnut begin to make their appearance and I know that the worst is over. I come to a barbed-wire fence that marks for me the first sign of my return to the world of below. Then I am led around a gentle curve and spy a beautiful fountain made of stone with fresh water spurting from its mouth. I must now be in heaven! I drop my backpack, hold my mouth up to the wide open tap and drink deep gulps of cold, minerally water, step back, stretch, remove my poncho and fold it up then tuck it inside the bag, fill my thermos, drink deeply from the fountain again and just rest there in complete, happy solitude. "I must surely be in Spain by now. It couldn't be much further to Roncesvalles from here," I assure myself. When I eventually return to the path, a bit beyond the fountain I find a large sign that I suppose is meant to offer me valuable information and perhaps even console me; it rather brags: "SANTIAGO: 780 KM." That number in its sheer factual hardness opens my soul to a wave of desperation. "This is impossible. I cannot walk seven hundred and eighty kilometers; I haven't even walked twenty yet and just look at me! I am crazy! I will surely quit . . . or die."

The next surprise of the road is one that surely comes sooner or later to every novice hiker: as painful as the uphill trek is, the downhill is even worse. The path through the beech trees soon takes a decidedly steep downturn putting a previously unknown pressure on my knees that shocks my whole body with every step. I experiment with my poles to figure out how to use them in this new situation and remember reading on the little tags hanging from them when I first bought them back in Belgium that they should be *lengthened* for downhill trekking, so I take a minute or two to loosen the lower segment from the upper, pull it forward and then re-tighten the whole, repeating the process for the other, making sure then that both are exactly the same length. As I take to the path again, I feel the difference immediately. The lengthened poles act like advance shock absorbers and soon enough come to feel like the front legs of a four-legged animal giving me a new agility as I pick my way downhill. They don't make me any less fatigued, though, and soon enough I am cursing the path on this downhill side of the mountain just as I did that of the uphill side.

I come around a bend and what do I find but the first fellow hiker I have happened upon since leaving Saint-Jean-Pied-de-Port. He is not hiking, though. He is sitting on the muddy earth, his legs sprawled out in front of him, his back leaning up against his own pack; he is damp, dirty, and looking rather dazed. He glances at me and I at him. We must be sights. He is a small-framed young fellow with long hair set in wild dreadlocks making him resemble a creature somewhere on Linnaeus's chart between human and arachnid. His brown eyes protrude from his slender face. He wears gray cotton athletic shorts and a well-soiled t-shirt. I ask him in English if he is okay and he indicates he doesn't understand me. So I try Spanish: "*¿Estás bien?*" Another shrug. He then asks me something in French. I understand the word *l'eau* and my keen observation of the pleading look on his face fills in the rest. I say, "*Oui,*" drop my pack, sit on the muddy ground nearby and offer him my silver thermos. After drinking, he takes out a pack of Prince Cookies with sticky jelly filling and gives me one. It is damp and tastes altogether too sweet. We exchange names, then stand, and for the next two or three hours we walk together through these descending woods, all the way to Roncesvalles, exchanging but a few words and a fair amount of hand signs as we go along. He keeps me going and makes it easier to finish the day's long walk. I suppose I might be helping him in the same way. Jean Luc is my first *camino* friend.

» *I've Been to the Mountaintop* «

Though we start out side by side, before long he's walking ahead of me through the beech tree woods that surround us in our descent; the distance between us increases with each turn in the path. Then in what seems to me to be an incredible act of generosity, whenever he gets ten or twenty meters ahead of me he holds up until I catch up, then with a smile offered to one another we start out again together. I feel like an old man as this wild looking little fellow with whom I can barely communicate waits for me turn after turn. I am filled with gratitude. Jean Luc is the strangest angel I have ever met.

Finally, finally, finally, we come out of the trees, cross a stream and behold the back wall of the great stone church of Roncesvalles. Jean Luc offers me his disposable Fuji camera and asks with gestures if I will take his picture on this very spot. I oblige him happily, getting down on my knees to shoot upward in an attempt to include in the small frame most of the massive stone edifice that looms above him. We then continue around to the front of the building looking for the *refugio* and there encounter some very kind *hospitaleros*, volunteer attendants who greet and care for the pilgrims; they lead us into a hall where for the first time I have the pleasure of dropping my backpack to the floor, unzipping the top flap, pulling out my *credencial* and having it indelibly marked with the unique seal of this particular place: a large black and white oval of medieval script surrounding the imprint of a bishop's crosier, some ill-formed *fleur de lis* and the *alpha* and *omega* that symbolize Christ. I am very proud to have gained this grand stamp for my pilgrim passport. I pay my four euros for a bed and together with Jean Luc head to the ancient, windowless building set up with what seems like a hundred bunk beds. I find an empty cot on the upper rank, a bed or two away from my new pal Jean Luc, throw off my bag and climb up onto the mattress where I finally have the pleasure of collapsing in a heap. It is hard to believe I have survived Day One but here I am. I take a deep breath of thanksgiving.

After only the briefest of rests, I sit back up, take a look at my watch, climb down and then with Jean Luc at my side, wander stiffly over to the great thirteenth-century church of Roncesvalles for the seven P.M. Mass and blessing of pilgrims. It occurs to me as soon as we enter the church that we are the only two present who have not as yet washed. I attempt to be discreet in my disheveled and sweaty state but no one seems to take offense: kindness upon kindness. Jean Luc dips his hand in the massive holy water font and I follow. The boy is a Catholic in some degree but there is no way to know what degree since our communication is limited to smiles, shrugs, and an occasional word or two. The several priests in the sanctuary celebrate a prayerful liturgy in Spanish and it is a pleasure to listen to a language I can easily understand. I feel at home. Even more touching is the medieval blessing they pray over us at the end of this grueling and impossible day:

> O God, you who took up your servant Abraham from the city of Ur of the Chaldeans, watching over him in all his wanderings, you who were the guide of the Hebrew people in the desert, we ask that you deign to take care of these your servants who, for love of your name, make a pilgrimage to Compostela. Be a companion for them along the path, a guide at crossroads, a strength in their weariness, defense before dangers, shelter on the way, shade against the heat, light in the darkness, a comforter in their discouragements, and firmness in their intentions, in order that, through your guidance, they might arrive unscathed at the end of their journey and, enriched with graces and virtues, they might return safely to their homes, which now lament their absence, filled with salutary and lasting joy.

Roncesvalles is a place steeped in European history, having seen the armies of Charlemagne, Charles V, and I suppose Napoleon pay probably less-than-happy visits, but I don't really care; the history of this place, rich as it is, is far less important to me than the rest and food and sleep Roncesvalles offers a rookie pilgrim who has just walked over the top of the Pyrenees. After eating and taking a shower, I chat with one of the *hospitaleros* and inquire about staying on the next day to rest up before continuing; I just can't imagine getting out of bed, putting on my boots, hoisting that pack up onto my back and walking another twenty or twenty-five kilometers in the morning. He demurs. "It may be possible but see how you feel when you awake." I know that he is gently telling me to get my ass down the road tomorrow.

My feet hurt. I go to bed.

Peregrino

July 10: Roncesvalles to Zubiri

What a surprise to wake up at six A.M. to the sound of almost everyone else in this ancient dormitory already awake and making ready for his or her day's walk. There is a rustle to this morning ritual: the soft patter of two hundred feet moving across stone floors, the slick sound of nylon sleeping bags being stuffed into their small sacks, the soft whisper of sleepy pilgrims coordinating their affairs with one another, rucksacks being packed, compacted, and clipped shut for the day, the sharing of the pilgrim's simplest verbal greeting: "*Buen camino,* Good way to you," as they go out the door and into the dark. It's not all completely pacific though. Interrupting the quiet rustle is the crackling sound of plastic grocery bags being handled by those without the foresight to consider how annoying the noise is to someone still lying in bed trying to decide if it is worth beginning another day.

While still deeply tucked inside my mummy bag, I take a reading of my body. Feet: a little sore but better than last night. Legs: not bad at all. Back: too early to tell but all in all, surprisingly free of agony. What a miracle seven hours of hard sleep is to the weary and worn! I crawl out of my sack, put my two feet on the floor, pull on my pants, rummage through my bag in search of fresh socks, put on my boots, head to the washroom and back again. Thus I greet the day. I then begin the puzzling game of secreting an oversize sleeping bag inside a very small stuff sack and am amazed that it takes about five precious minutes before I have the feather and nylon monster safely caged. I tuck away the rest of my belongings: toilet paper here, Swiss Army knife there, dirty clothes deep inside, sandals secured to the exterior. Ready. I'm going! The whole process has taken over an hour and I am one of the few walkers still in the place. It is already light and even Jean Luc has given up on me and taken off down the road on his own.

I take a quick look at the simple map on the back of my *credencial* and notice that the recommended hike for the day is almost twenty-seven kilometers. I can't believe I'll make it all the way to Larrasoaña so I set my sights on Zubiri, about four kilometers closer but equipped with a *refugio* just the same. I thank the *hospitalero* from the night before who told me so kindly not to give up so soon and so I walk out the door and into the new day.

Being a latecomer to the road I have it all to myself. I am feeling rather jaunty, actually. Within perhaps a half-kilometer the red and white blaze painted on a tree points me to a well-groomed walking path that cuts off from the pavement to the right and into a light wood. This is hiking at its best: fresh morning air, the scent of pine everywhere, and a road built especially for an amateur like me, level, graveled, and well-marked. Well-marked? No sooner have I thought the thought, than I come to an *unmarked* cross-path. I look up. I look down. I look every which way and see nothing besides a physical iteration of the famous Robert Frost poem about two paths diverging in the woods. I follow the advice of the poet and take the path less traveled but am not as fortunate as was he. *My* less traveled path is less traveled for a reason: it goes nowhere, but this fact can only be discovered by following it until it disappears into the underbrush of heavy woods about a half-kilometer further on. I turn back and with a commitment never to trust a poet for real-world hiking advice again, I find the main trail and continue down it past a farm and up to a small paved road that leads me safely out of the woods. Once secure in the route, I decide it is a perfectly good time to set a pattern for the days to come by gathering my rosary beads from their hiding place around my neck and under my shirt. I am alone. I am walking. I have nothing else to think about. The morning is still tenderly fresh. So why not? It seems the perfect time to pray this monotonous and altogether Catholic kind of prayer. I begin with the Apostles' Creed and work my way through the three little Hail Marys, a Glory Be or two, and then the five decades of Hail Marys with an Our Father before each and all with their accompanying Mysteries.

In point of fact, the rosary is a perfect prayer for a pilgrim; its repetitive recitation of the same few words over and over remarkably falls into time with my footsteps and my arms and the whole movement of my somewhat hunched body. With the rosary, I don't have to think, invent, or even really use my imagination. It comes from and rolls around within a place other than the front of my brain. It's not a mental prayer at all. It is a physical prayer, a prayer of rhythm more than words. Five fingers do all the work trundling beads through their paces while the rest of my body goes along for the ride. And it's all over in fifteen minutes or less and I rather feel sad that it is over and so I take another spin around the beads; after all, I've got all day. But after it is time to return them to my neck the rhythm I've gained in the praying continues to carry me along, making my footsteps lighter and my forward movement more confident.

This kind of prayer is so very Catholic. It is image-based, it is physical, it is rhythmic, and its "power" doesn't depend on feelings or creativity or a presumption of personal holiness. It is a good prayer for a sinner. We Catholics, even those among us who don't go to church much, experience our relationship to God much more through images, symbols, rhythms, and certainly flesh and blood than we do through what we experience as the wordiness of some other traditions. That part of our effort over the past forty years to renew our church that expressed itself as a preferential option for words over flesh has not gone particularly well. Once talk of being "a pilgrim people" replaced being a people who actually walk as pilgrims we rather lost our way.

And so it is that one of the grand patterns of my pilgrim life is pretty much set: first thing out of the gate, early in the morning, while still under the guidance of stars and moon, but also just as dawn begins to luminously announce itself on the eastern horizon, once I am away from other hikers, while I am still feeling perky and fresh, I say my rosary.

It isn't long into Day Two that the road begins to climb again. I begin to pass a few pilgrims also struggling upward even as others who had obviously started after I did are passing me by. A simple *bonjour* or *buenos días* is about all that is exchanged; so far I am finding a remarkable re-

» *July 10: Roncesvalles to Zubiri* «

23

spect for one another's privacy on the road. The red and white blazes direct us along what is quickly becoming another goat trail, making attention to the planting of feet and poles increasingly important. Loose rocks and roots are obstacles to be taken very seriously. The flesh of my feet, made tender by the previous day's efforts, begins to ache again. A flesh-ache is something new to me. More difficult still is my increasingly burdensome backpack, or as it is called now by nearly everyone out here: *la mochila*. I just can't get it to ride right on my hips. It pulls backwards against my shoulders, and a particular muscle to the left of the small of my back begins to pain me. I swear that before beginning another day, I will get the weight of that thing down to below ten kilos and find myself reprising variations of my monologue from the day before: I could ditch that second roll of toilet paper. But then again, t.p. hardly weighs anything and I will need that stuff sooner or later. Why put out good money for what I've already got? On the other hand the stainless steel Coleman thermos is way too heavy for what it's worth to me in fresh water; there are plenty of fountains along the way or so they say; but then again that container of cold, fresh water might be a life-saver out in the dry country up ahead a week or two. Throw it out. Keep it. Throw the stupid thing out. *Keep it!*

I am slowly beginning to sense that I have a rather personal relationship to this pack of the love-hate variety. Despite its initial store-fresh allure and its absolute necessity to me now, the backpack and I are not exactly friends. It is a burden borne grudgingly like an annoying and fat little brother I have to take with me just because he is my fat little brother and is therefore a part of me whether I like him or not.

A new problem arises this morning: heat. As the sun rises higher in the sky, the temperature begins to climb as well. Sweat drenches my shirt. The legs of my long, old, floppy Dockers pants begin to feel like they are made of sailing canvas. Actually, they might as well be made of canvas. I couldn't have picked a hotter material to walk in except perhaps for blue denim of the Levi Strauss variety; no smart hiker ever wears jeans out here, I discover. How lucky I am that I left mine at home. But so as not to crow too loudly over my foresight, I don't see many wearing winter-weight Dockers like mine either. At any rate, I also come to understand why those chirpy pilgrims in Roncesvalles had so quickly gotten out the door in the morning: the heat of the Basque country in July at midday, even if you are still in the foothills of the Pyrenees, can be stultifying. And so it is. Heat multiplies pain by fives and chops up available energy into mincemeat. I commit myself to become an early riser.

And yet another problem presents itself: hunger. My on-board cache of food amounts to nothing more than the second of the sandwiches I bought in Saint-Jean-Pied-de-Port, the bread of which is becoming tougher by the hour. With a long way yet to go before this day's walk will end, I ration it carefully. Hunger pangs and walking up mountainous goat trails do not good mates make. Nevertheless, like the day before, an occasional hearty bite of my sandwich softened up with a full swig of water seems to stave off death for an additional hour or two.

This day, somewhere along the way, I decide that this first week of pilgrimage with all of its ups and downs is to be dedicated to a simple cause: the flourishing of the little seminary I oversee. In Catholic piety we call this a "special intention." It must sound odd to those who haven't been suckled at the breast of the mother that is our Church, but most Catholics have this notion planted deep within their souls that they can give God a bit of a push to move on something important to them by offering to him their works and their aches and pains and all of their sufferings big or small. We tend towards a relationship with God that in character is less like that of a philosopher to an unmoved mover than of a child in the lap of a big-breasted mama (or a wide-armed father for that matter), who just can't do enough for her baby. We have the feeling that she loves it when we talk to her about our problems; she kisses our little wounds even as she reassures us in lullaby tones that she'll take care of it even if she was going to take care of it anyway. She likes to see us make an effort to help out around the house. And most of all, she loves it when we come bearing some little trifle as a gift, like an eight-year-old bringing home a hand-made crayon and construction paper birthday card for Mommy. We call such trifles as these, especially when they actually cost us something personal, "sacrifices." Are we bribing God to do our will? Not really. Well, maybe a little. But what we are really doing is just letting the Creator know that we are paying attention and we look forward to the Almighty coming through on promises made and, in the end, it is a way for us to say thank you. If we don't "get" what we've asked for with our little sacrifice, then that's okay, too; God knows best in the long run. But that little word "sacrifice" means a lot. It is Latin for "make holy."

» *July 10: Roncesvalles to Zubiri* «

We believe that by "offering up" something important to us even if it is a trifle, the trifle becomes holy because from then on it belongs to God. And in being explicit in that offering, and paying attention to God in a very personal way, and in crawling into God's big lap with our troubles, God can't help but tend to us.

So I decide my trifling ups and downs in this first week of pilgrimage on the way to Santiago de Compostela will be offered up for the little seminary that I have come to love.

It is a "little" seminary not at all in the sense of its physical size, for it is housed in a rather massive building, but because its students are few and it is little because for the moment it occupies a small place in the heart of the Church back in America. Nevertheless, I love the place for its history and traditions but most of all, for how it helps young men who want to be priests grow and deepen and mature; I'll do all I am able to keep it going. This includes walking to Santiago and enduring whatever I have to endure as a sacrifice on its behalf. Once there, I will wrap my sunburned arms around Santiago's thick neck and not let go until I have made him understand the urgency of my petition that this little seminary become just a little bit bigger. It is hardly too big a miracle for me to request, I believe, and so I will walk and sacrifice and beg for it.

I cannot adequately explain all this when fellow *caminantes*[1] ask me why I am on the road, but it is what motivates me in the first place to be out here and it is what is pushing me forward day after day and indeed it is what is at the heart of my walking prayer as I trek along. With each step I imagine the faces of each of our eleven seminarians and my three priest co-workers and I remember their quirks and their tics and all their various virtues that make them unique in the world: "This sacrifice is for you, men!"

At about one in the afternoon, I cross into Zubiri by way of a medieval bridge, a great rounded stone affair that is known locally as "the Bridge of Rabies" since farmers of old would drive their cattle three times around its central pillar as a way to get rid of the dread disease. Would that I might drive myself around that pillar three times to rid myself of two very hot feet whose very flesh aches with each footfall. Luckily, no

---

1. "Walkers on the road" might be the best translation of this alternative word for all of us pilgrims heading westward across Spain towards Santiago.

one ever told me this was going to be either fun or easy. The roadway leads me into a simple town, not particularly quaint or old-fashioned. I stop at a bandstand where several young boys are escaping the heat of the afternoon in the shade of its shell. I ask if they know where the local *refugio de peregrinos* might be; one gives me simple directions: up the street a block, take a right, go another block, right side. Easy. I must look awful, for another boy is laughing at me, but a third looks at me with some seriousness and calls to me: "*Vaya con Dios, Peregrino!* Go with God, Pilgrim!" That third boy's blessing at the end of a long day moves me. It is the first time I have been called *peregrino*, and it feels good even when everything else feels so bad at this sun-baked hour. I hope I do go with God and I hope that God goes with me. I expect he will. I am left speechless so I just wave *adios* to the boy and head up the street a block, turn right, go another block and there, baking in the hot sun, is a single level school building labeled *"Refugio"* and I'm home.

I am directed to the first of two large classrooms, the one labeled *"Muchachos"* and there I pick a lower bunk, drop my *mochila*, pull off my sweaty boots and socks, and flop onto the mattress. With my eyes closed, I calculate my progress: twenty-four more kilometers under my shoe leather today; seven hundred and some yet to go. God go with me, indeed!

After ten or fifteen minutes of down time, I slip on my sandals that are a heavenly change from boots, pull out my towel and a pair of briefs and head to the shower. There are no curtains on the shower stalls, but no one seems to care, except me, a little bit, but I'm getting over it. There is little room for American modesty here so I just go ahead and shower in the ice cold water, dry off, dress, wander back to my bunk and fall into a deep sleep, for all of five minutes. I'm awake again but I remain motionless for another twenty. Finally, I get up, go back to the shower room and wash my dirty clothes in a cracked plastic bucket then hang them outside to dry, stringing each piece over the bars of the aging playground equipment. Meanwhile, the *hospitalera* arrives with her rubber stamp, and after paying my four-euro rent I get my third proud seal of the pilgrimage. Then it's back to the bunk for another hour of restoration. It is remarkably quiet in this place. People are moving about here and there, but the respect for one another is impossible not to notice. Soft voices are used when speech is necessary but mostly no one is talking; sign language and weak smiles suffice. A few people are reading. Others are tending to their feet, anointing them, rubbing them, and poking at white blisters. Most are as quietly horizontal as I am.

About four in the afternoon, I get up and wander about the school-yard. I check on my clothes and pick up the socks and shorts that have fallen to the dusty ground. It is hotter than ever but I'm feeling better. I grab the long canvas Dockers pants I have been wearing for two days from the jungle gym, take them to the somewhat shaded porch of the school, dig out a very sharp blade on my Leatherman tool, and proceed to cut off the legs of those pants, making very uneven shorts out of them. Perfect. They are destined now to become a great pair of walking shorts and I love them.

I see a very pretty young girl discreetly laughing at my craftsmanship with the knife and so we quietly greet one another in Spanish. We recognize one another's American accents and then continue in English. She's working in Madrid, has a Spanish boyfriend, and seems to be a lot better hiker than most of the rest of us. She is perky and cheery and the day's walk doesn't seem to have left her dazed as we amateurs are. I admire her right away. Beth and I talk about hometowns and occupations and it feels good to chat in plain old American English for a while.

While waiting for the last of my socks to dry, occasionally moving them to catch a bit more of the afternoon sun, I pull out my breviary, a small volume holding within its pages a month-long course through the Psalms with an additional Scripture reading and prayers added to the mix. In this abbreviated version (the unabbreviated one is four volumes; not suitable for a backpack!), there is an "office" for the morning and one for the evening. I find a quiet place in the schoolyard and take care of my evening prayer. The Psalms quietly move me; they are earthy and speak to just the kind of experiences we are enduring on this road. They get it right:

> For he shall save the poor when they cry
> And the needy who are helpless.
> He will have pity on the weak
> And save the lives of the poor.[2]

2. Psalm 72.

We are poor, we are weak, we whine way too much, and in spite of our bellyaching, God is not all that far away and doesn't give up on us. I expect him to take up that boy's blessing and walk with me whether I remember to ask him or not.

By seven P.M., the *refugio* is full and about ten of us wander down the street to a hotel-restaurant for dinner. We all order the *menú del peregrino*, the pilgrim's menu, a few bottles of beer and some decent *Rioja* wine and we get to know one another across the long table we encircle. Though some of the table conversation is in English and a bit less in Italian and French, most is in Spanish. I observe with amazement the remarkable and seemingly natural manner in which Europeans are able to carry on a multilingual conversation without hesitation; links between those who know more than one tongue are found right off the bat and then mutual translation just happens without anyone hardly noticing it taking place. It is a remarkably generous experience in which to take part. After a slow amble back to the *refugio*, I crawl into my bunk and fall dead to the world.

» *July 10: Roncesvalles to Zubiri* «

Poor Fermín

July 11: Zubiri to Pamplona

My black Casio watch beeps at five thirty A.M. I awake feeling rather refreshed and by six o'clock I and everyone else in the Zubiri schoolroom
are up and getting our teeth brushed, taking turns at the toilet, and putting our bags back together. By six thirty I am out the door accompanied
by two new friends from the night before, Javier from Sevilla and Manuel
from Barcelona. Both are in their forties and a bit overweight so we all
move at about the same pace as we wander out of town and up the road
towards our next stop, Pamplona.

Javier is a gentle soul while Manuel is a bit on the aggressive side.
Javier is a true Spaniard while Manuel is a true Catalán. There's the rub.
There is little silence for the rest of the morning as they debate each and
every issue facing the conglomeration of ethnic and linguistic communities that make up modern Spain. What the fascist dictator Franco held
together by sheer force of arms, the modern kingdom has to hold together with consensus and diplomacy and plenty of political horse-
trading.

Few of us on the outside can understand the complexity of the inter-
relations, or lack thereof, among the Castilians, Catalans, Galicians,
Basques, and all the other somewhat autonomous peoples that inhabit
the Iberian Peninsula, but those very complexities give the modern citi-

zens of this fractious nation plenty to talk about and this they do with great passion, loud voices, and, often enough, little inclination to listen to one another before injecting a rejoinder into the discussion one on top of another. It can drive outsiders like me crazy; not just the issues, which are occult enough in themselves, but the manner in which they debate one another. It does not seem to be a discussion undertaken with the intention of arriving at some manner of mutual understanding; it is rather more like a political demolition derby with everyone talking over everyone else, no one listening, and absolutely no interest in arriving at any kind of common view on anything. Evidently, the point is the arguing itself. They love it and can engage in it for hours, and it never seems to get personal. As I said, it drives me crazy, and I get my first big taste of it from my new pals, Javier and Manuel.

It is not too long before I have tired of their arguing and either hang back or move ahead to let them go at it by themselves. They are nice guys and I have nothing against them. In fact when we stop for water or a snack they are altogether pleasant and amiable. In all that they have argued over the previous hour, clearly, there is not a hint of rancor or animosity. I have to admire that, even if the arguing itself annoys me to no end.

Getting back to the road itself, the first few kilometers are a snap. It is cool and there is shade. We quickly pass through Larrasoaña where most of the other pilgrims spent the night and there take a quick drink of water before continuing on our way. While leaning up against a low wall near the Larrasoaña bridge, Manuel asks me if I am a priest. I am a bit surprised but tell him plainly that I am. He then yells over to Javier who is a few meters away retying his boots, "Hey, Javier! This Kevin is a priest!" I am annoyed at the manner of the announcement but shrug it off. I then ask him how he knew and he responds simply that he saw me reading a little book with ribbons hanging from it last night. I just *looked* like a priest, he says. It doesn't seem to make much difference in our relationships and we move on through the village and back to the road, as always, the two of them arguing over Spain . . . and now the Church in Spain as well.

When I get a bit of distance from Javier and Manuel, I retrieve my rosary from a pants pocket and after untangling its links and beads, enjoy praying it while it swings from side to side out of sight of my yakking companions now several meters behind me. The pleasure of this first hour or two is not to last. The heat of the day is building and the ache in my feet picks up where it had left off the day before and the most dreadful of dangers to the pilgrim is beginning to make itself felt: a hot spot on the pad of my foot just below the big toe is threatening to become my first blister.

At about nine thirty, we come upon a small, rather modern village with a single bar at the far end of a long paved and curbed street. We roll in and find Beth and several others from Zubiri already there enjoying big cups of *café con leche*, croissants, or a slice of a curious almond pie that is typical, I am told, of Compostela. We lean our *mochilas* against a small retaining wall, put in our order to the friendly man tending the place, then relax in plastic lawn chairs under Coca-Cola umbrellas as we enjoy what is a mid-morning ritual for almost all pilgrims along the way. A coffee and snack seldom taste so good as they do after two or three hours of tiring walking. I try a slice of the almond pie with my *café con leche*, a sturdy shot of coffee outgunned by much more warm whole milk than we Americans would ever allow, turning the drink into a mocha colored mix that has enough fat, caffeine, and sugar to keep a pilgrim going for a couple or three hours more. The blend of rest and nourishment is extraordinarily delicious and laughter comes easily as new friends chat and old strangers become friends.

This particular morning I strike up a conversation with the bartender, a middle-aged man who seems to authentically enjoy the company of this day's raft of ten o'clock pilgrims. He asks me where I am from and is surprised when I mention that I am American but live now in Belgium. He begins to tell me that he knows a little bit about Belgium and in particular that there is a university there, a Catholic one, that is one of the oldest in the world and has a reputation for greatness. He even knows the name (in Spanish): *Lovaina*. I am astounded and after telling him that it is precisely this place where I live and work, I have to ask if he has been there since he clearly knows so much about it. "No," he responds simply. "I've never been anywhere really. I just read." I shake my head in wonder that there are still in this world people who come to know the world by "just reading."

After a nice coffee and slice of almond pie, there is nothing more to do except tighten my bootlaces, yank the old *mochila* back up over my shoulder, take in hand my hiking poles, or *bastones* as they are called here, and get back to the road. With every minute of delay, the sun only gets higher and hotter. The twenty-plus kilometers to Pamplona lead us through some interesting countryside but Pamplona, it turns out, is a big enough city that it takes some work to traverse it once we come within its folds. As we pass into its suburbs, the three of us are already very hot, aching, and foolishly presuming that we are almost home for the day. We are far enough into Spain and distant enough from France that the red and white blazes that guide us have now become yellow arrows, *flechas amarillas*, directing us onward. We follow the *flechas* as we work our way through some very wealthy but boring neighborhoods with most of the homes protected by high walls clearly meant to keep the unwashed and untrustworthy securely on the outside. We finally cross through the gates of the old city, the street running uphill just enough to make us feel the additional burden in our bodies as we make our way into the bosom of Pamplona.

As it turns out, we are arriving in the very heart of the *Sanfermines*, Pamplona's annual festival running for nine consecutive days in honor of its patron saint, San Fermín. These are the same *fiestas* made famous by Ernest Hemingway and which continue to attract young people from around the world for each morning's "running of the bulls." It will come as no surprise then that the place we are walking into is jumping, even in the heat of the early afternoon. We pass through a park where hundreds of dirty, hung-over, and often fairly naked young people are camping out. The landscape is dotted with plastic sandwich bags hanging from tree limbs and cyclone fences; they contain fermenting feces of the human variety. How thoughtful of these young revelers to collect their waste from the grassy lawns and hang it up for the tourists and pilgrims to admire as they stroll by. I am feeling cranky at the end of this day and the scene that is greeting me here pushes to the surface a sour burp of cynicism about humanity.

Now, San Fermín was a third-century bishop who had his roots in Pamplona, was mentored by the first great bishop of the place, Saturnino, went off to Toulouse in what is now France for further study there, and became a bishop in the French city of Amiens, where the locals eventually beheaded him. The cult of the local-boy-turned-martyr back in Pamplona eventually became the center of this Basque city's identity and

» *July 11: Zubiri to Pamplona* «

the annual celebration of the poor beheaded bishop has through the centuries grown and then degraded into its present state of debauchery and fun for all ages. Besides Fermín's name and the *Sanfermines*' red kerchiefs and white clothing that vaguely recall both Saint Fermín's purity and bloody death, there doesn't seem to be much of him left in the celebration. I doubt that he would be pleased with the scene in which we presently find ourselves. Poor Fermín. Poor us.

We move deeper into the heart of the old city and things go from bad to worse. We have to shoulder our tired bodies and bulky *mochilas* through rollicking crowds of even drunker drunks, streets slick with beer and piss, and goofy looks from those who can still look that say, "What the hell are *you* doin' here?" With a bit more trudging, we come to a main plaza in the old city that suddenly turns into a circus as giant puppets with huge *papier-mâché* heads come parading and dancing down the street hitting people with stuffed socks. This is more like it. This is actually fun. As I and my *mochila* are jostled to and fro I nevertheless enjoy watching the children squeal with delight each time they get whacked by a giant puppet dressed as a king. Their delight delights me. As I pass one middle-aged, very nicely dressed woman with a grandchild in tow, I hear her say to her husband as she nods towards me with her head, "*Mira: el pobrecito.*" I'm not sure if it is said with compassion or disgust, but it is the first time I have ever heard myself called a "*pobrecito,*" which in this case may be loosely translated as either "the poor little guy," or more likely, "the poor bastard." It is hard to believe I have come to this, and after only three days.

It is no easy thing to find the *refugio* in Pamplona. The ancient one in the center of town is too small for the summer crowds so it has been closed in favor of a large high school gymnasium somewhere beyond the old central area. Javier, Manuel, and I, once we regroup after getting separated by the giant puppet parade, simply lose our way in this buzzing city, that is until, quite by chance, we stumble upon Beth the American, who has with her some unidentified friend who knows the route through another, more civilized park and down a long street to the school. I am limping with what is now surely a full-fledged blister making every step an agony; my back is breaking under the weight of this damnable pack, and it is really hot now; one sign reads thirty degrees Centigrade. I gut out one last push forward towards the school building leaving Javier and

Manuel temporarily behind as I follow Beth to the schoolyard gate, go in, get my *credencial* stamped, pay my three euros for a bed, and collapse on a bottom bunk, one of hundreds in the massive gymnasium. Ah! Home! Thank you, Beth!

After taking some deep breaths, I sit up, pull off my boots and socks and take a look at my feet. The view is not a happy one. Just as I suspected: a big-daddy blister has perched itself in the worst possible place: on the base of the right foot behind the big toe where every step will hit it bang-on. This will call for surgery, but not before a shower and a bit more rest.

By and by, Javier drags himself in and takes a bunk across a small aisle from mine; Manuel follows and settles above Javier. Then to my surprise, my young French friend from the first day, Jean Luc, passes by my bunk and settles on his own bed, two aisles down. I nod to him and he nods back as he disgustedly examines a plastic bag full of well-smashed tomatoes and red-stained sandwich fixings. *"Merde!"* he mutters. I understand perfectly.

After cooling down and cleaning up in the cold-water shower, I wash my clothes, hang them to dry outside, then dodder back to my bed, take out my nail clippers and small bottle of Purell anti-bacterial hand cleanser, and prepare for my assault against the squishy bubble of in-flamed skin on the bottom of my foot. I cleanse the clippers with the Purell, pull my foot high up over my lap and angle myself for the best view of the *ampolla*. I snap the clippers' jaw at the skin and open a big enough hole for the liquid to dribble out. Perfect. Then I cut off a piece of Dr. Scholl's felt mouse skin from a bigger piece, rip off the glossy paper from its adhesive side, and apply it over the wound.

Almost as soon as I have finished I learn from more experienced pilgrims that I have done everything exactly wrong and have set myself up for a massive infection that could have the power to stop this pilgrim dead in his tracks for days if not a full week. The damage is done so I have no choice but to live with my open sore and tend to it the best I can with the wan hope that the fate described to me does not come to pass. I lie down again and just exist without formed thought for the longest time. Eventually Javier limps over and asks softly if I am hungry. It dawns on me that in point of fact, I am famished but cannot the restaurant come to me? After some dawdling on all our parts, I put on my sandals and Manuel, Javier, and I stumble back out into the blast furnace heat of the afternoon to a

» *July 11: Zubiri to Pamplona* «

nearby bar where I down a tender piece of cod smothered in tomato sauce accompanied by very limp fries, followed by a bowl of *pochos,* something previously unknown to me but highly recommended by Manuel: white beans cooked with *chorizo,* Spanish sausage. The flavor is rich though the texture and look leave something to be desired. I pick at them but can't consume the whole bowl by a long shot. We all have a couple of beers. Javier and Manuel argue. We are deep into male bonding.

Upon returning to the school and my humble bunk, a terrible temptation overcomes me. I come to believe for a moment or two that maybe this whole enterprise is a terrible mistake. The smartest thing for me, a fifty-year-old man clearly not in the kind of shape he thought he was in, is to just go home. A quick look at the map on the back of my *credencial* seals the case: after three days, I have covered only the smallest fraction of the route across Spain. The map is discouraging beyond words. I mutter a choice swear word to myself but then gain a bit of courage by remembering the knowing words of the *hospitalero* in Roncesvalles: "See how things feel in the morning." That thought is my only defense against the swelling tide of discouragement within me.

I idle away the afternoon on my bunk, then go out a second time with Javier and Manuel for another beer. With a bit of liquid courage making its way up to my brain, I feel slightly more determined about moving on in the morning if for no other reason than that, in its present state, this town might as well be Sodom and perhaps Gomorrah as well; it holds nothing of interest to me. I am not a tourist here. The bulls to me are just big and stupid bovines and I think running with them is the most ridiculous manner of which I have ever heard to commemorate a perfectly good third-century saint. The supposed heroism of those idiots in the run seems as phony to me as my dad's old plastic three-dollar bill. For me, at this juncture in my pilgrim life, heroism amounts to nothing more than getting up tomorrow and walking out of this place. I'm going even if I have to drag and claw myself down that road to Santiago.

There are fireworks over the city after night falls but I don't go out to see them; after all, I can barely walk. The evening psalm sums up the one feeling left to me as I crawl into bed: "O Lord my God, deliver me . . ."[1]

. . . from bags of *merde.*

1. Psalm 116.

» *Poor Fermín* «

Pilgrim Paella

July 12 and 13: Pamplona to Puente la Reina

My first Saturday on the road is not going to be an easy one. I went to bed hoping that my blister would be healed by the morning. It isn't. As I am getting ready for the new day, a nice lady from Madrid notices my pained gait and offers me a new kind of treatment for blisters, a little product called Compeed which is nothing more than a fairly thick silicone patch with a strong adhesive on one side; it is applied over the wound as a sort of second skin, giving feeble-footed walkers like myself a fighting chance at arriving at the next *refugio* without collapsing into a heap fifteen kilometers short of the goal. She kindly shows me how to use it: "You take this little piece of plastic, warm it up by rubbing it in the palm of your hands, pull off the glossy paper protecting the adhesive, and glue it right on top of the blister. See?" A great idea, but will it work for me? Even more than the Compeed, I appreciate her generosity in offering this small piece of silicone-based salvation to me.

I take the gift and return to my bunk to size up the situation. My blister has not become infected, thanks most probably to my small bottle of Purell, but even with that the wound doesn't look very good; it is large, open, and very tender. I clean around it with more Purell, and then apply the silicone patch as directed.

And so here I sit, on the edge of my bed in hung-over Pamplona at six thirty in the morning. I gaze down at my dusty boots whose open necks stare back at me in blank emptiness; daylight won't be long in coming and everyone else is heading out the door with visions of Puente la Reina dancing in their heads. I don't want to go but I *must* go; I don't know why but I *must go*. I suck up my apprehensions, pull on my socks and the boots atop them, close up my bag and throw its heft onto my back, grab my poles, and lumber out the door, accompanied by Manuel and Javier. The day has begun.

It is just not going to be a good day. I stupidly neglected to pick up anything yesterday to use as a breakfast snack today so I am hungry even before I begin. My pack is as burdensome as ever. My blister hurts even with the Compeed in place. Someone in the next aisle of beds reported before leaving that it is going to be even hotter today than yesterday. But none of this is as big a problem for me as that posed by Manuel and Javier in our second day of *camino* clubhood. It is clear as we leave Pamplona that the three of us have somewhat inadvertently bonded together as a band of pilgrim brothers, so we all leave the city . . . together. Leaving a city together can mean only one thing: it is eminently clear that we are committed to be there for one another for the duration.

As we walk the sun gently rises behind us, offering us, when I take a moment to turn around for a look, a display of pink and then gold light filling the sky that is about as pretty a dawn as I have ever seen. My companions do not turn around to look. Instead they talk and debate and chat and argue as they go along and I feel increasingly annoyed by my noisy brothers. Even worse, I know the problem is in me; they are perfectly good people having a perfectly good time doing what ordinary people do as they walk together. But I want, at least for a while, to be alone and to be quiet and not have to disguise the fact that *I am trying to pray a rosary out here*! I unhappily chalk my growing antagonism to them up to my own weakness as a human being, but even with that confession to myself, I am feeling as if *my camino* is being taken away from me. Why hadn't I known better than to get hooked up with a gang, even a small one, so soon in the walk? Nevertheless, here I am and there is no getting out of this fix except to plot in the darkness of my heart various strategies to ditch these boys somewhere along the way ahead. I feel like a fifth grader all over again. I *am* a fifth grader all over again. I hurt.

There is yet more to molest me as the day gets hotter and the road climbs higher and becomes rougher. Both Manuel and Javier are school-teachers; Javier teaches adults in a remedial program while Manuel teaches small children in an elementary school. Javier is gentle and kind and patient. Manuel, on the other hand, begins treating us as if we are his six-year-old pupils, directing us, correcting us, and indicating to us what we are going to do next and why. The constant yakking of the two takes a second place on my list of grand annoyances: I begin to hate being managed when what I really want is just to wander on, and to wander on at my own pace, resting when I want to rest, pushing on when I want to push on, and having quiet when I want some quiet. I don't like this crankiness in myself but I just don't have the energy to do much of anything to defend myself against the churlish feelings stirring around inside me. Well, as I said: I hurt. And I am hungry. And it is getting hot. And the discouragement of the day before has regained its footing in my soul. But I keep walking. I hardly know why.

Up a great side of mountain we labor towards a summit along a ridge of mountains called the *Sierra del Perdón*, the Mountains of Forgiveness. The particular peak we are climbing is called the *Alto del Perdón*. The effort needed to climb the rough-hewn path with the heat of the sun deepening by the minute slows down my companions, and for a while quiets them down as well. We each trudge upwards in our own little world. This part of the walk uphill is made slightly more interesting to the eye and ear by a file of massive wind machines, the blades of which fill the air around us with rhythmic whooshing sounds that grow ever louder as we climb ever higher. Presently a fountain makes itself available to the dry-mouthed pilgrim. It is well situated not far from the summit and a most attractive sight at this point in the road. It is called the *Fuente Reniega*, or Fountain of Denial. Of course there is a legend attached to any feature of the old *camino* route with a name as dark as this. It goes that a medieval pilgrim upon arriving at this very spot found himself in a rather parched condition. The devil appeared to him and offered him a spring of fresh, gushing water to slake his thirst if he would first deny his faith. The noble pilgrim passed the diabolical test, did not deny anything, and found himself then visited by Santiago vested, as was the man himself, as a faithful pilgrim; Santiago revealed to him the same spring promised by the devil whereupon he drank to his heart's delight from the apostle's own scallop shell. Well, there is a lesson in this story for me at this stage in the game. I think to myself that it is surely a reminder from Santiago of what a cranky ass I have been all morning. I have failed the test. With every step taken since leaving Pamplona I have denied the simplest tenet of my faith to forget self and love others. I take several big gulps from the Fountain of Denial and take a look down the hill as Javier and Manuel struggle up toward me. I size up the remainder of the route to the top of the *Alto*, then get back on the dirt track myself. I will meet them soon enough at the top and try then to start fresh with them.

In my aloneness on this last stretch before reaching the *Alto*, the image of those small plastic bags filled with human excrement hanging in the trees and along the fences of Pamplona's park comes to mind for a brief few seconds: what a perfect image of all that we human beings do to ourselves! How silly we are! The waste that collects in our hearts in the form of animosity, vengeful feelings, unrighteous anger, cantankerousness; all of it is in itself a normal byproduct of living. Our great stupidity is that we don't just dump it. Foolishly, rather than letting it go, letting it fall away from us so that the earth and wind and sun might quietly turn it into harmless dust, we seal it in bags, let it ferment within us, and even display it proudly for all to see. And the poor world suffers under the burden of so much *merde*, to borrow Jean Luc's perfect word. It is so ridiculous, but it also is so sad because the consequences are so disastrous for life. We are burying our world in our fermenting *merde*. And I contribute my share, witness my grim morning doing interior battle with Javier and Manuel's manner. So I suppose one of the reasons I am now rather painfully climbing to the top of this *Alto del Perdón*, this Mountain of Forgiveness, is to throw to the four winds my own *merde*. May it then go the way of all vanity and become nothing more than dust blowing out over the hills and valleys surrounding us.

Once gaining the summit I find myself surprisingly giddy as I join perhaps ten other pilgrims resting on the mountaintop. I throw off my *mochila*, kick off my boots, pull off my socks and let my feet breathe the fresh and delightful air of that height. I lean back against the stone base of a grand monument that marks the long-gone presence of an old *camino* hospital that once cared for exhausted pilgrims along the way. Others are doing the same, including my American friend, Beth. We exchange pleasantries and I stand in awe before her: the morning's climb seems to have hardly fazed her; she is as cheery as ever with only a hint of sweat about her. A German trekker asks permission to inspect my *bastones* and seems especially intrigued by the shock absorbers built into the handles. I am pleased he is impressed with my tools. I feel like an expert. A few minutes later, he shows me how to properly tie my bootlaces. I feel like a dunce. Perhaps out of spite, I don't pay much attention to his lesson of the laces and continue tying my laces the way my momma taught me.

I meet up here another American, after Beth only the second of my trip thus far. He is an older fellow from Texas, a Mexican-American who looks like the least likely candidate for an exercise like this. He is in his early seventies, a bit overweight, and, worst of all, his shoe and sockless feet look like hamburger. His blisters are massive, covering much of the skin of his feet and they look infected. My own blister looks like a pimple next to his. I strike up a conversation with Robert, a retired engineer. His wife is home worrying about him even though he's traveling with his teenage grandson. Though I feel pity for Robert out here with such raw feet, I also can't help but admire his gumption for having gotten this far at his age and in this kind of condition. After a while Josh, the grandson, appears on the scene and joins in our light conversation. While Grandpa rests and airs his feet, Josh decides to take both their *mochilas* and head down the hill toward Puente la Reina. It doesn't seem like the wisest of decisions to me but they are in agreement and I presume they have learned by now what they can do and cannot do. So Josh heads down the path and disappears beyond the crest of the hill, a double load on his back.

Javier and Manuel pull up to the top and we share water, snacks, and have a laugh or two while we rest with the whoosh-whoosh of the wind machines marking time in a most casual sort of manner. I don't hate them anymore. The *Fuente* and the *Alto* have done their work. I ask forgiveness from God for everything bad I have ever done, then pull the boots back on, tie them up (just like my momma taught me), lug the *mochila* up over my shoulders and with Manuel leading the way, Javier and I follow him down a very steep path to the plain on the Puente la Reina side of the *Sierra del Perdón*.

The early-morning prediction back in Pamplona of a very hot day ahead has indeed come true. It is, as my pop used to say, "hotter than a pistol" out here. Our walk continues nevertheless until the three of us arrive at the village of Obanos, some sixteen kilometers into the day's hike. A prominent sign on the road and notable indications in the tour book carried by Manuel urge all pilgrims to take a two-kilometer detour at this point to visit a small church of great architectural worth. They both are anxious to take the detour and urge me to join them. I demur. I am very hot, very tired, and those two additional kilometers might as well be two million. Manuel almost demands my company. I demur yet again. Manuel shakes his head uncomprehendingly as the two of them head to the right and I stay my less adventuresome course straight ahead. And so for the first time in two days I am gloriously alone.

The delicious solitude of these final kilometers into Puente la Reina and the increasing desire to just get there make me enter another dimension of *camino* reality; I become oblivious to my aches and pains, the heat and fatigue are lost to me. I am transformed into a walking machine. I enter some strange plane of consciousness in which thought and feeling are minimized while the unthinking desire of the body to just move forward takes possession of me. It is almost as if the most base functions of the brainstem have overthrown the much more lofty and reasonable operations of the cerebral cortex. I walk mindlessly, heedless of heat, pain, and exhaustion. I do not stop. I am a gut-driven, four-wheel-drive, *walking machine* that does not regain consciousness until it completes its mission for the day. Some neurological scientists must surely have studied this phenomenon for I am not alone in experiencing it; I have seen others go by with the glazed look in their eyes that is now in mine. It would be interesting to read what those scientists might say about it; all I know is that the repetitive bodily motion of walking, imprinted into one's flesh and bone a million times over, combined with exhaustion and too much heat and maybe a dose of desperation, does something to the brain and the body under its control: I find myself having suddenly clicked into a very low gear; I have become a human Jeep. Weird. Very weird. But effective. I get there. I arrive at my destination, the *refugio* of Puente la Reina. I arrive without having in the end collapsed in a heap as I feared might happen earlier in the day. In spite of everything, I have made it. Hooray. Now to my bed.

So different from the high school gym that housed us last night in Pamplona, the *refugio* of Puente la Reina has been built for just one purpose: to offer a homey and amenity-filled haven for worn-out pilgrims

» *Pilgrim Paella* «

like me. It is blessed with an expansive green yard and a few leafy shade trees to comfort us. The town strikes me as something akin to heaven after the orgiastic commotion of Pamplona. This is a small place, quiet and dotted with medieval churches worthy of attention. A young seminarian stamps my *credencial* and assigns me a bed. I unload my bag and tuck my poles beneath the bed. I head to the showers, then do my laundry in the deep porcelain sink designed just for this task, and finally I collapse atop my soft little bunk. The dozy not-quite-sleep of these clean moments after a long morning of hiking are one of the simple luxuries of the *camino* that a pilgrim grows to cherish and will surely miss once the whole adventure is over. The nap doesn't have to last long, but its pleasure drifts through the whole body leaving it limp and languid and it is just lovely. There is nothing quite like it in the workaday world beyond the *camino*.

Word drifts through the *refugio* that a little later in the day there will be *paella* and wine served in the courtyard of the *Iglesia del Crucifijo* right next door. Now *paella* is a dish not to be ignored, especially by a tired pilgrim. A great mash of rice, peppers, and seafood, it is cooked with plenty of saffron in plenty of olive oil in an oversize wok and is served up piping hot. The gluey, yellow mass fills any hole. The preparatory activity begins in the early afternoon with the arrival of a van and a couple of smaller vehicles. Out step several gents who begin the work of setting up the huge gas-fired wok as the women with them begin preparing the elements that will soon be thrown into its wide-open maw filled with boiling oil. A couple of cases of red wine are set out and before long the party has begun. We are all there; all the people I have been getting to know over three long days of walking: Beth and Jean Luc and soon enough Javier and Manuel trudge in and a number of others I have casually met along the way mill about. Everybody begins chatting with everyone. The *paella* fills our bellies as the wine warms our hearts, making it easy to overcome any residual reticence to introduce ourselves to one another. "Hola. ¿Qué tal? Where are you from? Where'd you start? How's it going so far? Me too." There is no charge for this wok of saffron kindness to a whole *refugio* full of pilgrims. It is a gift from these strangers, pure and simple.

As I am sitting on a curb with a plastic plate of steaming *paella* balanced on my knees and an equally plastic glass of wine in hand conversing with a Dutch lady, Josh, the grandson of Robert, comes over with a concerned look on his face. He asks worriedly if I have seen his grandpa along the way. I report that I haven't seen him since the *Alto del Perdón*. He should have arrived by now. We ask a few recent arrivals if they have seen Robert. One says that he had seen him some distance back, perhaps an hour and a half ago, resting on the porch of an old house but nothing more recent comes up. I get up off my haunches and approach one of the cooks explaining the situation to him. Without a moment of hesitation, he drops all that he is doing, grabs Josh, and in his vehicle the two of them head back down the road to look for the old fellow. I am learning something here about the *camino*: an expansive generosity and spontaneous kindness has been woven into this way that begins to touch us all, making us more caring ourselves and then more trusting. Step by step we are walking out of our fear. We are learning that it is easier to care than to not care. We are being softened even as our feet are being toughened.

Considerable time passes before Josh and the cook and old Robert come back to the *refugio* and our worst fears are alleviated. Nevertheless, the man doesn't look well and he is taken to a local doctor who without charge (again!) treats pilgrims for whatever ails them. When he returns to us Robert's feet are wrapped in pure white gauze and the doctor has ordered him to rest his feet by taking at least a couple days off from further walking.

While hanging around waiting for Josh and company to return, the Dutch lady I have been chatting with on the curb gives me wise advice about doing a better job of tending to my blister and even more, how to look at the rest of the *camino*. She is something of an expert in both areas since she has walked to this spot from her home in Rotterdam. She is the first *real* pilgrim I have thus far met along the way; not one like me who has taken a convenient train across half of Europe to get to my starting point, but a *real pilgrim*: one who has actually put on her boots, hefted her *mochila* onto her back, and stepped out the front door of her own home to walk *all the way* to Santiago. She has been on the road already for months. Now the kilometers between Rotterdam and Puente la Reina can surely be counted by a person with a good map and some handy tools. Perhaps now with a quick search on the Internet the exact figure can be discovered, but the number of kilometers is not nearly so important to me at this moment as the sheer gumption involved in attempting such a thing. To walk across a fair chunk of the Netherlands, across Belgium, across all of France, up and over the Pyrenees, and finally across Navarra to this little town, with more than seven hundred kilometers to go before landing in Compostela: that in my book constitutes the virtue of gumption in pristine form. Her "trick," she advises me, is twofold: First, don't look at maps of the *camino*, especially of what lies ahead, or you will discourage yourself by the impossibility of it all; instead simply take it a day at a time. Second, listen to your body and rest when you need to rest. Don't push it. Take Sundays off.

Concerning my yelping blister, she advises a fair dose of sunshine and of course fresh air so that it can dry out and heal itself. Ditch the silicone patch; that just keeps it soggy and sore. Sunlight is always the best medicine . . . and rest. Take tomorrow off, she encourages me; it is a Sunday.

I have no reason not to attend to her wise advice since she has an expertise in these matters gained from having hoofed it across a fair chunk of Europe; under her influence I decide to take the morrow off, rest up, expose the blister to plenty of sunshine and fulfill my religious responsibilities all in one quiet Sunday spent in this lovely town. A side benefit will be that I can then legitimately part from Manuel and Javier without any pangs of conscience; they will move on and I will stay behind. It will be almost impossible to catch up to them again. I'll be starting over with a fresh wave of pilgrims on Monday morning. With the decision made, I take to my bed for an hour of quiet and calm.

Javier and Manuel present me with an invitation to go out for a beer, so I put on my sandals and hobble with them down the *Calle Mayor*, the main street, to a noisy bar. Once seated comfortably around a small round table with three substantial beers among us, I tell them of my decision to hold back a day, wincing for emphasis at mention of my blistered foot. They take the news of the imminent break-up of our happy trio with a couple of discouraged looks but graciously accept the wisdom of it. Actually, I am feeling a bit like a piker in the matter, but what is decided is decided. I leave them to their second round of beer and limp off by myself to catch the Saturday evening Mass at the *Iglesia de Santiago*, located about halfway down the *Calle Mayor*. I take a seat inside its cavernous interior and enjoy its dark coolness for the few minutes before the eight o'clock evening Mass is to begin. I am pleasantly surprised when Javier quietly joins me on the old oak pew; we share a silent nod of mutual acknowledgment. I feel rather close to him now and a bit sad in

» July 12 and 13: Pamplona to Puente la Reina «

45

knowing that we will be going our separate ways in the morning. On the other hand, I also feel a breeze of relief at the prospect of a new beginning and the restoration of some protected time and space for myself in the days to come. Actually, I *need* that time and space. In the two days that the three of us have been walking together, I know, at the bottom of my petty annoyance with the two of them is a not-so-petty pull to walk not just *by* myself but *with* myself. I need solitude, not absolute solitude but just enough to blow the carbon out of my carburetor, to use another expression from my old man. I need to meet myself again, to pray for the people I promised to pray for, to get to know Jesus, pilgrim to pilgrim. So with that, the two of us shake hands at the sign of peace. The Mass ends and we leave church as friends.

Thus with a belly full of *paella*, several glasses of wine, a beer under my belt, and Holy Communion happily received, I wander back to the *refugio*, find a spot on the green lawn, carefully work loose and pull back millimeter by millimeter the very sticky Compeed patch from my blister, then enjoy the last of the day with my tender wound relishing the fresh air of evening until about ten o'clock, when I decide to tuck myself in for the night.

A few others have settled themselves into bed ahead of me and still others follow behind me, quietly preparing their things for the morning, then crawling into their sleeping bags themselves. Before I have fallen asleep, a man wearing shiny, skin-tight cycling togs comes into the room, turns on the bright overhead lights and begins preparing his clothing for the following day, deliberately folding each piece, even his shorts, and stacking them for efficient packing. He uses the toilet, returns, and repacks his bag a second time. He puts on his pajamas, then crawls into bed directly above me in such a way as to shake the bunk like a seven-pointer on the Richter scale. Now here is the zinger: the idiot does not turn off the lights he turned on twenty minutes earlier. I am amazed at this rather brazen breach of our still fragile *camino* ethic. So I say to him from below, "Would you like me to turn off the lights for you?" He says simply and without any note of shame, "Yes." So I get out of bed, waddle to the light-switch like a duck so as to keep my unprotected blister off of the dirty floor and turn off the lights on his behalf. No word of thanks comes from the man. He is already snoring. I hate him for a moment but let it go, for the healing comfort of sleep is far more important to me now than the gnawing aggravation that is hate.

» *Pilgrim Paella* «

46

I awake at five in the morning as others are already making their preparations for the day's hike to Estella, another nineteen kilometers further on. I have no reason to get out of bed since I'm not going anywhere today; there is nothing to do but lie here and watch all my friends from the road leave me behind. I feel a remorse that I did not expect. These folks, after all, have been my companions along the way: we have passed one another on the road with cheery *buen caminos*, we have washed clothes together, commiserated over feet issues together, consumed a mighty fine *paella* together, and all shared from the same bottle of wine together. I want to go with them. I don't feel up to the task of beginning again the process of coming to know a whole new bunch of *camino* acquaintances. But the gentle Dutch lady's advice comes back to me: "Listen to your body. Rest when you need to rest. Take Sundays off." Thus I stay behind, and though I can't fall back to sleep I put off getting out of bed as long as I possibly can. When I do get up, the bicyclist from the night before, the one who didn't turn off the overhead lights, points to my small pile of earthly possessions gathered around my bunk and asks me if I really need those sandals and would I not like to give them to him. He has to be kidding. He is not kidding. This guy *is* an idiot. I say no as coldly as I can and hope to never see him again in my life here on this good earth.

Robert and Josh are also staying behind, and so we take up as companions for the day. Robert has planted himself, his feet wrapped in gauzy bandages, out on the front porch of the *refugio* where I join him and we kill some time chatting about bits and pieces of our ordinary lives. I eventually take my leave and wander across the small plaza to the *Iglesia del Crucifijo* to see what I might find inside. It is a lovely place, consisting of husky Romanesque arches, domes crafted of perfectly fitted stones, each one holding the other in place, and then as if intended to be the perfect finishing touch, small round-arched windows set deeply in the walls, each one fitted with a single alabaster pane which casts a soft golden light into the dim space. After a brief wander through the interior gazing at its ancient features, I slide into one of its simple wood plank pews to gaze more seriously at one particular feature of the church: a large crucifix that has its origins in Germany. The cross is unusual to my eye, for its crossbeam extends upward in a radical "V" shape, forcing the arms of Christ's otherwise sinking body upward in an almost impossible reach towards the sky. Since I am going nowhere today I have all the time in the world to contemplate this unsettling scene. The crucifix is an image as familiar to me as my own hand; most of the time I hardly pay attention to it. But this one catches me off-guard; it disturbs. The way the feet cross at the bottom and the gashes in those feet left by the nails are wrenching. Those arms of Jesus stretching achingly upward seem to be grasping at heaven yet the gravity of earth seems even stronger as it pulls him down into its dusty crust. The utter earthiness of the image and the physicality of this dying body pull me out of myself. In him I see myself as I don't think I have ever seen myself before. His wounded feet take into themselves my blistered ones. The heaviness of his body being pulled down, down, down is an image of the daily weight of the *mochila* on my back which bends me over and turns me into an old man whose gaze is now almost permanently locked into a downward cast as he walks. His utter aloneness echoes the emptiness I am feeling this morning as I straddle this strange stoop between my friends who have moved on and the new wave of still unknown pilgrims who will sweep into this town a few hours from now. He and I, we are in this together.

This *camino* is the most utterly physical thing I have ever done; it has put me into a new relationship to my feet and to the earth upon which they are treading. This earth is dirty, rocky, slippery, brambly, and even with all that, it is lovely. There is something in it that is more than dirt and rocks and brambles. It is too lovely to be stupid. And these feet about which I have complained so much to myself and to so many of my *camino* friends, here they are, working, barely, but working nevertheless. I love them for putting up with me and carrying me forward. And this crucifix that makes me know who I am and what I am doing here: it breathes as I breathe. I have a sense of being accompanied in all this. No more than that: just accompanied. Accompanied by the good earth, by my feet, by the icon of Jesus up there. I get up from my seat, waddle up into the sanctuary, go behind the altar and kiss those feet.

I wander out and find almost by accident a small parish church a little bit off the tourist track that is no showpiece but a real parish with ordinary locals filing towards it purposefully. I file in with them and am given a small booklet with the texts of the Mass in Euskara, the Basque language. The people are a mix of young and old; they are animated and welcoming. I'm staying for this one. The ceiling above the sanctuary is scalloped like a shell, making it reminiscent of Santiago's trademark conch. A

» *Pilgrim Paella* «

48

gentlemanly priest enters the sanctuary from a sacristy door and begins the usual Roman liturgy in the usual way, except that the language is something I've never heard before. There is not a word in it that is recognizable, but the ritual gestures and the flow of the liturgy allow me to feel really quite at home. The hymns that dot the prayer do their part too; I join the community in song. Happily, the melodies are easy to follow and I do my best to pronounce phonetically the written words from the small hymnbook that was handed me as I entered. In a provisional way I feel as though I belong to this Basque country. For a moment, it seems to me that I and the happy people surrounding me in this church are all of a piece. Communion is what I feel here. Communion it is.

After Mass in Euskara, I wander back towards the *refugio* but stop in for a second time at the Church of Santiago on the *Calle Mayor* of Puente la Reina. I take some time sizing up a statue of the church's patron, Santiago himself, and decide I like its sturdiness as well as the fact that to my eye he is beginning to look less and less like a figure out of another age and more and more like me; or I am beginning to look more and more like him. I ask him to get me down the road tomorrow. I then surprise myself and kiss his feet too. This is becoming a habit. It feels right and just to reverence these feet so.

I meander into the town's central plaza where the only thing open on this Sunday morning is the local tourist office. I finally buy myself a guidebook. I choose the more traditional one by Millán Bravo Lozano.[1] Finally, I find a bar equipped with e-mail and after paying a euro or two send out to a number of friends and family my first electronic report from the road. Among many other things I write:

> One thing I notice out here is that everyone is equal: language, nationalities, and cultural differences seem to disappear or at least recede in importance as we all go through the same experience day after day. Everybody is in this together yet everyone is really doing it alone and is experiencing it alone. It has its effect on us, I think. The *camino* is doing something to us interiorly but we don't know exactly what — we sense it — but can't put our finger on it yet.

1. Millán Bravo Lozano, *A Practical Guide for Pilgrims: The Road to Santiago* (León: Editorial Everest, S.A., 1993).

» *July 12 and 13: Pamplona to Puente la Reina* «

There is so little to do this day that I hobble back towards the *refugio* but stop once again at the *Iglesia del Crucifijo* to see if I can feel again what I felt earlier in the morning in this great old church. Well, it isn't the same, of course; that seldom happens in life. But something slightly different is waiting for me here on this second visit into the crucified one's world: this *camino* is already more than a road for me. It is a way. It is his way. I'm on it with him. In spite of so many indications to the contrary, when all is said and done, I realize now, I actually like this way. It is simple and true and, I now know, it is a way that can only be understood by walking along a road such as this *camino*, walking as he walked, gazing at rising suns, passing through sunflower fields, tending to aching feet, eating and drinking with strangers, one step at a time but a million steps all in all. Steps that get me there.

Once I am back at the *refugio*, the new crew of pilgrims is already arriving and settling in, sweaty and exhausted and complete strangers. I know not a one of them. I feel a certain regret that my old pals are now an uncatchable day ahead of me and I now must start over with the social part of the *camino*; a new beginning but no less sad for it. I size the newcomers up, and feel odd in their presence, aware as I am that I am clean and rested while they, with their sweat-drenched clothes, drawn faces and limping gaits, are the very image of the weary pilgrim.

There is a Brazilian fellow about my age wearing a very tight sky blue t-shirt with handwritten messages inscribed on it in heavy magic marker; the messages make it clear that he is happily gay. A tall slender man with scruffy beard accompanied by a pretty lady dressed in a red and white checkered blouse, like a tablecloth, come in together and offer each other a slight kiss. A stocky young fellow wearing a real hiker's shirt with lots of pockets and snaps and matching shorts swoops in, barely sweating; his accent gives him away as British. A couple of young girls, one with a blond pony tail, the other with hair cut short, pass by and greet someone else with an Australian "G'day!" Two French Canadians, one young and muscular, the other scrawny and considerably older, settle into their new bunks. They come in ones and twos and before long the newcomers fill the place. Many have already made friends among themselves and I feel all the more like an outsider among them. I take refuge in my one established relationship: that with old Robert and young Josh. We dither away the afternoon and evening and before long, once again, it is time for bed.

» *Pilgrim Paella* «

Hospitality Is Everything

July 14: Puente la Reina to Estella

At five A.M. I am awake; I blink open my eyes and take a few moments to orient myself and take stock of my body's condition: feet, legs, and back seem strong this morning. Good. I get up, use the bathroom, put on my boots, swill down a yogurt from its plastic pot, tighten up my pack, and by five forty-five I am out the door and completely alone. I head down the *Calle Mayor* toward the ancient bridge that gives the town its name, cross it, then look back just long enough to appreciate for a moment the graceful form of this medieval structure illuminated at this early hour with massive lights. I nod a heartfelt *adios* to the little town behind it, the town now famous to me as the place where my first blister healed. God bless you, Puente la Reina! No dust to shake from these feet as I leave you behind! The solitude and silence of this cool morning departure is like heaven. I pull my tangled rosary out of a pocket, tug at its knots for a moment, then begin my morning pilgrim prayer: Hail Mary . . . Hail Mary . . . Hail Mary . . .

I can hardly believe it, but I am really walking well now and I'm fast and I've got rhythm and it's in my whole body: Click clack foot step, click clack foot step, click clack foot step. My hiking poles are now part of me. For the first time on this road, my back doesn't ache, my feet don't hurt, and my blister is almost forgotten. I even find myself passing some pilgrims who had gotten out the door earlier than I. This is unheard of! The *buen camino* greetings we share are particularly happy ones for me as I pass by these pilgrims with a smile and a wave. Our few words of greeting are absorbed into the silence of the still-dark morning. The moon hanging above my left shoulder is a great yellow globe, the soft light of which allows me to see the roadway ahead with only the slightest strain. The moon is my *flecha amarilla* this morning. I am getting stranger, even to myself, for I greet this moon and thank it for showing me the way on this fine morning and then in a wild jump of imagination and without any forethought, I see it as my father, my long-dead Pop, who was not the best father in history but a good father nevertheless. With limited emotional resources he did his best to raise his eleven children. We never suffered any memorable want in our childhood; to the contrary, his hard work put something on the table every day of our lives. His moods and temper got the best of him much too often, but he could not help that really. At his death, I forgave him his faults and I hope, I trust, that after his death he also forgave me mine. From his position above my left shoulder, he silently cheers me on and assures me of the rightness of my way. I say then to the moon, "I love you, Pop." The dark of the night is ever so slightly making way for morning and my moon, my father, finally sets behind a distant hill; for a brief moment the silhouettes of pine trees are magnificent against its subtle light coming from behind them. This is Pop's answer: "I love you too, Kev." I am really happy. Hail Mary . . . Hail Mary . . . Hail Mary . . . click clack . . . foot step . . .

Day takes possession of the way ever so smoothly. The low sky over the eastern horizon begins to glow, it is touched then by a hint of rose which in just a few moments almost unnoticeably grows into full pink which then transforms itself into an aureole of orange, and finally, just before the leading edge of the sun itself rises out of its nocturnal hiding place, great rays of white transparent light shoot up into the sky like spotlights. It is very much like the image schoolchildren draw with crayons when teacher asks them what a sunrise looks like, only, with all due respect to child artists everywhere, this is better, a lot better, infinitely better. It doesn't take my breath away exactly, it just stops me and I have to look at it because I know that in a minute or less these ascending rays will be gone and they are too beautiful not to behold. This is like new love. You just have to behold it. Well, I suppose it *is* love. For a grand moment I love the earth and the sun and the whole big-banged universe from the smallest quark to the grandest galaxy. Then the vision is gone and the leading edge of daylight creeps quickly across the landscape, touching the western heights first and then spreading eastward across the lowlands as the sun gently rises and this too is sublime to behold. Day catches up to me too and I can feel the sudden warmth of its blanket of light. Hail Mary . . . click clack . . . foot step . . .

I hit a very rough patch of road that climbs up over a steep hillside. Actually, the way is not much more than a washout with boulders and rocks to be clambered over or around as I go up, up, up. But today I am strong and I am mighty and I don't hurt so I climb that gully like a billy goat. I catch up to a young guy who is struggling but he's got a tremendous smile as he wishes me a *buen camino*; I pass him by but as I look down on him from a little higher up the trail I notice that his smile has disappeared into an aching frown.

After passing through the hilltop town of Cirauqui, which is still very much asleep and where a broken rubber stamp and dry ink pad have been thoughtfully left outside the door of the small city hall for passing pilgrims so that they might give to themselves their *sello*, the *camino* goes back downhill but does so following an original Roman roadway. Now this is not just where a Roman road used to be many centuries ago. It is the actual thing, its worn paving stones still in place after all these centuries; then I cross over an original Roman bridge to complete the experience. The feeling of being accompanied that I had the day before in the Church of the Crucifix comes back again, but this time in a different way. The hard work of the morning is making my imagination take flights of fancy and I can almost hear the footfalls of the hundreds of thousands of pilgrims from times gone by shuffling in time with my own footfalls. They are with me. There is a duke to my left, a cobbler to my right (a good man to know out here!), and a priest wrapped in a threadbare cassock just in front of me. A dry crust of bread is passed from the duke to the cobbler to me to the priest and we each take our bite. The priest pulls out a skin of cheap wine from under his moth-eaten cassock and passes it back to me for a swig, then I pass it to the duke who passes it to the cobbler who passes it back to the priest. Such is our way. I am grateful to be walking with them across this old stone road. Dirty, bearded, sweaty, suffering far more than I, they are my pals for this moment. What a motley bunch they are, sinners all of them yet saints too in their own way, at least most of them. Thank you for welcoming me to your rough company, boys. I'm grateful to be walking with you. Do I stink as bad as you? I laugh to myself and keep on walking.

The final hour into Estella is no easy walk. The heat is building by the minute and surely the temp is well up into the thirties by the time I draw close to my day's goal. I drink water like crazy to keep hydrated and move to whatever side of the road offers some hint of shade. Even with the heat of this last hour, I feel great. I amble into Estella at about noon, find the *refugio* closed until one P.M., and so gladly plop my *mochila* and myself down on the stone sidewalk in front of the place. There are four or five other pilgrims here already. After a few moments of rest, I get back up on my haunches and, leaving my *mochila* in their care, hobble stiffly further down the street to a nearby market. I buy a nectarine and some grapes and as I return to the *refugio* I cannot resist the temptation tendered me by my nectarine so I bite into its skin with gusto and cannot help but let out an audible "Ahhhhh!" as its juicy flesh fills my mouth. The scrawny Canadian I met the night before enjoys my enjoyment, so I say to him, "Tastes like heaven!" He laughs. I have had enough of solitude for one day so introduce myself to Guy and make a new friend.

Estella is a town that easily engages the eye, with medieval touches abounding all around, and the folks that I meet in the shops and on the street are altogether kind and welcoming to this particular day's wave of pilgrims, but the *refugio* is something else. It is shiny and clean and modern and altogether beautiful. The floors and staircases are made of polished stone; the bunks are almost new and have no sway in their mattresses (and what a blessing that is after a long day on the road!). The toilets and showers are as clean as clean can be. The town put a lot of money into this place for us. All the greater the tragedy that the *hospitalero* who opens the door at exactly one P.M. ruins it all. The problem begins with the very opening of that front door. By chance I am the first one in and cheerily greet the fellow. He doesn't respond but directs me to the makeshift desk on the other side of the lobby, where he takes a seat for business. I make my way to the desk while the young man prepares his rubber stamp, inkpad, money-box, and sign-in sheets. I pull out my *credencial* and greet him again. He does not look up from his desktop. He takes my *credencial*, stamps it, takes my three or four euros, then waves me on up the stairs towards the dormitory. Just as I turn to head up the polished stone staircase past a substantial statue of Santiago, I am startled by this same *hospitalero's* sharp voice demanding to know who is responsible for spilling almonds all over his clean floor. Don't we know that he has just washed this floor? I turn back around and sure enough a few stray almonds are strewn here and there below me, then I hear a few more fall to the ground, and *then* I realize that the offending nuts are falling from my own *mochila's* rear pocket. I tucked them in there earlier in the day but obviously the small plastic bag has split a seam. I hurriedly begin picking them up off the floor, this with my pack still on my back and my *bastones* tucked under one arm. As I do so, yet more nuts fall to the ground and I feel for just a moment like a minor-league Sisyphus struggling with one of those awful tasks that can never be completed. No matter how many I pick up, more fall out. Moreover, all this is taking place in a small space congested with a raft of tuckered pilgrims. I take off my *mochila*, set down the poles to do the job right, and in a jiff I scoop up most of the almonds off the otherwise squeaky-clean floor. The fellow gives me a pathetic look. I take my equipment and head upstairs to my bunk, led on by a much kinder *hospitalero* than the one manning the desk.

By day's end, other pilgrims have found themselves similarly treated, ordered about, given injunctions about where and how they should behave, and told what they can do and not do on the premises, all in a tone of voice that is not what any of us have grown accustomed to in our previous *refugios*. I hear others say that this *refugio* is pretty but one of the worst places they have stayed so far — and this because of one inhospitable *hospitalero* who cares more for the pretty stone floor of that building than for the people for whom it was so kindly built. What is also true is that we are slowly but surely becoming real pilgrims while hardly noticing the transformation; this is the sign: none of us care that much about the marble floors and firm mattresses of this *refugio*. After five or six days on the road, what we care about is care. Hospitality counts for everything; appearances for nothing. I hope I can hold onto this obvious life lesson once I return to the big world where shine and newness so often trump humility and kindness.

I am learning another curious lesson: the process of coming to know people on the *camino* begins as a matter of chance but always ends feeling much more like a matter of design. At first, like those hours in Puente la

» *July 14: Puente la Reina to Estella* «

55

Reina when the new pilgrims began arriving on my second day there, there is just a crowd, and anonymity reigns. Then I begin noticing certain people within the crowd. There is a randomness about this: a particular voice or smile or manner of shrugging a shoulder catches my eye. Then somewhere down the road or at some odd moment in *refugio* life, a nod or a simple word is shared, then a name, then a bit of food, then before I know it I have made a friend and all his or her friends become my friends as well. It is then not long before I feel that our lives were *meant* to touch and intertwine and enrich one another.

I have already met Guy but other than this one friend, on this hot afternoon in Estella I am adrift in new faces and voices and body smells: none of them with names or personal histories accessible to me . . . *yet*. As we settle in, do our laundry, share the showers, quietly greet one another, I begin to see people and remember that I noticed them the night before in Puente la Reina when they were not yet so very distinguishable one from another. I remember some as having passed me on the road a few hours earlier. One lady talks loudly with a singsong accent and has very thick black hair and a slightly indigenous quality in her face, probably a Latin American. Ahead of me in the queue for the shower is the young guy I passed scrambling up that gully in the second hour of today's hike; he's smiling again and has lots of friends with whom he happily chats. The two twenty-something Australian girls are tending to one another's feet as they rest on a lower bunk next to my own. The mob slowly forms itself into a community.

While washing the day's dirty clothing in a patio basin, I introduce myself to the guy with the smile who is doing his laundry at the basin next to my own. His name is Fermín. He is from Patagonia in Argentina. He came to Spain just last week with the intention of running with the bulls in Pamplona, fulfilling a life-long desire to join in the bash celebrating the memory of his patron saint. He tells me that he first heard about the *camino* only after he arrived in Pamplona and immediately decided on the spot to walk. He had to do it. No other reason. Fermín is friends with Alfredo, the tall guy with the delicate woman friend who dresses in white accented with red-check tablecloth material; she is Lola. They too are Argentinean. I don't really get to know Alfredo or his lady friend, but at least I know *who* they are. They have names now. I say hello to the Aussies and they laugh and say hello back; I give them my name and they tell me that they are Kylie and Anne, and that is that for the time being. The Latin American is Lucía María. An older French gentleman, much older than I, with badly beaten feet, is a couple of beds over. He speaks only French so seems a bit alone in the midst of the rest of us with our dominating Spanish and English. He wears lightweight nylon running shorts and tank-top which seem out of place on a man his age, but maybe clothes like his are the way to go and it is the rest of us who are missing the comfort boat with our much more serious hikers' gear. For the second night in a row I notice a young Spanish girl and her boyfriend who juggle together. They toss colored balls high above their heads in wonderfully repetitious arcs. She in particular smiles and laughs as she does so. Her long, straight hair swings across her back as her whole body keeps the rhythm of the game. It is wonderful to behold and I am not alone, for a gang of kids from town gather to watch them as they perform on the stone street in front of our building. With each passing day, all of us strangers enter more and more into each other's world. At some point, no one knows when or where, after conversations are had, jokes are shared, food is divided, we realize we have become *camino* friends. It is a singularly subtle and wonderful thing. The juggler's name is Eva.

There is too much noise in the crowded *refugio* to relax, so before settling in for the night, I take a walk through town. I find a nice plaza in front of a large church where young people dressed in medieval clothing disembark from a horse-drawn wagon and begin playing drums and flutes and dance. Several centuries roll back in an instant. It might as well be the 1500s as the 2000s. I enjoy watching them for a while, then climb the steep staircase to enter the church for the evening Mass. The church is that of San Miguel, a fundamentally Romanesque affair but with plenty of baroque clutter shoved uncomfortably into its dark interior. While an old couple begins loudly reciting the prayers of the rosary, a young priest slips into a wooden confessional. One old lady takes a lot of time with him while I debate whether to go to him myself. Time runs out for a decision as he slips out of his box just as quietly as he slipped in. Through the door of the sacristy I can see him vest himself in the white undergarment of the priest, the alb, a green stole placed over his shoulders with both ends hanging down in front as a symbol of his ministry as a priest and the old Roman overcoat, the chasuble, laid over the top of everything as the final preparation for Mass. He solemnly enters the side

» *July 14: Puente la Reina to Estella* «

57

chapel and the liturgy begins. I take my place among the old-timers. For a while, I don't know what to think of this young priest. His "style" in the liturgy is quite formal and stiff and his voice wavers with nervousness. On the other hand he seems brimming with sincerity and a desire to do well. In his little homily after the Scripture readings he shares his name and explains that he is temporarily pitching in for the pastor. Even more importantly he reveals to us that he was ordained just last week. Now I understand! I remember now the novice priest's nervousness and sincerity and desire to do well all rolled into one from my own first days. He asks all of us for our prayers as he begins his life as a priest of the church. After the Mass ends, I step into the sacristy to greet him, priest to priest. I introduce myself and explain that I too am a priest. As we shake hands, I promise that I will pray for him in my next day's walk. I also ask him to pray for me while on this road to Santiago. He assures me that he will and we part with a handshake and a slight embrace. Oh, if I could start my life as a priest over knowing what I know now! What mistakes I would avoid! I cringe at the memory of some of my worst failures. I should have gone to confession to him after all.

I go home, read my psalms, and pack my bag for the morrow, a process at which I am becoming a pro: fill camelback water bag first, double-check screw-top for tightness, wrap in sports towel in case of leak, stuff whole in special pocket, run tube through the right-hand shoulder strap, fill rest of pack with Leatherman, Swiss Army knife, glasses, journal, prayer book, then stuff clothing into all remaining space. Done. Now I am ready for a good night's sleep and a quick six A.M. start. A very substantial electric storm rolls over the town and presents a ferocious light and sound show as I crawl into bed and settle down for sleep. Storm or no storm, tomorrow I march on Los Arcos.

The Eighth Day

July 15: Estella to Torres del Rio

A new record: I am out the door of the *refugio* at five thirty A.M. I am proud of myself, but this doesn't make finding my way out of town in the dark any easier. I miss a *flecha* or two and so wander a bit before getting back on track in this still-sleeping town. The air is clear and cool; the storm from the night before has dampened everything. Though there is the delicious peace of the early morning to cheer me, even from these first steps I can tell that this is not going to be a day like the one I enjoyed yesterday. No flying today. I must have worked too hard then, for today I am very low on energy. Along the way I take up with Anne and Kylie, the two Australian girls, and enjoy a bit of chatter with them before they divert for an early coffee while I choose to push on. I now have two full hours of almost complete aloneness, but they are hours that are becoming increasingly uncomfortable. The weight of the *mochila* begins to annoy me and in particular a nerve on the left side of my back, just atop my shoulder blade, begins to zing. Yet I remain motivated and so I keep walking even as the heat of the day rises. Some three hours into the day's walk, I find a very substantial haystack in whose shade I can take a brief nap. I drop the pack to the ground, lay it sideways against the base of the hay bales, and then lie down on the loose and still slightly moist hay strewn about on the ground around the entire base of the stack. The softness of the hay beneath me is in itself a refreshment. So this is why Jesus was born in a hay-filled crib! I eke the maximum pleasure out of the moment by untying my boots and taking off my socks to let my feet and toes have a breath of fresh air as well. They rejoice.

While I'm reclining against the haystack, only one or two pilgrims pass by, but I go unnoticed to them as I rest in my open-air stable. Finally, the young French Canadian, Guy's pal, bounds by at breakneck speed. I mean really *breakneck* speed, for this fellow is actually running down the road with his *mochila* bouncing up and down in time to his running gait. I can't believe what I am seeing and wonder how long this can last; it must surely be getting close to thirty degrees out here by now. This young man has a problem with hubris, which is just not a good thing out here; this road sooner or later will humble him. Woe to you vain; for the *camino* shall take you down more than a few notches. And then he is gone. I drink and nibble on my remaining almonds and then close my eyes. I doze for ten or fifteen minutes, restore my feet to their Coolmax inners and leather outers, stretch, then pick up my bag and poles and get back on the road.

There is not a lot to look at as I hike this day. Wheat fields extend from the road to either horizon; they have already had their crew cuts for the summer and so are not very interesting. There are occasional vineyards as well; the grapes hanging from the vines are still small, hard, and green. I suppose it would only be a priest who would consider the thought that now arises within me: what small portion of the wheat that only a few days ago waved in the breeze in these very fields might make it into one of the hosts we use at Mass? Will one or two of these grapes eventually end up in someone's chalice? These are pointless questions, certainly, but they show where a mind like mine sometimes wanders when it has little else to chew on. I imagine the face of the newly minted priest I met the evening before in the Church of San Miguel; I hope he is in the end a happy man. Not that he never suffers, but that *in the end* he will say that it has all been worth it. By the end of his days, may he have kissed Jesus' feet at least a few times. May he find as he holds those small hosts of wheat in his hands and peers down into the wine-filled cup *real* blood and *real* flesh. May he see the flesh and blood of Jesus, yes, but also the flesh and blood of all of us in our confused conditions and ambiguous situations, living as we all do with one foot on the earth and another somewhere amidst the stars of heaven. Yes, may he come to know that flesh and blood as his own flesh and blood in all of its grace and agony. I remember as I walk through these fields the first time and maybe the only time that I looked into that cup and saw, *really saw*, what it held; it was the morning that several Jesuit priests were hacked to death in El Salvador by a right-wing death squad under orders from the country's top general and soon-to-be president. I knew of one of those priests by name from one of his books, and even more, I had worked in nearby Guatemala for a year, so I knew many priests in Central America like them and indeed had tasted a bit of what it is like to live in a place overrun with government-sponsored murderers. When I awoke to the news of their brutal death on the radio that grim morning I felt the sadness and horror of their ends very personally, as if they were my own co-workers and friends. An hour later, I was at the altar in our parish church leading my people in our best and deepest prayer and there it was, right in front of me: their blood, the blood of so many victims of other human beings' aggression, my blood, in the end, the blood of Jesus. There it was. What more can I say? Amen. In the end, in the end, yes, in the end, may that freshly hatched priest of San Miguel *see* and *know* this at least once in his life. That is my prayer for him today.

I walk on in the oppressive heat. These memories and prayers move into the present and it dawns on me that life on this road is remarkably free of humanity's propensity towards aggression. To the contrary, I am so grateful that even after only this first week out here, I have experienced extraordinary concord among my pilgrim colleagues. Whatever aggressiveness there may be in us seems to be focused on overcoming the trials of the road, not on one another. Maybe our contemporary cultures just don't make us walk enough. These are just random thoughts as I pass through these shaved fields of wheat and an occasional vineyard of still-green grapes. Will any of this fruit of the earth surrounding me now make it into my chalice or onto my paten one day? It is pleasant to think it might be so.

As the morning wears on I am being passed by the younger pilgrims quite regularly. I'm slowing down and back to my old self again. Even the senior Frenchman in the running shorts briskly overtakes me and that is a bit harder for my ego to take.

Just before entering the town of Villamayor de Monjardín, I and a couple of other pilgrims pass a remarkable *fuente*. In a land filled with drinking fountains, this fountain is like no other. Called the *Fuente de los Moros*, it is not just a fountain but an *edifice* with a double-arched entrance, barrel-vaulted ceiling, and a large cistern of black water sitting completely still at the bottom of a wide set of stairs that span the length of the building's face. I have read up on the *fuente* in my small guidebook and so have the privilege of briefly explaining it to the two other pilgrims who join me at its steps. I enjoy being their tour guide for a moment. In a small way, this fountain is a reminder of the very complex history of the Iberian Peninsula and the bellicose pushing and shoving between Muslims and Christians that transpired on this land for so many centuries. The Christians eventually won out under the leadership of Isabella and Ferdinand (of Christopher Columbus fame), but not without lots of blood on both sides being shed. I wonder if any of that old blood made it into the vine branches and stalks of wheat growing about me and from there onto some priest's paten and into his chalice? I stop for a *café con leche* and ponder for a moment such mysteries as these over the rich brown liquid laced with sugar and cream that is now a staple of life every morning along the way. A slice of Spanish *tortilla* (the egg and potato omelet served like a pie) accompanies my coffee and it all goes a long way to restore my strength to take on the road ahead.

From Villamayor de Monjardín there are no more villages or towns until Los Arcos, so my morning coffee and *tortilla* serve me well as I push on. I walk first down a paved road and then soon enough I'm onto a farm road that leads me along the remaining twelve kilometers to Los Arcos. About halfway down that dirt road I am overtaken by a young couple who, after a kindly *buen camino*, continue on their way. After a few turns in the road, I come upon them again, he standing idly in the road and she barely tucked in behind some bushes off to the side taking care of nature's call. A second pass in such a short time on such an isolated road calls for more than a simple *buen camino*, so I go a social step further and offer as well a friendly *¿Qué tal?* "How are you doing?" And so it is that I meet Javier, a young executive from Madrid, and Isabel, an elementary school teacher from France. After she returns to the road well relieved, we continue walking together and I am glad for the company after walking by myself for the better part of two days. After a couple of hours of pleasant companionship along the way, we approach my destination for the day:

» *The Eighth Day* «

Edmonton Public Library
Mill Woods
Express Check #1

Customer ID: ************3091**

Items that you checked out

Title:
 Slaves of obsession : a William Monk
 novel
ID: 31221097718683
Due: July-09-18

Total items: 1
Account balance: $2.25
June-18-18
Checked out: 7
Overdue: 0
Hold requests: 0
Ready for pickup: 0

Thank you for visiting the Edmonton
Public Library

www.epl.ca

Los Arcos. Javier advises me that the two of them are going to continue on another eight kilometers to a small village noted for its warm and cozy *refugio*; and the extra kilometers will also set them up for a push ahead that would cut a day or two out of the usual pilgrim itinerary. I am invited along. I make no commitment since there are two conflicting issues here: on the one hand the eight kilometers is something to consider since at my pace that means another two hours of hiking, most of it probably in the open sun, and it is already almost noon. On the other hand, these are really nice people and we have become rather friendly and I am interested in hanging on to their good company at least for a bit longer. Once we find the *refugio* in Los Arcos, my mind is made up. This *refugio* seems from the outside to be another school gym set up as a bunkhouse for the summer. I have a bit of a rest in the schoolyard, enjoy a bite to eat, restock my water supply, and with Javier and Isabel, I take a bye on Los Arcos. We are joined by Ana, a compact and cheery Basque girl, so together we walk on to our new goal for the day: little Torres del Rio.

The heat of the afternoon is more oppressive than I expected; it is pounding me down and these additional eight small kilometers turn into eight very big kilometers. Even worse, the extra wear and tear on my feet is making my old blister hot again. My stride becomes far more labored. Ana walks under a small umbrella that gives her appearance on the road a comical cast. She gives me instructions on how to better use *bastones*, showing me how to make them click-clack at a faster clip and with a chirpier synchronization, all the while making my body move to their rhythm rather than the other way around.

We arrive at a small town called Sansol and then move quickly down into and back out of a rather deep ravine toward the village of Torres del Rio. In the short distance between the two villages, we meet an old man who stops us to talk, a rosary twirled among his fingers. He does not hesitate to introduce himself as a long-retired Franciscan priest who is helping out in the neighborhood parish. He congratulates us for having taken up the life of the pilgrim, then moseys on his own way while we continue up the track into Torres. The *refugio* is even nicer than expected, a small and quaint place, a private home remodeled and newly opened to house pilgrims like ourselves. Best of all, it is quiet and there are no more than a handful of us here. The *hospitalero* greets us warmly, stamps our *credenciales*, and shows us the bathrooms and showers, then leads us to the stairway that goes up to the open-beamed dormitory above. This place feels just right after the previous evenings of much larger and busier operations.

Removal of my boots and socks reveals a very full blister adjacent to if not actually on top of the old one. I just about die; this is not what I need in my life right now. After my shower, I move outside with my nail clippers and small bottle of Purell, intending to treat it as I had the one before. I remember what they told me about treating these things back in Pamplona, but I don't take the time to learn another way. Ana in her kindness stops me from cutting into the blister and gives me new instructions on how to *properly* tend to these menaces of the road. First, grab a bright yellow bottle of a disinfectant confected with an iodine base called Betadine. Spread this reddish fluid over the blister completely. Then get a sewing needle and a long piece of thread, disinfect them thoroughly by passing both through your fingers liberally daubed with the Betadine. Finally, pass the needle and thread through the heart of the blister, avoiding the tender meat underneath (you'll know if you hit it), take a second pass forming a small cross pattern in the blister, cut off the needle and tie up the ends of the thread so that it doesn't fall out. Leave it in place; it will eventually fall out on its own. The advantage of this small surgery, I am informed, is that it allows the blister to drain for an extended time, the thread serving as a wick for the fluid to follow out. In no time, I will be fit as a fiddle, I am confidently advised. I can't bear to do the sewing on myself, big chicken that I am, so Ana does it for me. She adjusts her plastic chair so that it faces my own, hauls my tender foot up onto her lap, and performs the surgery in less than a minute. I don't feel a thing and then proudly hobble around in my open sandals with my happy little thread flapping in the wind as a pilgrim badge of honor.

There is almost nothing in the tiny village of Torres del Rio, not even a respectable store. The only object of interest for the occasional tourist or pilgrim to this small spot on the map, of course, is the local church. In point of fact, the Church of the Holy Sepulcher that graces this small village is a jewel worthy of a detour from anyone's well-beaten path. The small twelfth-century sanctuary is a pristine example of pure Romanesque architecture. It is a beauty. From the outside it is wonderfully proportioned; but when the little neighbor lady with the key opens the door at six in the evening for one hour and one hour only, it is a revelation of how sublimely we human beings can express the things of heaven in a simple arch, portal, or column all tied together in hand-hewn stone.

First of all, the church has eight sides: perfect. And perfection is exactly what those eight sides symbolically represent. Follow the math here: there are seven days in our worldly week. The *first* day, Sunday, is very important for Christians, for it is the day that marks the resurrection of Jesus Christ. The *last* day, Saturday, the Sabbath, is very important to our Jewish ancestors in faith because it marks the day God rested after creating the universe. Now Christians push ahead here just a bit speaking of an *eighth day of the week*, which is the *day after the last day*, which is in a spiritual sense the *first day beyond time* and is therefore really the first day of all eternity, the first day of the "Kingdom of God Come in Its Fullness." This is the spiritual day on which the "New Jerusalem" descends to earth as described in the highly symbolic language of the final book of the Christian Scriptures.[1] The octagonal shape is repeated over and over again within this church: its cupola and lantern also have eight sides and if it had a baptistery, it would almost certainly be octagonal as well. So all this spirituality is intimately written into the very architecture of a Romanesque church like this one. The church building itself is meant to teach and proclaim the mysteries of faith and our medieval brothers were great at doing just that when they designed their churches.

The second feature of Romanesque architecture that teaches and proclaims the mysteries of our faith comes from the very nature of Romanesque. Unlike its Gothic younger sister, Romanesque architecture is very earthbound. It doesn't soar because it can't. Its masters did not yet have at hand the secret of the flying buttress without which large columns and very thick walls have to do the heavy lifting necessary to hold the structure up. This keeps the whole thing very thick, low, and dark. To walk into one of these churches is akin to walking back into your mother's womb, if such a thing were imaginable. Windows cut in its outer walls have by necessity to be small and are often glazed in alabaster, making the light inside dim and otherworldly. Support of the upper ranks of the church come from the interior columns; from column to column there is a sort of reverse-garland of round arched stonework with a

---

1. Revelation/Apocalypse 21:1-9.

» *July 15: Estella to Torres del Rio* «

keystone set of course in the central position of each arch. Shapes in a Romanesque church are simple, clean, and softly focused.

If you ask young people which church style they prefer, Gothic or Romanesque, most will tell you they like Gothic more. If you ask older people the same question, most, I would hazard to guess, would respond that they prefer the Romanesque. Gothic shoots our eyes upward and makes us dream of a heaven we are yet to see. Romanesque enfolds us like a warm blanket draped over our shoulders on a chilly night and makes us feel at home on this good earth that God created for us and that we can feel under our feet, run through our fingers, see with our eyes, and even smell with our noses. Gothic proclaims that God is *up there* while Romanesque murmurs that God is *down here* on this earth with its wheat fields and vineyards and dusty roads, and, of course, all its fleshy joy and bloody pain. Both are right and beautiful, but at this stage in my life, I must say, I gawk at Gothic but I pray in Romanesque.

In this small *refugio*, new people are noticed. The energetic Englishman has a name: he is Matthew and so we visit a bit out on the stoop. Ana, Isabel, and Javier become my pals for the day and we laugh and tell stories as we hang around passing away the final hours of a hot, twenty-eight-kilometer day. A young Basque fellow eats and smokes at the table next to us in the small bar set up next to the *refugio* but he keeps to himself for the moment. Clouds are building again at day's end so I head for bed with hopes for a cooler morrow. I briefly fall into temptation and take a look at the small map on the back of my *credencial*; I've covered a hundred and eighty kilometers since Saint-Jean-Pied-de-Port. Only six hundred more to go.

I also count up the days since I first caught the train in Leuven: this is my eighth day as a pilgrim.

Life Measured in Feet

July 16: Torres del Rio to Logroño

I suppose it is time to offer a word about one of the plagues facing the contemporary pilgrim as he works his way slowly from east to west across the Iberian Peninsula. It is not a new affliction to the human race but for that it is no less troublesome. The problem is that of snorers. The racket they can raise is really rather incredible. Whenever two or more gather for a good night's rest, there is bound to be at least one of the two or more who snores. More often than not they can be detected even before one tucks himself into bed: watch out for men over thirty who are also overweight. The second thing worthy of note about snorers is that they are always the first to fall asleep, leaving the rest of us to contend with their wheezing inhales and snorting exhales. It is almost as if they have been placed purposefully among this world's pilgrims as a specific test of our patience and a challenge to our love for the least among us. It is easy to hate them. The third thing about the snorers of the *camino* is that no matter what you do to avoid the most likely candidates when choosing a bunk, one among them always seems to find you and tuck himself into the bunk directly above your own. You can then not only *hear* him, you are also given the extra gift of actually *feeling* the bed shake with each breath he takes. I must say that as a celibate I am not used to this kind of treatment at night; I do not know how wives put up with it for a lifetime; this must surely be one of the graces that comes with matrimony. One of the most interesting mysteries of snoredom is that when two or more snorers occupy the same room, a rhythm develops among them and they find themselves unconsciously snoring in time with one another. *Snorkkkkk — Snirkkkkk — Snraaaaph-ph-ph-th* — (pause to the count of three) — *Snorkkkk — Snirkkkkk — Snraaaaph-ph-ph-th* —; and so it goes.

What should by all indications be a very good night of sleep in a very pleasant little *refugio* with warm and good new friends after a very long walk becomes for me a night of tossing and turning and cursing to myself, knowing that with one sleepless hour after another passing me by, the next day is not going to be an easy one. A late-arriving German bicyclist, over thirty but uncharacteristically thin as a rail, provides tonight's recital. As he comes in, there is only one bunk still available in our cozy dormitory and it is the upper level of my bed. His physique does not match the usual typecasting so I don't think to make handy my little yellow foam earplugs that have saved me from disaster on previous nights. Once in bed and with all lights turned off it is impossible to find them hidden deep in one of my *mochila's* great pouches or pockets. The horror begins immediately. As soon as my bunkmate's head hits the pillow the most ghastly sounds begin to emanate from his nasal passages, having commenced their travels from somewhere deep in his trachea, past his tonsils, around his teeth, and through his whistling lips. What can capture the almost diabolical sounds that issue from this happy camper above me? He rattles and whistles and snorts throughout the entire night so that I am blessed with only an hour or two of sleep before rising at five thirty A.M.

In spite of the mostly sleepless night and a still-tender blister the morning's walk actually goes quite well. Before the day is over I manage to cover another twenty kilometers and this in just less than five hours. With about eleven of those kilometers under my belt I meet up with Javier and Isabel in the beautiful old city of Viana where we take our morning coffee and enjoy a thick slice of potato *tortilla*. Joining us is another young woman by the name of Susanna, a German whom I have only just begun to distinguish from the crowd. After my coffee I take a bit of additional time out on the ledge of a large fountain to pull off my boots and tend to my now-blazing blister. Susanna comes over, asks how

I'm doing, looks over the situation, pulls my feet into her lap, and tenderly applies a Compeed silicone pad to the affected area on the ball of my foot. I thank her for her generosity and as she moves on I re-imprison my feet inside my dusty boots and limp out of Viana falling increasingly behind everyone. Such small but kindly gestures as Susanna's give a pilgrim courage to go on and to go on not only with the *camino* but in a deeper sense, to go on with life and the world. If I were God looking down on our embattled and selfish world, what would keep me from having old Gabriel blow the final trumpet blast to put an end to this mess? Exactly such small and unnoticed signs of compassion and generosity as Susanna's or Ana's the night before when she sewed up my foot with a needle, a piece of thread, and a little Betadine. The simple act of another person holding my sweaty foot, tending to it, even massaging it a bit, gives me hope that this race of ours might actually be redeemable. I suppose that the tender humility and unexpected care and love that fills this gesture is what Jesus must have experienced when the lady sinner in Luke's Gospel anoints his feet with her tears and wipes them dry with her hair.[1] This is almost certainly why Jesus' most profound gesture of love in John's Gospel, saved for the most profound moment in the whole story of his life, is the washing of the feet of his twelve apostles one by one.[2] It saddens me to know that to the best of my memory I have never held anyone's feet in my lap, tended to them with ointment, or washed them except on Holy Thursday, when Jesus' act is celebrated ritually in the liturgy of that solemn day. So what kind of priest have I been across these twenty-four years without having done so? I don't know. Perhaps it is as a belated acknowledgement of this lack in my life that I have felt moved over the past days of pilgrimage to covertly kiss the feet of the crucified Jesus or the pilgrim Santiago when I have come upon them in the *camino's* churches.

Now Logroño is no small town. It is, on the contrary, really quite substantial. It takes a fair amount of walking to get through its industrial and suburban areas. Industrial areas in particular are never pretty sights for the sore eyes of the pilgrim whose reserves of energy are pretty much sapped by the time he reaches them. Suburban neighborhoods offer

1. Luke 7:36-39.
2. John 13:1-11.

» *July 16: Torres del Rio to Logroño* «

more visual interest, for at least there are homes, yards, and other signs of domestic life to pay attention to. In both situations the *camino's* yellow *flechas* get painted on curbs and lampposts in these areas and a keen eye has to be kept to stay on track. I manage, nevertheless, to get into the heart of the city, cross a very substantial bridge, then arrive at the town's *refugio* at about eleven in the morning. Though I haven't really been aware of it, I have made pretty good time. The *refugio* is still closed when I arrive and won't open for another two hours. There is no one else around so I find a small store, buy a yogurt and a nectarine, find a park bench along a shady side street, snack, then set my *mochila* on one end of the bench as a pillow, take off my boots, and stretch out on the bench for a nap. I fall hard asleep and have a vivid dream that I promptly forget as soon as I awake again, perhaps only ten minutes later. A light breeze is blowing down the street that feels delicious in its own right; such must be the breath of God, I suppose. People walk by. Some of them nod to me (in sympathy?). One greets me with a *buen camino*, marking him as a veteran of the road himself. A very old lady in very ragged dress and moth-eaten shawl limps up to me with two aged canes holding her upright and two completely deformed feet attaching her body to the earth below. It seems that she is actually walking on her ankles while her feet themselves look like nothing more than knots of purple flesh and gnarled bone. Without a moment's hesitation, she asks me if I know how old she is. I haven't a clue so I say simply: "*¿Muy vieja?*" "*¡Si! MUY vieja!*" I am very old! I have ninety-three years, she tells me in a Spanish garbled for lack of teeth. I become the one-person audience of a lengthy sermon about things I can only barely understand as she recounts to me with great animation events from her long life, most of which seem to center around the deformation of her feet. I have nothing else to do so I listen with attention, missing most of the point if there is one, but recognizing that her feet are with justice the central fact of her life and that in comparison my own foot issues are as minor as can be. My blisters will heal in a day or two, unlike her absolutely deformed appendages. The *vieja* completes her talk with a flourish of her canes as if to say simply: "So there!" and then walks on down the street atop those deformed feet. As the old lady disappears around a corner, the encounter with her seems like an apparition; she becomes another one of those strange angels sent by God to teach me a thing or two about life. If the breeze of this street was the breath of

» *Life Measured in Feet* «

God, then this strange lady with the deformed feet has been his word for me today.

Yet another lesson is about to unfold. Even as I lie back down on the park bench after my visit with the *vieja* I glance up and spot a very familiar figure walking down the street toward me. It is none other than Javier, the very Javier from my first days on the road, the schoolteacher from Sevilla. He is walking now with a decided limp, that distinctive side-to-side gait that is so typical to us whose feet are hurting. Javier does not notice me as he walks by so I call his name just before he passes me completely. He does not stop so I call more loudly a second time. He turns with a quizzical look on his face, then a great smile widens across that same face, his eyes light up, and he quickly hobbles over to me and with an excitement that truly surprises me he greets me and tells me of how he and Manuel had missed me since Puente la Reina, wondered often how I was faring, and had even phoned back to various *refugios* to see if I had passed through or not. Manuel had gone ahead the day before while Javier had decided to hold back in Logroño due to ongoing aches and pains in his own feet. He decided to ditch his hiking boots, blaming them for those aches and pains, and is just about to look for a shoe store to buy a new pair. As we sit on our bench I advise him that I am not so sure buying new boots midway in the *camino* is the best idea; everything I have heard is that tight and unbroken-in boots are a recipe for even more blisters. My argument makes no great impression on him and he tells me he already has found a shoe shop with just what he needs and will make his purchase this afternoon. He spent the night before in this *refugio* but has since found that not far away is the convent of a community of nuns who rent out individual rooms to pilgrims for ten euros a night. That includes, he tells me excitedly, a real bed with sheets and blankets, a washbasin, hot water, and free access to the Internet. Wow! He was just on his way to collect his belongings from this *refugio* and move over to the nuns' house when I called to him. I agree to go along, the image of a private room after the previous night's sleeplessness at the hands of the German snorer is just too good to pass up. A small splash of luxury does not seem an altogether unforgivable sin under the circumstances.

We make our way over to the convent, a characterless modern building along a pedestrian-only street with a multitude of tony shops lining both sides. With the help of a passing nun we find our way to the nondescript and unlabeled entryway and there are warmly received like true guests into their home by these good sisters. The rooms are small but everything advertised is there and best of all we are virtually alone in the place. After settling in, I have a pleasant visit with the sister who serves as our *hospitalera*. Her community is dying, with no young sisters coming in while the remaining sisters only grow older. Nevertheless, they continue to dedicate themselves to their mission as best their resources allow: they work with women who are marginalized in society, prostitutes mostly, and women who are being abused and beaten by their men. It is tough work that these ladies do yet they smile and their eyes twinkle and they pray.

I have an engagement for lunch with the young Brit, Matthew. Though I invite Javier to join us, he decides to go in search of his new shoes instead; I meet Matthew back at the town *refugio* and we wander over to Logroño's *plaza mayor* for a *menú del día* with its typical three courses: salad or soup, big cut of lamb or beef or pork, and a cheap dessert. I have known Matthew over the last few days mostly as a youthful pilgrim who has consistently passed me by on the road; this fellow marches at a clip that can only engender admiration or envy. I choose admiration as the better of the two options. This is our first real visit and I take advantage of the time at a table out on the *plaza* to be a bit bold and ask him why he is doing the *camino*. Like so many others, the "reason" is hard for him to articulate. Somehow the idea grabbed him, captured his attention, and it kept coming back to him as something important to do. It was an internal pull; something drawing him on, but other than that, there is not much more he can say about it.

This kind of answer, which I hear often as I walk along with these young people, touches one of the inscrutable mysteries of the contemporary *camino*. Though many if not most of the young people out here walking day after day belong to what is now called the "postmodern" era and are really quite secularized as far as institutional religion is concerned, there are nevertheless some kind of "receptors" within them that pull in spiritual signals. They are not closed to spiritual realities at all, or they would not find themselves, as Matthew puts it, "grabbed" and "pulled" into the *camino's* field of gravity. The vagueness of their answers makes it clear to me that the real issue is that, unlike their forebears, they just don't have much in the way of vocabulary to describe what goes on spiritually within themselves. Perhaps even more to the point, they don't have much in the way of symbols and myths to help them make sense of what is moving inside them. In previous times pilgrims knew precisely what they were doing and *why*; for them a pilgrimage was a way to do penance, ask a favor of a saint, or fulfill a sacred promise. Today's pilgrims for the most part know little if anything of that kind of language or mythology; they just feel pulled. It could not be otherwise, I suppose, considering the state of society and religion in these times; indeed our old myths, especially our Christian myths that made sense of the world in those former times, have quite crumbled, for who among these young people believe in a real heaven as distinct from a real hell? Who among them really believe as their grandparents did that the meaning of life can be found in a man who was God and who died a nasty death on a cross two thousand years before and rose to tell about it and in so doing took the sting out of suffering and death for the rest of us? Who among them understand a language that says things like "suffering redeems"? Yet they know how to share bread, pass around a bottle of wine, tend to another's feet and let themselves be pulled by something they do not know. The old taproots are still here; this *camino* evidences the possibility that, in spite of everything, new shoots may be springing up out of those old roots.

As I return to the convent I am taken by the sound of the sisters' communal voices coming from the house chapel; they are singing one of the most beautiful of hymns in the Catholic repertoire: the *Salve Regina*. The sweet melody drifts out of the chapel and down the hallways and through our thin doors and into our waiting hearts. Incense for the ears is what it is like. Later, I rejoin Javier, we enjoy a small *cena* and a beer out in the town, plan our morning march, then retire to our very private rooms ready for a restful night of sleep with not a snorer in a mile. In point of fact, I sleep as deeply as a man can sleep and still remember a dream: Santiago the Pilgrim is smiling and opening his arms to us and without a word says to us: "*¡Vengan!* Come!"

» *July 16: Torres del Rio to Logroño* «

First Tears

July 17: Logroño to Nájera

Javier and I are up and ready to go at five forty-five and already waiting for us is one of the sisters, ready with a pot of coffee, warm milk, sugar, and a couple of pieces of cake. Such is the very definition of charity: getting up at five forty-five in the morning to offer a cup of *café con leche*, a slice of cake, and a gentle *"Vayan con Dios,* Go with God," to a couple of strangers who spent the night in your house and whom you will never see again. These sisters are the most hospitable of *hospitaleras* I have yet come to know.

Javier and I have to walk quite a ways to get out of the city. We follow a couple of arterial streets with their traffic lights blinking yellow and red as they do at this hour of the morning. Even from the first step, the newest blister is paining me and forcing me into a lopsided limp. Discouragement is not a welcome frame of mind with which to begin a day's walk and I try to keep it from overtaking me, but the physical pain does not allow me the freedom to ignore its antagonizing presence. As with snoring, there is no completely full description in words of just what this small cross on the front ball of my foot feels like as I begin a twenty-six-kilometer day, but let me take a stab at it: speaking of "stab," it is very much like a stab, a small stab certainly, not unlike the tip of a knife poking straight in and twisting just a bit. But that is not the end of it; the pain then takes a fast-start sprint up your leg, reaching to maybe about the knee. But that is not the end either; the rest of the body responds by instinctively tilting just slightly to the opposite side of the wound to take the pressure off the point of origin and this in turn causes you to walk off center, tipping you sideways just enough to throw your *mochila* slightly off center as well. And all this repeated with each step a thousand times across a morning results in muscles and tendons straining as they should not have to and this then sets you up for even more problems further down the line. It is a real form of suffering; though not on the scale of Jesuits being murdered in El Salvador or an old woman walking on her ankles or millions of people dying slow deaths from AIDS, still and all, it hurts and it takes its toll and in the end a pilgrim has to decide if it is worth it all or not. Quit or keep going? Is this suffering, small as it may be on the scale of world suffering, somehow *meaningful?* If there is no personal philosophy that takes in human suffering as a part of life, that *makes sense* of it, then just quit. As I knock off one by one the twenty-six long, hot kilometers from Logroño through Navarette and on to Nájera, the temptation to call it a match is threatening to overcome my will to go on. For the moment there is no way to stop. I am nowhere where I *can* stop. Javier has moved well ahead of me. I, for my part, enter into my automatic walking mode, the one I described some days ago wherein the base of the brain takes over from the more cerebral part and I plow ahead one step at a time like an old Jeep. In blankness I walk and walk and just keep on walking.

At about two in the afternoon I come to what I believe must be the entrance to the town of Nájera, a place called the *Jardín de Poesía,* or "Garden of Poetry," which at this time of the year is little more than a dried-up and overgrown picnic area with garbage strewn about, chipped concrete tables and benches here and there, and, most significant of all, a large cement retaining wall to one side of the path, all of which conspires to make the area seem more like an industrial dump than a garden. Worst of all, a small sign painted on a post along the path indicates most clearly that this is *not* Nájera; Nájera is still two and a half kilometers further on. At two in the afternoon on a very hot day with little shade, little to look at, and twenty-four blistery kilometers already notched on my boots those two and a half kilometers *more* seem impossible to conceive. The sign is experienced as a blow to my very soul, an attack against my person by some unseen trickster. I am being beaten down and I cannot go on. I'd rather die here and now than walk those additional two and half damnable kilometers. I quit.

I turn to the large concrete retaining wall and realize the wall itself has given this grim place its name: the Garden of Poetry. There is only one poem painted on it, looking something akin to graffiti. It is in Spanish of course, but also in Italian and German. Nobody has thought to take the time to do an English version, I suppose. I lean against my sturdy *bastones* and read:

> Polvo, barro, sol y lluvia
> es camino de Santiago.
> Millares de peregrinos
> y mas de un millar de años.
> Peregrino: ¿quíen te llama?
> ¿qué fuerza oculta te atrae?
> Ni el campo de las estrellas
> ni las grandes catedrales . . .

Loosely translated:

> Dust and mud, sun and rain,
> Such is the way to Santiago.
> Thousands of pilgrims
> And more than a thousand of years.
> Pilgrim: who calls you?
> What hidden power attracts you?
> It's not the field of stars
> Nor the great cathedrals.

> It is not the beauty of Navarra
> Nor the wine of Rioja
> Nor the seafood of Galicia
> Nor the fields of Castilla.

> Pilgrim, who is it who calls you?
> What unseen power attracts you?

» *First Tears* «

Not the peoples of the camino
Nor their rural customs.

It is not history nor culture
Not the rooster of the Calzada
Nor the palace of Gaudí
Nor the castle of Ponferrada.

All that is seen in passing,
And it is a joy to see it all,
Is still less than the voice that calls
The feeling that is yet so much deeper.

The power that pushes me
The force that attracts me
I know not how to explain it.
Only He who is above understands it![1]

From a literary perspective, it is not a work that will ever rival that of Cervantes or Saint John of the Cross, I suppose, but at this point, I start crying. I can't explain why or how or what even I am crying about really, but here I am, as alone as alone can be, exhausted, hurting, hot, and two and a half kilometers away from my destination for the day and I am sniffling and weeping and hardly able to see through the water in my eyes. He who is above knows why. He who is above calls, pulls, attracts, I dare say, seduces me onward and I cannot resist. I am not alone at all, I am seen, and so I cry. This one who is above knows me and I know him, and so I cry. I was dead but now I am alive, and so I cry. My watery eyes turn away from the poem and back to the road. I don't quit. I walk. As the tears pass, strangely enough, I feel more relaxed and firmer in my intention than I have ever before.

I cross those two and a half impossible kilometers into Nájera and after the usual duties of checking in, washing clothes, washing self, eating, and napping, I take a needle and thread and my bottle of Betadine in

1. I later learn that the widely reproduced poem is attributed to one Eugenio Garibay Baños. The barely adequate translation into English is my own.

» *July 17: Logroño to Nájera* «

hand and undertake surgery on my latest blister. As I am finishing my sew job on the blister the sound of a nearby church bell ringing a *llamada,* call to Mass, comes my way, so with thread flapping from my sandaled foot I hobble down the street to the church. While at Mass, I start crying again. Either I'm going nuts or this is what is supposed to happen on the pilgrim's tenth day on the road.

I get back to the *refugio* and help my Canadian friend, Guy, string thread through his own blisters, which are considerably worse than my own. This treatment is new to him and he thanks me profusely for sharing my medical wisdom with him. At one point, Guy looks down at his feet and says to me, "Well, to borrow a phrase, I really carried my cross today." It strikes me how even for these supposedly postmodern and secular young people the language of older times, of my times, is in the end about the only language they have to express themselves even if it has to be "borrowed." Yes, when all is said and done, we did carry our crosses today.

As I pass among the bunks of the crowded dormitory upstairs, a young girl advises me that the backs of my calves are very sunburned. Without a second thought she offers me her blue bottle of Nivea cream. "Here, put some of this on. It will keep the skin from drying out. Take as much as you want." As the day began with the charity of a nun offering me a coffee and cake so now it ends with the charity of a young girl sharing with me her bottle of Nivea cream.

As I prepare for bed after a hard day with two good cries in it, I feel grateful to be out here. It surprises me to feel this way. I'm not crazy. Something fundamental is happening to me out here and *I* don't have words for it either. Yet.

In the Spiritual Heart
of the Camino

July 18: Nájera to Santo Domingo de la Calzada

My guidebook advises me that Santo Domingo de la Calzada is the spiritual heart of the *camino*. I would have thought that Santiago de Compostela itself might lay claim to that honor, but looking back on what happened yesterday with its double dose of tears I know now that indeed I am getting deeper into this odd *camino* world than I would ever have guessed. The daily routines, the walking, the physical pain, the solitude, the kindness of strangers conspire to wear down my defenses so that, like yesterday, I quite unexpectedly find myself, a grown man, sniffling like a child at the most simple and fundamental postulate of my faith: God knows me. It is wonderful, really. So even though I am still hundreds and hundreds of kilometers from Santiago, somehow I suppose, as the guidebook says, I am indeed already in the heart of Compostela. The *camino* is now something much more than a physical and mental challenge, more than something to check off my life's list of "to do's," and more even than the accomplishing of my personal goal to seek the help of a grand old saint for the great cause of my life. This is now life itself. The *camino* has become my world inside and out.

And so I walk on toward Santo Domingo de la Calzada. The way today passes through a few vineyards but mostly through as-yet unharvested wheat fields; the heavy golden heads soak up the morning sun and loll this way or that whenever a slight breeze passes above them. At the same time, the straw stalks make a silky noise as they rub against one another. It is a beautiful sound. In just a day or two, I suppose, a monstrous combine will decapitate them all with a roar and send their grainy heads off to bakeries and pasta factories and church altars around the world. That is beautiful too.

After about seven or eight kilometers, the road splits and I am given a choice of paths: one that stays close to the highway and is more true to the medieval way, but the other, so I am advised by the guidebook, is more attractive, running up and around some hills before it drops the pilgrim down into Santo Domingo. The guidebook indicates quite clearly that the more authentic route is also the more difficult since it gets lost from time to time under the fields of wheat. While most of today's pilgrims take the high road, I decide to follow the authentic route, figuring that even if all does not go well, at least I'll be close to the highway and will not be able to get too very lost. For quite a while as I go my own way I can see Javier and the others following the modern path off into the gentle distance while I have my own rather severe hill to climb. The yellow *camino* arrows disappear from view not long after the "Y" in the roadway. Soon I am left to my own devices, which amount to nothing more than guesswork as I choose which of several connecting and interconnecting roads through the vast fields might be the *camino* path. I guess wrongly and then compound the first error with further guesses that are just as wrong, sending me along roads that simply piddle out or that drop back down the very hill I have just climbed up. The one thing that keeps me from complete desolation as I wander aimlessly across this plateau is the fact that indeed the highway with its speeding trucks and cars is clearly visible to the north and so I know that I can indeed never be *that* lost; if worse comes to worse, I can hike over to the highway and walk its shoulder into Santo Domingo. After meandering stupidly along the farm roads atop this plateau of wheat land and using up the better part of an hour doing so, I finally give up and take a cross road through the wheat over to the big, roaring N-120.

There is much to be said for highways and their role in the economy of today's world. They are wide and smooth and make possible extraordinary speed for all manner of transportation with one exception: that of the humble pilgrim who must rely on his own two feet as his only mode of conveyance. For the pedestrian pilgrim, pavement is tiring to walk on for any great distance. It is hot. It has no give under foot, as dirt does. Even worse, the *whoosh* of huge semi trucks as they pass by lifts the hat off the pilgrim's head and sends it flying into ditches full of thistles, wild vines with thorns, and half-hidden piles of disagreeable refuse thrown from passing cars and trucks. The mighty wind that the semi trucks make as they pass at one hundred and thirty kilometers an hour just a meter or two off the right shoulder of the humble hiker is enough to make his hair stand on end as he braces himself against its immense force. These enormous vehicles appear on the horizon as anonymous beasts bearing down on him at breakneck speed with what seems to be complete disregard for his life. Sleek automobiles are less fearsome but they travel even faster; through their windshields can be seen the vague outlines of drivers chatting on mobile phones and smoking at the same time, which, needless to point out, does not give one confidence in those drivers' attention to pilgrims occupying space on the shoulder of their highway. In fact, along the *camino* where it crosses major highways, monuments to pilgrims presumably killed by such vehicles as these are not unknown. It is easy to see how it could happen: pilgrims are tired and sometimes their judgment suffers as a result. Distances can be deceiving on a hot highway, and evaluating speed of oncoming traffic is at best a risky business. Moreover, feet hurt and legs do not always move as fast as one thinks they should. Finally, there are those packs on their backs making them much closer in spiritual kinship to turtles than to sprinting hares. One bad choice at a bad moment and, *bam*, the pilgrim is toast. So that is the sort of thing I ponder as I walk the shoulder of this major highway over the course of seven or eight kilometers. It is sobering and when truckers pass too close for comfort all I can do is turn, shake my fist in the air, and yell at the top of my lungs, "You stupid *ass!*" And so I spend two hours in highway hell as I push my way into Santo Domingo de la Calzada. Such is my punishment for the vanity of choosing the more authentic route, a route that I had been warned was not well marked in spite of its historical pedigree.

I eventually walk into the outskirts of modern Santo Domingo and as with so many of these *camino* towns, I must first pass through the semi-industrial gauntlet of tractor shops, tire stores, and cheap hotels with their dirty parking lots. The last half-kilometer consists of one such banal building after another. The transition to the stone heart of the city with its medieval streets, houses, and churches is all the more welcome when it finally embraces me in its granite shade.

Now, Santo Domingo is a town whose significance for the pilgrim is revealed in its name. There is a story in this name, of course. It goes that a young man from the area, Domingo by name, desired nothing more than to spend his life as a religious and so went to the nearby Monastery of San Millán, but upon requesting admission was rather unceremoniously thrown out on his ear. He thence became a hermit at the site of the present town of Santo Domingo and here he devoted himself to assisting the increasing flow of pilgrims on their way to Santiago. In the year 1044 he constructed a bridge over the river Oja and later built a pilgrims' *hospital*, an early cathedral, and after that a very important road from Nájera to Redicilla del Camino, part of which, the modern guidebooks tell us, exists intact to this day and over which I will walk tomorrow. The holy and charitable man died in 1109 and was buried in the village on the shoulder of the *camino's* route through the small town. With the body of the holy man so close to the *camino*, it was not long before pilgrims were stopping to pay him a word or two of gratitude for his valuable roadwork and to ask him for the additional favor of heavenly protection as they continued on their way. To this day, his tomb is only a few short meters from the *camino* as it passes by the doors of the cathedral that bears his name.

I believe that when the good guidebook writer indicates this place as the very heart of the *camino*, he is doing so because of this Domingo's extraordinary dedication to the service of the pilgrim, offering him a place to sleep, protecting him from robbers and murderers, providing him with bridges and roadways, tending to his sore feet, all of which he learned from Jesus; this is the "true spirit" of the *camino*. By this point in the march to Santiago, this spirit has seeped into our bones too and so here we are, being kinder than we've ever been in our lives, treating others as we would like to be treated, yes, even massaging one another's feet. We share what we have without second thoughts and just as importantly, we no longer flinch at other people's attentiveness to us; it is just fine if someone sews a thread through one of our blisters and it is great if a stranger picks up the tab for our morning coffee, and we now readily say yes when another offers us half of their dry, unsalted almonds as a snack along the way. We do not fear one another out here; that is perhaps most remarkable of all. That old hermit, Domingo, the fellow lying in that dark sarcophagus just over against that church wall, encourages us with his spirit of charity. He is an icon of selfless and compassionate care for the poor and burdened and sick among us. He did a great job. He is our teacher and his lessons allow us to survive the rigors of this pilgrim life. To make it we have to care for one another. It is that simple. Pilgrim: kiss Domingo's feet as you pass by.

As with every day now, I contentedly settle into the town's *refugio* and am surprised to find Robert and his grandson, Josh, arriving on foot an hour or two after me. It is both hard to believe and wonderful to know that these *camino* friends are still out here, pounding away at this road with a determination and faith that I know I could never match in my life even if I lived to be one hundred. We have a genial little reunion after so many days lost to one another. They hint that they have had occasion from time to time to make use of public transportation in their pilgrimage but there is no shame in that, for the old man continues to suffer from blistered and swollen feet even after all these days.

After the usual afternoon rituals and rest, Javier and I go to the eight o'clock Mass in the Cathedral of Santo Domingo. The priest who says the Mass gives the pilgrims present a warm blessing at the end of liturgy and then offers to take us on a walking tour of the cathedral. He is a priest perhaps ten years younger than me and very gracious to us all. He begins his little lecture by telling us the story of Domingo and pointing out his tomb off to the side where the *camino* passes close by and then leads us to many of the features worthy of note within the church. He points out, in particular, an extraordinary high altar with a gilded Spanish baroque reredos as exquisite as any I have ever seen. Within its niches and fretwork is written in wood much of the story of humanity's on-again, off-again relationship with God. In a time when most people did not read, works such as these were their Bibles and catechisms.

The priest leads us to the other side of the church; not far from Domingo's tomb but high up on a transept wall, is the *gallinero*, a wrought iron cage built into the wall that holds a hen and a rooster, both looking, from this perspective at least, rather sickly. They commemorate a *camino* miracle that is surely more fable than history but is a great tale nevertheless. It seems that a troop of foreign pilgrims (variously described as French, German, or even Greek) spent a night in the town somewhere around or about the fourteenth century. Among them was a family with a very handsome young son. A local maiden took a fancy to the lad and encouraged him in not so subtle ways to join her for a bit of a tryst. He, being virtuous, spurned her advances. Not the type of damsel to be put off so, she hid a precious goblet in his traveling pouch and then, as he and his family left town, accused him of thievery, for which he was duly hanged. To emphasize the injustice in the boy's unfortunate end, our priest guide points to a substantial chunk of the wooden gallows suspended from a wall high above our heads.

At any rate, the boy's grieving parents chose to leave the unhappy place, but before they left town, their son miraculously spoke to them, assuring them that he was not dead but that at the moment of his perceived demise good Saint Domingo stood beneath him, holding him up by his feet so that the noose did not have its intended effect. The parents ran back to the hanging judge who was dining on, you guessed it, a rooster and a hen. They protested to the fat magistrate that their son was still very much alive, at which the judge chortled something to the effect that their son was no more alive than the two well-roasted chickens upon which he was feeding. Well, at that very moment the well-roasted fowl jumped off his plate, alive as alive can be, grew feathers, and began to flap about, crowing in delight at their resurrection and that of the just and chaste young man. The son was of course reunited with his parents and off they joyously continued to Compostela, and after arriving there and paying their prayerful respects to the apostle, they presumably lived happily ever after. The testimony of those chickens has been commemorated ever since by the living hen and rooster nesting even to this day in the *gallinero* high above us. There is a moral to all of this, of course; well, actually, there are probably several: Stay virtuous; it pays in the end. Don't cheat and lie; the truth outs. And don't mess around with Santo Domingo's pilgrims, for he takes care of his own.

Finally, the priest points out something extraordinary: also up on the wall are heavy chains and manacles. At some point in the history of Spain some royal decree, made by some duke or king, declared this place to be a "free town" wherein no one could be held against his will. Any slave or prisoner of any kind who made it into Santo Domingo had his manacles opened and was released from his duty or punishment forever. Scot-free, no questions asked, they left their chains behind and began new lives.

The presumption behind this act was that the very generosity and liberality of it would be enough to convert any miscreant so freed to a life of virtue and the town's citizens would have nothing to fear from those so released from their chains. This is something that happens only in fairy tales and children's books, isn't it? Yet these chains and manacles we now see proclaim that it in fact happened here in this little town inhabited by the spirit of our hermit, Domingo. Sad to say, we cannot even imagine such a thing nowadays, except here on the *camino*; here it makes perfect sense. Out here trust trumps fear and this too is part of the "spiritual heart of the *camino*," I am sure.

In the end, there is only one prayer to Domingo that bears saying as a pilgrim passes through this town: Unlock these chains! Open these manacles! Free me, old man, so that from here on I might walk justly and uprightly!

» *July 18: Nájera to Santo Domingo de la Calzada* «

On Sin and Suffering

July 19: Santo Domingo to Belorado

Free me from what? Oh, plenty, let me tell you.

It may seem that up till now things have been going along swimmingly with my companion from Sevilla. Not quite. As before, my dark side is acting up even here in the "heart of the *camino*." In this place where compassion and care are so deeply written into the stones upon which I walk, I am feeling again that sense of being subtly imprisoned by this pal who scuttles my solitude and whose very pal-hood is limiting my freedom to come to know others along the way. I'm not so cruel as to actually "ditch" him, but inside my head I'm hoping we'll be separated again, that we'll go our separate ways, that I'll be free of him sooner rather than later. It is not that I don't like him, not at all. I *do* like him. He is a very good person and I have nothing against him, it is just that I don't want to give up my independence out here; I want to be free to be alone when I want to be alone and not be constrained to always have to take him into consideration as I make my plans for this or for that. The previous two mornings at that exquisite time when night gives way to dawn, that moment when I would have most loved to have had to myself the sublime transition from the world of stars to that of pure sun, I have had Javier at my side — *chatting*.

Morning number three with Javier has begun. It is five forty-five and

I am ready to head out the door of the Santo Domingo *refugio*, but Javier is still tending his feet, rubbing them with Vaseline and getting his socks and boots pulled together. *But I am ready to go.* So I tell Javier that I'm heading out and will meet him for coffee at the first town down the road, Grañon. He looks up at me quizzically as if I have just betrayed him: *Et tu, Kevin?* He says nothing as out the door I go. Now there are two routes to Grañon from Santo Domingo. I choose the longer and hillier one. When he finally leaves, Javier takes the more direct but less interesting path closer to the highway. I have a pleasant walk by myself; my rosary gets prayed, I watch the sun rise over the fields right and left, and I am walking well in spite of the most recent blister. As I arrive in Grañon and make my way to the local bar, I am surprised to find that Javier is already here well ahead of me and almost finished with his large *café con leche*. He is cheerily chatting with a couple other pilgrims. I greet him but he ignores me. He continues talking with his new friends, then makes a quick good-bye and off he goes down the road with one of them, a fortyish lady of rather grand style whose light cotton ankle-length dress swings with the breeze. This time he is the one leaving me behind. He is doing to me what I did to him. I figure he has made his point, and it is one well made at that, and once we meet again the lesson will be over; we'll be friends again. However, at the next town, Redecilla del Camino, he and his new companion are at the town fountain and as I approach, he looks up and upon seeing me, makes haste to leave.

I take a quick draught of fresh water and follow Javier and his new companion out of town, hoping they'll hold up a bit for me so that we might walk together. They push ahead, widening the distance between us with every meter; the two of them never look back. I am being completely disregarded. This irks me. I realize I have been reduced to a jealous grade-school kid, so I give up trying to keep up and just return to walking my own *camino* at my own pace but all the happiness has gone out of my day's work and I feel cheap and immature. When finally I arrive in Belorado and stop at the still closed *refugio*, Javier excuses himself from my company and advises me in his most soft and serious voice that he will be continuing on another five kilometers to the next village so as to get a head start on the next day's walk. He does not explicitly say he is doing this to teach me a lesson but he teaches it anyway. So off he goes and that is that. Javier has just taught me that friends shouldn't treat

» *July 19: Santo Domingo to Belorado* «

friends like I treated him and he is right. Of this kind of slavery to my-self, *free me!*

While I am sitting on a curb against the wall of the *refugio* of the Church of Santa María with a growing crowd of incoming pilgrims, my Canadian friend, Guy, comes walking in from the town center and hap-pily tells me that just a few blocks further on there is a private *refugio* that is already open and very, very nice inside. It even has a yard with a small lawn and a fountain for cooling tired feet. Best of all it is only seven euros for the night. I put my boots back on and hobble down the street to the new place and it is all that Guy has made it out to be: small, clean, mod-ern, and attended by an amiable family who treat us all as honored guests in their home. After settling in and cleaning up I find my way out to the grassy backyard where lovely music is playing through small speakers set under the house's eaves. Vivaldi's strings are accompanied by the cheering sound of the fountain and pond where bees sip and people like me mas-sage their feet on the gravelly bottom. As the splashing water cools me the gentleman of the house comes over to me and unknowingly pays me a much-appreciated compliment when he asks me from where in Mexico I might hail. I tell him that I am an American. He then suggests that surely my parents must be Mexican. Again, I tell him no, that my parents were both Americans as well. I then ask him why he has presumed me to be a Mexican and he says simply, "You speak like one."

Among the other guests for the day are two German men whom I have seen on the road for several days and whom the night before I had spotted at Mass in Santo Domingo. We begin conversing and after a while I have a sneaking suspicion about the nature of their career choices in life; I ask them then if they are priests. They look surprised and with shy smiles acknowledge that indeed they both are priests, but how had I known? I respond, "It takes one to know one," but they don't understand the English expression. I reveal to them that I too am a priest and with that we spend most of the afternoon sharing our *camino* stories and dis-cussing the state of the church. They are the first pilgrim priests I have met on the road up to this point and that seems really quite amazing; it is a sadness that after so many days and so many people, there have been so few of us supposed pastors out here where so many of our supposed sheep are to be found.

This must be my day to meet Catholics, for later in the afternoon I take a brief walk back to the Church of Santa María to take a look inside when I meet Susanna, the young German girl who tended my feet back in Viana. We have not really talked much before this, but in the cool of the day's end we stand in the street for quite a while and just chat. She has heard that I am a priest and asks if it is so and, as always, I acknowledge my life's work as long as I have been asked. She then shares that she has just finished her studies in religion at the university in Freiberg and is certified to be a teacher of religion back in Germany. In September she will begin her first job as a church catechist. She tells me about how she came to this profession having felt her previous career to be unsatisfying. This seems to me to be a rare and special treat: a visit with a young person on the road who is a committed believer and actually choosing a career in sharing that faith with other young people. Delighted though I am to get to know Susanna much better, I can also feel a piece of my theory about her generation's postmodern secularization falling out of place. The generalizations I propounded a few days earlier don't always meet the test of particular experience, and in the end I am grateful for that.

And here is another piece of the puzzle that only fits awkwardly if at all into my theory of the times. Earlier in the day when I had just arrived at the *refugio* to the side of the Church of Santa María but before I had hiked up to the new *refugio*, I had taken off my boots and socks and was tending to my still very sensitive blisters. A Spanish gentleman of about my own age, and one who obviously was a very accomplished walker, was also standing about, barely showing a sweat after the day's walk. Another pilgrim asked how my feet were faring and I said, "Not so great, but I'm surviving." Then I added, "But such is the *camino*; it wouldn't be the *camino* if suffering weren't part of it." To this the older gentleman responded with a finger shake: "*Nada de sufrimientos. Si no es un placer, no lo haced.*" Which simply put means: "No to suffering! If it's not fun, don't do it."

Now this is an interesting take on the *camino* and, I suppose, on life. How could either *not* entail suffering, for God's sake? Out of my eleven days of actual walking out on this road thus far, only one or two have been even remotely pleasurable. Out of all the people I have ever met in my life as a priest, ninety-nine percent of them or even more have had to bear more sufferings in life than anyone should have to bear in life. According to his logic, if life involves suffering we just should not get involved with it. "Excuse me, I have a headache, would you be so kind as to put me out of my misery?" But we human beings, at least most of us, don't say that and we don't quit and though some can't bear it well, most take their sufferings and work with them and find some kind of place for them in their lives and in the end find good coming out of them. I don't know what this guy was on when he invented *his* theory but it certainly isn't the same road I am on or the one most people I know are on in their troubled and beautiful lives. As a Christian on this *camino*, it is precisely the images of suffering either in the beat-up knees on the statues of Santiago the Pilgrim that adorn so many churches or that of Jesus on his ugly cross that are most important to me. The whole point is to learn how to make *sense* of the suffering, to find *victory* in the humiliation, *healing* in the pain. So it dawns on me this day that it is not just the young who no longer speak a language that has as its central grammatical feature a personal relationship between a comprehending God and a hurting humanity, it is my own generation as well. We are probably the culpable ones; the young haven't *heard* what this faith has to say about such things as suffering because my generation makes pronouncements like "*Nada de sufrimientos. Si no es un placer, no lo haced.*"

I began the day sinning against a friend and end it challenging a view of life that has no room for either sin or suffering. I head to bed with my conscience hanging low for what I did to Javier who is five kilometers down the road now and whom I will probably never see again in my life, muttering to myself, "*Nada de sufrimientos?* Give me a break."

Paella Redux

July 20: Belorado to San Juan de Ortega

The Sunday stroll from Belorado to San Juan Ortega, a journey of about twenty-four kilometers, marks my second Sunday on the road. The world I left behind in Belgium now pertains so deeply to the past that it is difficult to believe that only twelve days have passed since I left Leuven to take my first step into this world apart. I am becoming aware that each day of the *camino* is in itself a *camino*, a small pilgrimage from one place to another, rather complete in itself with its own adventures and mysteries and lessons to be learned along the way. This particular day, as with all the others, is a mysterious mixture of people who become persons, turns in the road opening onto unexpected vistas of new country, doses of physical suffering mixed with flashes of gratitude for being here. This small *camino* unfolds in bits and pieces, with an hour here and a few hours more there, a coffee and tortilla in a bar, a ten-minute rest in the shade on the side of the road, a visit with another pilgrim as we walk together for a brief time before one or the other moves ahead or lags behind, increasing heat and fatigue, thoughts peculiar to a passing moment, flatlands here and a mountain looming there, arrival, then rest and washing and food and more rest and laughter and beer and then it is bedtime and my eyes close and another small *camino* is complete. But only tentatively complete, for once this *camino* day gets taken by the hand by all the other *camino* days, they join together to form something more grand. In communion with one another, they form a growing family having its own wholeness, its own identity, its very own being; they become *El Camino*.

On this eleventh day of walking a new blister appears, this time on the back of my right heel within that tough skin that is very difficult to pierce even with my small sewing needle. But as if in compensation for the pain on my heel, the way on this day leads me into a land of fresh textures and colors and I find myself walking into a new world that is as beautiful as any I have yet seen. The rolling fields of wheat that have dominated my field of vision over the past days, becoming the very background to my nighttime dreams, finally give way to leafy trees with green underbrush everywhere and a river rushing and roiling through its irregular bed and the smell of damp earth fills the air with the sweet odor of moss and mud and slimy slugs.

I walk this morning's first eight kilometers mostly by myself, but then come into the village of Villafranca where I find many of my companions already enjoying their morning coffees and tarts. As always I lay down my *bastones* and drop my *mochila* and with sweat completely dampening my shirt, join the crew for my own refreshment at the local bar. Susanna, Fermín, Kylie and Anne, the elderly Frenchman in the running shorts, Alfredo the Argentinean, the jugglers, and a variety of others are all here and it is a pleasure to now know them and to be welcomed among their company as everyone chats animatedly about the increasingly diverse countryside and the steep mountain which we are about to start up as soon as we set foot outside this bar.

The first few hours up to Villafranca have been slow ones for me, the kind in which I am conscious of just how fatigued my body is, and each step forward has seemed like an effort I have had to individually will. After my rest at the bar in Villafranca I shake off my lethargy and start up the path ahead with new steam in my engine. The route rises steeply and becomes wilder. Pines and massive oaks grow in quantity on both sides of the road. I now find climbing uphill to be easier than walking on the flatlands and I fairly scamper, stopping occasionally to take a look at the spacious vistas spreading out below me. With the increasing elevation, the views out over the hills and plains become ever more breathtaking. I delight in how one mountain range overlays the other, each having its distinctive blue cast vary in intensity depending on its distance from where I

» *Paella Redux* «

stand. Turning my attention back to the roadway, I notice that the path itself is decorated on either side not just with mighty trees that make restful conversation among themselves whenever a breeze passes through their branches but closer in and down, delicate yellow flowers balancing themselves atop tall and slender stems are interspersed with low-growing heather adorned with intensely purple flowerets; these random dashes of life are simply magnificent to behold. Out on a road like this, the eye pays attention to such details as the brilliance of a flower petal or the iridescence in the wings of a fly. That same eye follows the path of ants as they march across the roadway in a steady stream, one right after the other, each one carrying a load three times its size. And yes, my eye even marvels at the shape and texture of the shell of a snail as it lumbers along its burdened way.

The rise upwards over the *Montes de Oca* lifts us to over one thousand meters above sea level. Somewhere near the peak, a gushing spring has been converted into a fountain and a small rest area. Alfredo is reclining in the shade as I approach. We happily greet one another and after I have bent down and taken a great swig of this fresh mountain water he advises me that I should fill up now because this is the last source of water until San Juan de Ortega, some ten kilometers further on. I drink again. The water too is a delight to the senses: cold, liquid, gushing. I drink again and then I immerse my whole head into the flow from the fountain. As I let the water rush over my skull, down my neck and across my face I realize that I am falling in love with the earth and that the earth obviously loves me too. I refill my Coleman thermos with this precious gift to me from the depths, and after wishing the still-recumbent Alfredo well I continue up the road.

My guidebook informs me of the sobering history of this stretch of the *camino* so captivating to me today. In former times, these woods that I so happily pass through without a worry were the favored hiding places of all manner of thieves, brigands, and murderers, making this one of the most feared and dangerous passes the medieval pilgrim had to negotiate on his way to Santiago. I am grateful to be a *modern* pilgrim!

I eventually pass by a large stone cross set deep into the ground at the roadside; it is a monument to *Los Caidos*, the Fallen of Spain's gruesome Civil War of the 1930s. It is a reminder that this land has often had the blood of its inhabitants smeared across its face. The kind of ferocious and mindless violence that we modern pilgrims self-servingly presume to belong to others is not only the evil of ancients or medievals; it belongs to us moderns as well, the cross tells me. I have long doubted that substantial moral improvement has been part of human progress across the millennia and the commemoration of this twentieth-century bloodshed reminds me of my skepticism in the matter. I shake my head in sadness and move on, descending now through the forest to a very small chapel in the middle of nowhere, the *Ermita de Valdefuentes;* the chapel is closed and locked so I continue on towards the town of San Juan. There is little in the guidebook to prepare me for the first view of San Juan. As I come around a bend, I leave the woods behind and find myself in the midst of wheat fields. Above the softly rolling fields arises the *torre*, the bell tower of the old San Juan Monastery church. Unlike most other churches along the way, this tower is one of those light and airy gables rising up over the roofline of the church with open spaces cut through it allowing the bells to freely swing, very much like those seen on old mission churches in California. After almost twenty-four kilometers of hiking over the top of a substantial mountain range the appearance of those bells, silhouetted against the sky and nesting so comfortably in their open niches does my soul good. They welcome and invite and almost call my name even without having sounded a single note.

I walk into the town and find hardly a town here. Outside of the old monastery and church there are only a few houses scattered about here and there. We have to wait a while for the *refugio* in the old monastery to open, but when it does, my hopes for the kindly welcome advertised by the bells of the church are unfortunately not met. An elderly man orders us into line and then with the crankiness of an old bureaucrat he takes our euros and stamps our *credenciales,* then commands us into the building as if we were cattle to be pushed through chutes towards his barn. Even worse, the old fellow complains loudly about the elderly lady who is supposed to be assisting him and, as a variation on that theme, he whines to all who are trapped in his presence about women in general and their native incompetence in all things practical. It is unpleasant and embarrassing. I pass through the gauntlet of dark words, climb the stairs to the floor above, and find my bed in a wide-open dormitory dating from a distant century. A few of us grumble among ourselves about the grumpy old *hospitalero* below and then go about our business of showering and washing our clothes as always.

» *Paella Redux* «

94

As I finish these daily duties Guy the Canadian arrives and is greatly concerned about his companion, the athletic and macho young man whom I had seen some days ago actually jogging down the road, *mochila* and all. His name, I finally learn, is Alexandre. He fell sick back up the road, vomiting and dizzy; he is barely able to walk. Alexandre the Great is now a mess as Guy assists him into the monastery *refugio* and onto a bed. Guy asks for help with translation since neither of them speaks Spanish so I come to his aid. As it turns out, a young doctor is among the newly arrived pilgrims and he gives a preliminary diagnosis of either heat stroke or dehydration or both. This is serious business. A taxi is called to take Alexandre to the nearest real town for a more extensive check-up. The sickness of this strong and perfectly built model of a young man is unsettling among the pilgrims and an object lesson in taking care of ourselves out here. Walk, don't run. Rest when the body asks for rest. And drink, drink, for heaven's sake, drink on these hot days! I remember too the lesson of the mountain goats from my first day: "Woe to you vain . . . the road will humble you."

Even before *l'affaire Alexandre* has been fully resolved, word spreads like wildfire among the pilgrims that something special is going to happen this afternoon. A great *paella* is going to be prepared for the pilgrims, and there will be plenty of wine and bread to accompany it! I am surprised to hear of it and wonder if this could be the same group of folks who had cooked for us in Puente la Reina. It isn't long before the *paella* crew arrives with their huge propane-fired wok, their cases of wine, and their boxes of fresh bread. Those manning the wok and pouring the wine are indeed the very same people I met in Puente; I recognize the man who went out looking for Robert when he failed to arrive exactly a week ago. Before long they have created once again a festive atmosphere that fills the courtyard of this monastery; wine is flowing, *paella* is steaming, and everyone is entertaining everyone. As before, the feasting makes a family out of this company of pilgrims. There is nothing quite like bread, wine, and a mountain of saffron-yellow rice laced with chunks of fish and shrimp to bring people together; food and drink do a community build. I visit with some of the chefs and inquire about how often they do this and why. They explain that they belong to a *cofradía*, or confraternity associated with the church and dedicate themselves to ministering to pilgrims on their way to Santiago. About two or three times a year they take up a collection from among their members, buy their supplies, load up their equipment, and just drop in at places like this to make up a great meal for pilgrims like us. It is a gesture of support for us as we struggle along our way, pure and simple. They want us to know we are not alone. The scene of conviviality founded in bread, wine, and plenty of food shared with no price tag attached that is created by their good work strikes me as one lifted from the Gospels with Jesus right here in the middle of it all.

Surprisingly, Beth, the American girl I first met back in Zubiri, shows up looking as fresh as ever. She is a day ahead of me on the road but her Spanish fiancé is visiting her for the day so they have driven back here just to see the place. Anyway, she too has the luck to be in the right place on the right day twice in a row, for here we both are once again, with plastic wine glasses in one hand and paper plates loaded with rice and seafood in the other, eating and drinking and babbling on about our adventures over the past days.

The old man who so unhappily greeted us at the door of the *refugio* earlier in the afternoon makes the rounds too. It is only now that I learn he is the pastor of the place and the moving force behind its recent restorations and development as a modern *refugio*. On the basis of his good work I figure it is worth giving him a second chance and I also want to thank him for providing to us this place in the middle of nowhere to pass the night. So with wine in hand and feeling increasingly warm inside, I amble over to the *padre*, present myself as a fellow priest and offer my right hand for a cordial shake. He shakes my hand perfunctorily. He barely makes eye contact with me and seems singularly uninterested in knowing me. He walks away.

As the fiesta in the courtyard winds down, a young German man comes up to me with an interesting invitation: would I like to join several others in the crypt of the church, where San Juan (a disciple of Santo Domingo) is buried, to sing some songs? I ask what kind of songs and he says in his unsophisticated English, "Just songs, religious songs." I agree to come down. At the appointed hour I wander into the crypt where four pilgrims are situated, one in each of the four corners of the dark and cool space. They are already singing in beautiful harmonic tones the hymns of the ecumenical monastic community of Taizé, France. These hymns possess very simple melodies that are repeated over and over again, allowing the words to be sung in almost any language, including Latin. The hymns possess a capacity to lead people into a centered and tranquil prayerfulness that has made them very popular in recent decades. They are now familiar and well known to Christians of many stripes and colors all around the world. The hymn they are singing as I enter is a simple version of the famous prayer of Saint Teresa of Avila:

Nada te turbe.
Nada te espanta.
Todo se pasa.
Solo Dios no se muda . . .

Let nothing disturb you.
Let nothing frighten you.
All things are passing.
Only God never changes.

I sit down on a cold stone step and join in, careful not to upset the others' glorious harmonies. This too is a Gospel scene. I remain quiet and prayerful with these hymns echoing about me, echoing *through* me, echoing *within* me. After about forty minutes or so the cool damp inside the crypt creeps into my bones and I find myself shivering. Imagine shivering in the middle of the hottest summer recorded in Spain in over one hundred years! I get up quietly and return to that hot summer outside just as the bells of the church ring the *llamada* for the evening Mass. I take a quick walk around the courtyard to warm my bones, then return to the church; even as I enter I can hear the Germans downstairs still singing their hearts out to God. The priest comes into the sanctuary and begins Mass, but does so with such haste and rote recitation of the prayers that I am deeply bothered from the inside out. I find myself not praying here but only critiquing my confrere in ministry. Once he finally directs us to "Go in peace," I go in anything but peace; I shiver with cold anger. I need to get outside so that the sun might warm my heart anew and so I am one of the first out the big door.

It is hard to believe that after all that *paella*, bread, and wine there might still be the desire to eat anything else for the remainder of the day and night. Nevertheless, pilgrims are a hearty lot and their appetites are really quite voracious. After Mass, I amble out to the small bar that has been installed at the far end of the old monastery building and where a large crew has gathered on the sidewalk and is having a great time continuing the feast. I am welcomed into their midst: "*¡Mira! ¡El Gringo! ¡Kevin, vente! ¿Qué tal, hombre?*" I greet the gang, buy myself a beer and a sandwich, one made of a blood sausage typical of the region, then sit with the group under a red Coca-Cola umbrella. A most animated discussion among the Spaniards follows about where the best of this sausage is to be found. They sound like kids arguing over whose mom makes the best apple pie. I am happy enough with the local variety; this gringo actually likes the sausage, to the surprise of the others, and I feel a small swell of pride for my cultural and culinary openness. Alas, the sandwich is just too rich for me so I cut it into pieces and share it among those who are sitting around. That shared out blood sausage becomes then a small symbol to me of the amity and camaraderie that has been maturing like a good wine over our days on the road; we are now quite like brothers and sisters who can tease and laugh and enjoy one another's company as if we have known each other all our lives.

Night falls as we carry on; after a while I excuse myself from the group, return to my bunk, prepare my *mochila* for the next day's journey to Burgos, the first big city since Pamplona. I finally lie down on my swayback bed but before sleeping I examine my conscience concerning my feelings toward the old *padre*. I suppose what has annoyed me most about this priest is that in my three encounters with him today he has failed to look at me even once. The French existentialists write much about *le regard*, the look, as a fundamental principle of human relationships. If I remember my philosophy classes from years ago, good *regard* makes another person or thing a subject in relationship with me. The other is no longer then just an object, an "it," something outside of me, the existentialists say. It makes you and me an *us*. Bad *regard* or no *regard* keeps us trapped in a loveless and meaningless world where no one ever knows anyone. The old priest, perhaps because of a hard day or a hard week or a very hard life, is no longer regarding, beholding, seeing the other, at least as far as I have met him today. Regarding is one of the best lessons I am slowly learning on this road. Truly looking at things, beholding, appreciating, pondering, allowing them into me: this is what happens when I notice a flower or a person or talk to an old statue of Santiago in a niche somewhere. I also know that disregarding, not beholding, not really seeing, especially when I'm tired, is one of the great faults in my life. I don't regard God, I don't regard others, I don't regard life. So in one way, the old priest and I are in the same boat. He reminds me of me and that is actually why I don't like him. We both fail in what Jesus was so extraordinarily good at. I am sorry for both of us and promise, for my part, to do better tomorrow.

I close my eyes and drift into this night's dream. This "little *camino*" is complete for the day. Amen.

» *July 20: Belorado to San Juan de Ortega* «

A Vision of Light

July 21: San Juan to Burgos

There are three distinct routes from San Juan de Ortega to Burgos for
the pilgrim, two that follow highways and one that goes more directly
through the countryside until it meets up with one of the highways about
five kilometers outside the city limits. I choose the middle route, the one
with the least highway and the most nature. Despite the ongoing struggle
with blisters, one completely healed, one almost healed, and the most recent one on my heel still hurting but beginning to mend, I have a great
day walking through all this countryside, much of it rising again to a
thousand meters and at one point near some tall telephone towers opening onto a magnificent view of the plain below and the great city of
Burgos in the far distance.

By the time I arrive at the outskirts of the city the morning's work
has taken its toll and I am losing energy quickly. As with Pamplona, but
even more so, the venue for entering the city of Burgos for the pedestrian
pilgrim is one fraught with industry, busy arterial streets, railroads, characterless suburbs, and surprising distances. After the hours and days
spent in the countryside all of this strikes me as dismal. Also, it is to be
noted, the yellow arrows that guide us on day after day are much more
easily overlooked or misinterpreted ("Is that a *full* left or just a *half* left?");
it is much easier to get lost in the city than in the countryside.

Unfortunately, after a few twists and turns around factories and underneath train tracks, I and the young pilgrims I have hooked up with in the last hour or two are pretty hopelessly lost. The arrows have disappeared completely and we are left to rely on the directions of passers-by to guide us forward. The natives direct us towards a large park that follows the Río Arlanzón through the modern city toward its medieval center. The park makes for pleasant walking but it is not the route indicated in my guidebook. For fear of being not only lost but lost and alone I am determined to keep up with the youngsters who are leading the way but my body just won't carry me as their bodies carry them. I fall further and further behind. From time to time, they stop to rest and I catch up only to fall behind again once they continue. We finally take a chance on a major intersection and cut to the right out of the park in hopes of finding a street leading to the central plaza and cathedral. We have guessed right, but when we arrive in the plaza we are told that the *refugio* in Burgos is not in the central area at all. It is located, rather, in a large park not far from the other end of the city and requires another couple of kilometers of walking to find. Some of the group decide to stay in town and eat, while I join a few others in moving directly on to the *refugio*. Such additional stretches of walking at the end of the day when all a pilgrim's hopes of imminent arrival are dashed are terribly deflating and these final unexpected kilometers, especially in a city, are accomplished only through the exercise of sheer gut force. There is nothing fun or interesting or worthy of note in them. In fact they are the most awful kilometers of the *camino*. But what can I do? I must walk them so I walk them.

The park, when I find it, is suffering under the persistent heat of the summer, making it look tindery. The *refugio* is a rather improvised place: log cabins set down here and there and packed to the gills with bunk beds. When we sign in and have our *credenciales* stamped, we are offered free tickets for a tour through the city to see its highlights later in the afternoon. I gladly accept the ticket, figuring it will be a way to see Burgos without having to put my boots on and hike those two kilometers back from where I have just come. This has become one of the primary rules of my own pilgrimage: never go back, always forward. Never go back even a little. Such rules have to be broken by necessity at times, but the rule itself is still important; it keeps me going in the right direction and makes decision-making simpler in those moments when I suddenly discover two kilometers down the road that I have left my shorts hanging on a laundry line. Forget them; don't go back. Ahead, only ahead.

I rest, shower, then collect my dirty clothes for their daily washing. While doing my laundry I make a new friend. For days and days, a trio of young people, two men and a lady, have been walking in the same wave as I; we've passed each other often on the road and of course have been sharing the same toilets and showers and washbasins in the evenings. Curiously, the three of them never mix with anyone else. They have seldom greeted anyone on the road, even with the *buen camino* everyone else happily shares, nor have they sat down for meals with anyone but themselves. The young lady wears a long cotton dress at all times, which is very distinctive out here. One of the men has a high-quality camera that he uses to take pictures along the way. Other than that no one knows anything about them except for the single fact that they are Hungarian. We all presume that they speak neither Spanish nor English and perhaps that is why they are so reserved.

So here I am washing up my socks and shirt and undershorts and hanging them onto an improvised clothesline to dry, when out of a cabin comes one of the Hungarians with his own pile of laundry. We are sharing space now so I nod to him and, miracle of miracles, he responds in almost perfect English; he asks if I have seen his companions earlier on the road. He explains that he moved ahead because the girl is so slow, but now, a couple of hours after they should have arrived, they have not yet shown up at the *refugio*. I report that I saw them on the outskirts of the city perhaps two hours earlier. He seems relieved and then begins yakking up a storm with me, asking me all kinds of questions about myself and sharing with me the details of his work, his family, and even his country; quite unexpectedly this Peter has become a friend. As we tell stories of our experiences on the road, it is as if a dam has broken and he can hardly stop himself from chattering away with me; perhaps he has just had enough of being tied up in a world of three, and with the other two still out there, he now finds himself free to precipitously fall head over heels into amiability. I look forward to bumping into him again in the coming days — but as sometimes happens on the *camino*, after this one visit I never see him or his companions again.

Another young pilgrim, an Italian named Marco, takes a bunk near my own and begins talking with me so we go to lunch together at a nearby restaurant where many others of the group have also gathered. He is an artist, an oil painter specializing in Baroque and Renaissance styles. He is between things in his life. At one point in our conversation I ask him why he is doing the *camino* and in his simple English he answers, "I just need to wash my mind before the next thing in my life."

So the little tourist bus, cleverly disguised as a choo-choo train, arrives on the street in front of the *refugio* and in it we climb, an altogether happy and convivial group, taking along with us several bottles of Rioja wine to make the experience all the more pleasurable; we chug off in our little train to see the city of Burgos. Alfredo and Fermín direct the fun by passing the wine bottles to the rest of us, each of us taking a grand swig before passing it on to the next person. Soon there is enough of Rioja's best in us that song and laughter and grand cheer are pouring out of our silly choo-choo as it carries us through the avenues of Burgos.

There are only two stops that impress me: The first is a viewpoint at the top of a hill overlooking the central area of Burgos. We disembark from our train and move to the patio overlooking the city and its environs. What is interesting is that from here I can look back into the past and make out the very telephone towers set high on a distant promontory that I passed earlier in the day and from where I first spied Burgos in the distance. To look back at those towers now, only a few hours later, gives me a sense of perspective on what fifteen or twenty kilometers look like and what I am accomplishing in marking off these daily passages, one after another. It is really something to have walked all this way and I feel proud of myself.

The second stop is the cathedral in Burgos. We are given a half hour or so to visit before the tour bus will continue on its way. The interior of this Gothic church is a revelation and something the likes of which I have never seen before anywhere. What takes my breath away are not the soaring columns and arches; it is that the ceiling is made of alabaster! What in most Gothic cathedrals is stone or brick, solid and dense as can be, in this place is *alabaster!* The effect of this is extraordinary: from among and around and above the lacy gothic ribbing of this ceiling there flows a gentle and soft light that seeps into the space not from the sides but from *above*. To this pilgrim's eyes, it is not only breathtaking, it is like a vision of heaven: all light and delicacy and sheer grace. I still love Romanesque, but this cathedral makes me see Gothic in a new way. I can hardly believe it: an *alabaster* ceiling. Imagine!

One final moment from our wine-happy ride through Burgos touches me more even than the alabaster ceiling: Eva, the young juggling lady who has been with us for days and days, is ending her *camino* in Burgos. She makes her sad farewell to the rest of us in front of the cathedral; from here she will catch a bus back home. Her leave-taking is emotional and affecting as one by one we hug her and make our goodbyes. What would the *camino* be without a juggler or two to amaze wide-eyed children in village squares and delight the rest of us tired pilgrims after a long hike? Much less than it has been is all I can suppose. I am grateful for her life and what she has given to us over the past days at odd moments. I give Eva a hug and say *adios*. Such is the *camino* and life: people come and go even though you love them.

Sometime between arrival and the tour of Burgos, Kylie and Anne, my two Australian friends, tell me that they are getting very worn down by the road and the endless string of *refugios* night after night. They want just one day of rest and one night of privacy. Tomorrow morning, they admit to me, they are going to move to a hostel in the center of Burgos and spend a day in the city and an evening enjoying private rooms and long, hot baths. I for my part have been walking every day for a week without a break and am getting to the point where I can hardly remember where I have been from one day to the next, what I have done where, and what the name of which town is. The *camino* is beginning to blur. A rest would be good for me too and so I decide to follow their example and take a day off in Burgos.

Once we get back to our log cabins in the park, something wonderful begins to take place. Pilgrims go off to nearby stores and return with plastic grocery bags filled with everything from wine to cheese to bread to *chorizo* to grapes to olives to watermelons to whatever. They then begin to gather in loose groups out on the lawn and sitting on the dry grass, they begin to share it all one with another. Laughter and talk and friendship fill the air. This goes on until bedtime. In spite of the dark of night coming on in Burgos, this gathering of friends and the sharing of food is pure light. To this pilgrim's eyes, it too is a vision of heaven: all light and delicacy and sheer grace.

» *A Vision of Light* «

Brothers

July 22: Burgos to Hornillos del Camino

With my decision to remain in Burgos firmly made, I sleep in until six thirty, get up, leisurely wash, and then meander outside to see off the few pilgrims who have not already left. We make our goodbyes and one after another they head across the park to the path that will lead them out of town and eventually on to Santiago. I am feeling again what I felt in Puente la Reina, this terrible sadness at losing a *camino* week's worth of friends. This time I do not even have a very good excuse: my remaining blister is not incapacitating. I dawdle and feel the dilemma eat away at me. I really do like the idea of a rest day, but I hate the idea of staying behind, losing my pals and losing a day on the road to empty luxury. Finally, at seven thirty, I have had enough of the indecision. I decide. I quickly fill my water bottles, throw together my *mochila*, jerk it up onto my back, and head across the park to the path where the ever-faithful yellow *flechas* reappear to guide me out of Burgos and onward to Compostela. Unfortunately, because of my intention last night to stay in Burgos, I didn't buy anything for my breakfast, but I figure I will surely find a market along the way out of town and all shall be well. No such fortune is mine. No stores, not a single one, not even a closed one, greet me as I walk further and further away from the center of town and closer and closer to the open countryside. There is nothing to do but rely on the energy from last night's snacks to get me through the morning, drink lots of water, and hope for the best. I call on my beads and as the city is stirring back into its fast-paced life, I say my prayers, and before I know it, the big city of Burgos is behind me.

My guidebook suggests a walk today of over thirty-eight kilometers, all the way to Castrojeriz. With a late start and one blister still bothering me, that kind of a walk is an impossibility. I shoot instead for a midway point on the route, a place called Hornillos del Camino. With such a late start and being as always one of the slower walkers, it is unlikely that I'll meet up with many of my companions on the road today but perhaps I'll see at least a few in Hornillos. Yet as the occasional pilgrim, having started even later than I, passes me by, I realize just what a slow walker I am. I do not like being slow, but I have no choice, my body will only go so fast and these young people have huge advantages over me: their tendons are lithe, their muscles repair themselves quickly, and their backs are still strong. I have never been so aware as I am now of what fifty years does to a body. Nevertheless, I am moving, and I am moving *ahead*, and I've come this far, and I will get there all the same. And so I walk.

Except for that occasional pilgrim quietly coming from behind, greeting me and moving ahead, perhaps no more than one in an hour, I am almost completely alone on the road today. Most of the time I do not think about much as I walk along, but there are moments when the mind jumps out of its hiker's coma and back to life, something akin to an old idling car that suddenly has its first gear engaged. Some of these times are for remembering. Odd and fairly random moments from my life appear; a scene comes back to mind with clarity and immanence and the feelings surrounding that moment, sometimes sad, other times pleasant, return to visit as well; a few are accompanied by shame but most with gratitude. One memory leads to another and then another and so on an on and the hours pass. Very often these memories turn into prayers; as naturally as day follows night I hope for blessings upon the principal person within the memory, its star, wherever he is and whatever need she might have this day: each of my brothers and sisters (all ten of them), my mom and dad (both now gone to God), old friends, parishioners, our seminarians, they all have their turn. My mind wanders again to the flowers beside the road or the cawing racket of a crow high in a nearby tree or I bat at a fly that won't leave my face alone and I'm back on the *camino* marching on to Hornillos.

» Brothers «

There are other times on the road when a different kind of prayer happens. The click-clack of my *bastones* sets up a rhythm that catches my attention and pretty soon I'm chanting and breathing the Jesus Prayer in time to my *bastones*. "Lord Je-sus have mer-cy on me a sin-ner. Lord Je-sus have mer-cy on me a sin-ner. . . ." This is a form of prayer practiced by Russian Christians; for those who are faithful to it over a lifetime, the prayer becomes the very breath they breathe. I'm not nearly so holy or committed as they, but for a while I can do it and like doing it. I don't have to think, consider, or analyze; I just breathe it in and out: Lord Je-sus have mer-cy on me a sin-ner. Lord Je-sus have mer-cy on me a sin-ner. . . . In the end, both memory and prayer remind me that in my life I've accomplished some good and done more than my fair share of bad and there's no way to figure out how much of either or how they might balance out in the final weigh-in, so I have little choice but to leave this small life of mine in the hands of the Lord of Pilgrims; in the end I have no choice but to trust in his care and hope in his mercy. Thus, for an unknown amount of time I walk along, my *bastones* keeping time: "Lord Je-sus have mer-cy on me a sin-ner."

At other times I sing. I must have learned this from my dad. He enjoyed singing when only Mom or one or two of us were around, usually at the breakfast table, and Pop knew plenty of songs but only the first three or four words of any one of them. "I'm dreaming of a white Christmas . . . boo boo boo boo. . . . DAY-o, Day-ay-ay-O, du du DUH duh, du du du duh. . . . Yell-oww bird, laa la la la laaa la la. . . ." I am my father's son so I find myself doing the same out here with some of his songs but also with a multitude of hymns from church added to my repertoire. The first few words are firm in my memory but after that, I have to improvise. "Whatsoever you do to the least of my brothers, that you do unto me. When I had blisters, you sewed up my feet. When I was hungry, you gave me a peach . . . Now enter into the refuge of Horn-i-llos." It is a silly diversion that in the end turns into its own kind of praying.

So the road is good for me. Out here I see. Out here I sing. Out here I pray like crazy.

By and by I eventually arrive at Hornillos. This is a one-street and one-bar town, which pleases me, for these small places fit into the world better than the big cities. The contrast between Hornillos and Burgos couldn't be greater. No city lights, no hundreds of pilgrims, no great ca-

» *July 22: Burgos to Hornillos del Camino* «

thedral here, just a very small dot on the map with an occasional tractor chugging by and a few old-timers sitting on green park benches passing the time looking at us looking at them. It is perfect. I am pleased too that I guessed right this morning and a fair number of my *camino* companions have chosen to stop here for the day. The long walk all the way to Castrojeriz is just too much for most of us to bite off under the hot conditions of this summer weather. It is good to be with them after all and I am very glad that I did not remain in big Burgos.

The *refugio* in Hornillos is an old house next door to the parish church and it has been renovated into a very modern and pleasant building. In front of the *refugio* is a monument to a priest who was a native of the place. The plaque on the monument gives no details but offers the village's communal accolades to one Brother Servando Mayor García who gave his life for the faith in the Congo. An olive tree nearby is also dedicated to him. A little later in the evening, the elderly *hospitalera* comes by and joins me on a small bench in the cool shade under the portal of the old church. We talk casually for a moment, then I ask her about Servando and his fate. She nods sadly, then tells a grim tale of this young Hornillos man who joined a missionary order, the Marists, and was eventually stationed in Africa. In 1996, he and three other priests were brutally murdered by Tutsi militants. I vaguely remember hearing of this horrible incident and feel a sense of privilege to have stumbled into the village of Servando's youth. This insignificant little dot on the map consisting of only a few houses, barns, a single bar, and a church is actually a community of families, filled with love and faults and faith, that had the power to raise up one of its own to a life of self-giving even unto death. I am privileged to stay in his village for a night. The *hospitalera* tells me that Servando's sister still lives in Hornillos, just around the corner, and that her own husband's family is related to her.

After she finishes her talk with me, I walk back down to the monument and notice that Servando was born in 1952, the year of my birth, too. This touches me. He and I are contemporaries. If a few facts of geography and history had been different we could have been brothers, Servando and I. But like Santiago, he is a martyr, while I yet bumble along my pilgrim path here on this earth. I once attempted to live as a missionary, heading off to the *altiplano* of Guatemala and a small indigenous village named Santa Catarina in 1988. It was tough duty and I did not last long; after only about ten months in Santa Catarina, on Easter Sunday after the last *aleluya* was sung, I sadly drove out of our deep valley back to Guatemala City and a caught a plane to Spokane, where I continued my life as a more ordinary parish priest. Servando went to the Congo and never returned. Though I didn't make it as a missionary, at least while in Guatemala I got an inkling of what must animate a soul like his to stay with his people even to the point of being hacked to death with a machete. Though I don't have that kind of courage and faith, I wish I did and so I claim Servando as my blood brother. I hope a small portion of his spilled blood might mingle with mine in the next Eucharist I celebrate. May the mingling make me a better brother, a more courageous priest, something of a missionary even back home where machetes are not swung at priests' necks but where there are still plenty of challenges calling for as much courage and faith as can be mustered from folks like me. Servando, help me.

After the old *hospitalera* has moved on I remain on my bench reading the evening psalms to myself. A slender young fellow whom I have seen from time to time in the previous days but not yet met comes to the cool shade of the church portico and asks in excellent if slightly accented English if I would mind if he shares an end of the bench for a while. I welcome him of course. He sits and opens a small paperback. I glance over and notice that the book he has in his hands is one written by one of the monks of Taizé, the same monastic community in France that composes the hymns we sang in the crypt of San Juan. I ask him about the book and if he is enjoying it. He answers that he is enjoying it very much and tells me that in fact he himself has spent time at the monastery in Taizé. And with that we begin to get to know one another. Ivar is Norwegian; he is also a Lutheran seminarian preparing for ministry back in Oslo. It comes as a surprise for him to learn that I am a Catholic priest. With our self-introductions taken care of we begin to converse. I ask him about his experience at Taizé and what moved him to go there. He responds that the spiritual writings of the monks attracted him. While there he found that their manner of prayer was both very contemplative and inviting, both mysterious and accessible, both ancient and modern. The prayer of the monks manages to overcome the differences among the various Christian communions. The convergence of young people of so many nations and tongues from all over Europe at Taizé gives him hope for the world. De-

» *July 22: Burgos to Hornillos del Camino* «

spite the differences in age, culture, and even religious traditions, Ivar and I become friends, and even more because of our common desire to give our lives each in our own way to the work of Jesus, we become brothers as we quietly sit on this bench in Hornillos.

Even as Ivar and I visit, two brothers from Santander in Basque Country come dragging into Hornillos and join us on our park bench before moving into the *refugio*. They tell us they are just finishing a *doble etapa*, two stages of the *camino* in one day, a walk of over forty kilometers. They are making up time because they had to lay low for two days due to serious intestinal problems that hit both of them. Two things strike me as we visit: the first is that they are doing this pilgrimage as a team, as brothers. It is obvious that they care about each other and have a bond between them that is rich in respect and love. I would guess that one would die for the other if the need arose. The second thing that impresses me is more physical. Many of the Basques have very distinctive facial features: black hair, sharp noses, dark eyes. The face of one of the brothers in particular could be the model for innumerable mosaic images of Christ in Byzantine churches throughout the world. It is an exact match. I feel as if this Byzantine Jesus has just walked into Hornillos and what really touches me is that he has appeared in the form of a brother.

The Basque brothers leave, then Ivar gets up and heads to the *refugio* as well. I am left alone on the shady porch of the old church. My eye wanders to the olive tree that commemorates the village's martyr. How lucky I am to have so many brothers today: Servando, Ivar, the Basque boys, Jesus.

Cures, Crusades,
and Dancing Stars

July 23: Hornillos to Castrojeriz

As I depart Hornillos in the dark of a new day I pass the olive tree and monument to Servando, the martyr, my brother; I stop and ask his blessing on me today.

I leave town with weariness in my bones; of all the mattresses I have slept on over the course of this pilgrimage none has been as profoundly swaybacked as the mattress I have just had the displeasure of sleeping on in the Hornillos *refugio*. After some hours of struggling to find a comfortable position I considered putting the mattress on the floor but the tight quarters filled with *mochilas* and boots made that tough to do without raising a ruckus in the middle of the night. To make matters worse, the dormitory housed one very great snorer. I just could not sleep and this always makes me cranky and impatient the following day.

The sun rises as always, but today its light reveals the all too familiar vistas that have become such standard fare for my eyes along the way: wheat fields, wheat fields, and as far as the eye can see, yet more wheat fields. They offer nothing to alleviate my dark mood. I am bored by all that surrounds me.

Boredom of course is an interior matter. It has little to do with what actually exists in the world outside any of us. The world is just fine; it is full of beauty and miracles abound even in the most desolate of deserts.

This morning, I am the one who is desolate. I have on occasion scolded teenagers in my church youth groups or religion classes for whining that they are bored. "How can you be *bored?* Look out that window! Step out that door! Examine any blade of grass, for God's sake; it is a marvel! Behold that dandelion growing out of a crack in the sidewalk; it is a miracle! Hold your hand to your own chest and feel your heart beating inside you; you are ALIVE! Bored? How dare you!" Yet here I am, bored with my wheat fields because I did not sleep well. I am failing to see, to look, to regard as I promised myself I would. But for the moment I can't shake my interior lethargy so I will have to be more patient with myself than I was with my teenagers. A better hour will come, I am sure. I can only await it.

Not far from my end-point for the day, Castrojeriz, I pass by an ancient monastery, the *Convento de San Antón*. It is not altogether correct to use the word "by" in referring to this passage, for in reality, I actually pass *through* the place. A most imposing archway extends out from one wall of the old convent and the paved roadway that serves for the moment as the *camino* passes under this archway. After so many hours of plain-jane walking it is a rather remarkable experience to find my gaze lifted upward by this graceful stonework above my head. The monastery was built by monks of the Antonine Order. This group, now largely forgotten, was famous in former times for their widely heralded cure for something called "Saint Anthony's Fire," a highly contagious skin disease whose primary symptom was large, leaking, burning blisters covering the skin of its unfortunate victims. It was a scourge in Europe throughout the tenth and eleventh centuries and complicating matters further was the fact that the same disease was also found in pigs. The Antonine friars were equal-opportunity healers, so they took care of both human beings and their porcine beasts. Part of their healing rituals mysteriously involved the use of their order's insignia, the Greek letter *tau*. Not much more about their methods is known any longer; their secret has been lost forever. As I pass by and through this building, the *tau* is clearly emblazoned in the stonework of the place. It is a tragedy that we do not know what their curative secret was, for there surely is need for it in today's world; perhaps it could be used to help the millions on our earth dying from AIDS, or heal that freckle on my friend's chest that decided to turn itself into malignant melanoma, or even just calm down my own annoying blisters which continue to pester me day in and day out. I take my spiritual temperature and find that I am feeling worn, hopeless, and churlish as this day wears on.

It is not long before this day's dry walk comes to its end as I approach with relief the town of Castrojeriz. My destination today has been famous among pilgrims for centuries for two things: first, it is extraordinarily long and thin for a city and, second, it has a great castle, now in ruins, set on a high hill just to one side of the town. Since the medieval flow of pilgrims began to pass this way the town has grown up accommodating itself to their road; hence its shape, something akin to a long, slightly curved sausage with the castle hill nestled into that curve. The area suffered much in the tenth and eleventh centuries as the wars between the Saracens and the Christians moved back and forth across its lands and so, as in so many places in Spain, and I suppose in the world, the dust of this place must still carry the residue of the blood that once soaked it. The fact that this blood was spilled for the cause of Christ disgusts me. I cannot help but think that when my president referred to his battle against Iraq's Saddam Hussein as a "crusade," he obviously didn't understand the dark resonance of that word for those whose ancestors suffered under the blades of Christian warriors in previous centuries. The word "crusade" is not a noble word, for it has been the cause of unspeakable violence done by true believers against true believers. If I might be allowed the briefest moment to preach, in places like Castrojeriz where so many died brutal deaths in the name of both Jesus and Mohammed, it is important for the pilgrim to stop, shut up, and solemnly pray for forgiveness among us all, living and dead, past and present.

There are two *refugios* in Castrojeriz and so our band of pilgrims is split between them on this night. Our communal life is diminished for it, but there will always be tomorrow for renewing our pilgrim bonds. I choose the house on the lower road, then wash up and after a brief nap go out to explore the old town. I come upon a bustling crowd of locals, mostly old women, sizing up the fruit and hosiery on display in the town's weekly open market, and to my great surprise I also spy my old friend Robert and his grandson, Josh, sitting on a small retaining wall. They are enjoying sandwiches made of kipper snacks and looking as happy as can be as they slip the oily little fish between hunks of fresh bread and swallow them with delight. I am truly amazed to see them and even more to see them looking so fresh and cheery. I walk up to them and we have a grand reunion. It has been days since I last saw them on the road and I figured our paths would never cross again. Robert offers me a kipper snack, but the things look awful to me. Rather than just hint, this time they admit without any hint of shame that in fact they have been making occasional use of public transportation to get themselves down the road when necessary. Robert's feet are looking much better. I tell them a few of my own experiences over the past days, then take my leave and wander about the market on my own. I buy some fruit, and then a new pair of very inexpensive walking shorts, having left my Zubiri cut-offs hanging on the laundry line back in Burgos.

I also meet Ivar again and with him two of his friends, teenage cousins, Martin and Michel, from somewhere in France. Both these French boys are as skinny as rails, wear the thin cotton clothing we associate often with hippies, and most distinctive of all, both Martin and Michel sport extraordinarily wild hair. To look at them I am put in mind of Saint-Exupery's Little Prince having grown into rebellious adolescence. Though this is the first time we have met, I have indeed noticed them over the past few days, for their comic coifs make them stand out as rather unusual characters on the road and in our evening camps. The younger of the two, Michel, reports that he intends to climb the hill to the castle and camp out tonight within its ruined walls; he wants to sleep under the stars for at least one night along the way. He wants to see stars as he cannot see them in the city where he lives. I am glad for Michel, for the seeing of stars is a great thing in life.

Stars are everywhere in our imagination: We picture the Creator strewing them across the universe's vast fields of nothingness on the Fourth Day. We wish on them when they seem to fall. They guide wise kings from the East to the crib of a Savior. Cartoon characters see them when they are bonked over the head with flowerpots. They are stuck to grade-school spelling exams to indicate success. They dance over the graves of long-dead apostles. How can you not love them for all of that? Even modern science, with its discoveries of galaxies and the big bang, only makes them all the more wonderful to us. I have long imagined that when old Abraham became a monotheist he did so not because he reasoned himself to it, but because he walked out of his desert tent one night, looked up, beheld the display of light above him in all its stellar glory, and saw unity in all that infinity. God winked at him that night and

Abraham must have smiled back at his new friend. That is what the seeing of stars can do to us.

The sad reality of modern life is that stars are not so easy to see anymore, even on the *camino*. City lights are mostly to blame; the delicate shimmer of a star just can't compete with the glare of a million halogen streetlights. To get away from those lights is very difficult nowadays; to see the stars of the night sky as our ancestors saw them, or even as our grandparents saw them, is a rare thing in these modern times. Nevertheless, our dreams and our imagination and the spirits within us make us *want* to see them and dearly so.

This skinny kid's willingness to spend a cold night shivering in a ruined castle just to see stars is the clue I need to finally open up in words the greatest mystery of the *camino*, to put a name on that gravitational force that is pulling us so inexorably down this road. With Michel's wish to see stars in mind I want to posit a new theory as to what has led so many of us to do this. I want to suggest, and I ask my fellow pilgrims to help me verify if these are adequate words or not, that what is urging us forward on this road, is the longing to see real stars again. In a world filled to the gills with a billion meters of twisting and turning neon tubing and trillions of flashing and winking liquid crystal diodes and only God and Sony know how many zillion television sets casting their phantomish blue light throughout every room of every house, we want to turn off the switch on it all, *click*, if even for just a minute or two, so that we might look up, blink, and then behold in the night sky above our heads a single real star. We want to see there one little sign that there is more to us than just us. We want that one star to reveal a twinkle in the eye of God for us. Well, actually, we want to see far more than just one star; we want to see them all, strewn, cast, dancing away in their galactic pinwheels. We want to see there an extravagant God who does not count or measure but just pours and pours and pours, grace upon grace, stars upon stars, into our sky, into us. We hope against hope that before we die we might see what Abraham saw: a universe shot through with sparkling care. Then everything will make sense. To witness all this, to see the stars dance, to dance with them ourselves, this is what attracts us, this is what has grabbed us by our souls, and this is what is pulling us down this crazy road. Ah, yes, the seeing of stars is indeed a great thing in this life.

» *July 23: Hornillos to Castrojeriz* «

Girasoles

July 24: Castrojeriz to Frómista

If the previous day was a tiring one, then this new day walking from Castrojerez to Frómista is almost glorious. There is no explaining these things: some days are mostly grief while others are filled with energy and delight. It's a mystery that all pilgrims experience and comment upon but that none of us quite understand. The lucky thing is that not everyone is low on the same day or high on the same day. On my low day, I am cheered by another; on her low day, I do the cheering. We carry one another in this way.

After walking the length of the Castrojeriz sausage and leaving town in the dark of six in the morning, I have to climb a steep hill that takes me high above the plain where Castrojeriz and the castle hill nestle together. The path is thin and rocky but I climb with gusto, feeling like a mountain goat as I master the way up with the assistance of my ever-helpful *bastones* ably serving as my front legs. I arrive at the top of the hill just as the sun rises over the distant horizon behind me. The sun comes up over the lip of the earth like a great golden light and once again it is a grace to see it illuminate first my own hilltop, then its lower reaches, then the steeples and rooftops of the buildings below and finally all the surrounding fields. I behold it from above and rejoice in the return of day. As I continue on my way across my newly achieved plateau I find myself composing a prayer for the time of sunrise:

» *Girasoles* «

Blessed are you, Lord God of all Creation!
    For the waning night and the rest it has brought us . . .
    For the last star still shining as a guide into the new day . . .
    For the small white moon high above my right shoulder,
        quietly fathering me along my way.
Blessed are you, Lord God of all Creation!
    For the rising sun which will soon warm us . . .
    For the sunflowers which raise their heads
        to greet the Creator in praise and admiration . . .
    For the light which makes clear the way ahead . . .
    For the pink and blue of the new sky,
        decorating the dawn with a bounty of color.
Blessed are you, Lord God of all Creation!
    For the earth beneath my feet,
        an earth you welcome me to tread upon . . .
    For the road stretching out before me and behind me . . .
    For the thistles and reeds and weeds on its shoulders
        that keep me from wandering off the right path.
Blessed are you, Lord God of all Creation!
    For my feet and legs and lungs . . .
    For my heart, my soul, my mind . . .
    For my family, my friends, all pilgrims on this road . . .
    You have made us all.
Blessed, blessed, blessed are you, Lord God of all Creation!

I've written about stars and sunrises along the way; now let me add something about those sunflowers, or *girasoles*, as they are known in Spanish. There are stretches of the *camino* where the endless fields of wheat are interrupted by smaller, but far more interesting, fields of sunflowers. I suppose the owners of these fields sow them for the oil in their seeds, but their true value to the pilgrim is the happiness that they sow in his heart even on the most difficult of days. In themselves, the flowers are not the prettiest in the world, and the leaves and stalks are a bit on the husky side, but when you come upon a rolling hillside covered in neat rows of sunflowers stretching from the edge of the road out to the horizon, the delight is immense. These are flowers with faces. No eyes, nose, or ears adorn them, but their seedy central disk surrounded by the daisy-

» *July 24: Castrojeriz to Frómista* «

like yellow petals make about the happiest faces one could hope to imagine. Even better, as their Spanish name, *girasol*, implies, is that these same faces follow the sun in its daily course. They can't get enough of the sun and so even before the first ray of new light has peeked over the eastern horizon, they have their faces pointing east, ready to soak up that first beam with joy. As the sun rises, then traces its high course toward the west, these flowers follow it moment by moment, gradually turning their heads to the west until the day is done and the last bit of light has slipped into dusk. By the next dawn they are at the ready again with their faces already turned east. How do they do it? I have no idea but rejoice in their mysterious ways all the more because of my ignorance. I can only say that it is such a simple, graceful, and altogether wonderful phenomenon of nature that you just have to forget your own problems and say to yourself: "Now, isn't that something!"

There is one more thing that fascinates the pilgrim on his way: these flowers do this in unison. Since they are sown in orderly furrows their yellow-rimmed faces by necessity also line up in orderly file, row after row of them, extending off to the blue horizon. Moreover, all those flowers are pointing exactly the same way at the same time. They appear as the most joyful churchgoers you have ever seen, praising the Lord from their assigned pews with faces lifted high and silent voices singing hymns of thanksgiving. So they look to me, anyway.

As today's path leads me through these wondrous fields I think of my mother and how she would have delighted in these great flowers. And since I am delighting in them, our delights mingle and I have seldom felt as close to her since her death than at this particular moment along the road to Santiago. I hear her voice: "Do you see that, Kev? They look like they're *praying!*" And of course using my imagination as her voice of choice, she does say it. Thus it is that Mom and I, out here on this sunny morning among the *girasoles*, pray and praise and thank God for such wonders as this earth's sunflowers.

It is, all in all, a great morning. I am fit as a fiddle and happy as a lark as I wander down my road towards Frómista. For the first time since Pamplona, I have no blisters to molest me, my back doesn't hurt a bit, and I fairly bounce down the *camino*. For this I am grateful beyond words; finally, I am getting a taste of what other people seem to enjoy day after day: hiking as sheer pleasure!

» *Girasoles* «

But I speak too soon. At about five kilometers outside of Frómista as I pass through a small town called Boadilla, I begin to feel a strange tightness in the front of my lower right leg. It doesn't ache or hurt really; "tightness" is about the only way to describe it. I stop and stretch my foot a bit by lifting it and giving it a few twirls, first to the right and then to the left. The roadbed changed a ways back to a sort of uneven stone pavement that has made me step more carefully than usual so maybe this is the cause of my new problem. Nevertheless, I keep going on, for what else can I do with only five kilometers left in a great day of walking? The tightness increases and does so rather quickly, getting more and more troublesome with each passing few meters or so. I sit down on a retaining wall and take off my boots to air my feet a bit, again giving them a few more twists and offering my leg a rubdown; I reboot, hope for the best, and amble on. There is no great relief after the brief rest, and so I harbor a suspicion that perhaps Santiago is something of a trickster and may be having his way with me: one good morning to show me what it *could* be like, and then, bang, he afflicts me with a new disability just to teach me that the importance of suffering is not to be underestimated.

By the time I limp into Frómista, I know I am really in trouble. I now understand for myself what others have been experiencing when they have moaned about sore tendons. This is the real McCoy, I am very much afraid. I also know that it doesn't go away in a day. Ice, aspirin, anti-inflammatories: they are to become my new physiotherapeutic friends.

I settle into the clean and modern *refugio* in this fairly modern little town. I request some ice and aspirin from the understanding *hospitalera*, which is happily offered, then I begin receiving advice and assistance from any number of fellow pilgrims. Fermín shares with me some leftover anti-inflammatory pills with the serious caution that only one should be taken in a day and only on a full stomach. Another pilgrim brings me some cooling gel in a tube that he liberally spreads over my foot and lower leg and massages in. Others caution that I should take it easy for a day or two, stay off the leg altogether if possible so as to let it heal. I get contrary advice from yet another who warns me in a most grave tone that it could be a day or it could be a week before the tendon heals, but in either case there is nothing to be done so I might as well plan on continuing my walk unless the pain really begins to kill me.

After my shower and round of laundry I am feeling quite in the dumps, so by myself I hobble out for lunch in a bar, read a newspaper for the first time in over a week, and then wander over to see the Church of San Martín, another Romanesque jewel along the *camino*. Well, actually, it is more than just another Romanesque jewel; it is, my guidebook notes, "the climax in the development of European Romanesque along the pilgrims' route." High praise, for sure, but seeing is believing: this is a deeply beautiful building. San Martín is more sophisticated than the church in Torres del Rio, yet it does not lose its feeling of wholeness and integrity as it expands the Romanesque form into a triple apse and a triple-aisled nave. Its interior carvings are exquisite. Those images in stone atop their columns, as in all good medieval churches, were intended to assist an illiterate people to learn their Bible stories and religious doctrines more than they were designed to please the eye of those more interested in the artistic side of things. But they serve both purposes for me. Images of sin and grace abound. Taking a bit of time with a polychrome wooden statue of a barefoot Santiago the Pilgrim makes me feel at home, as if I am spending time with my brother. The much more ancient figure of Christ crucified in the central apse makes me sigh, it is so beautiful; it almost speaks. My spirits have been raised in this quiet place, *by* this quiet place. Feeling refreshed, it is back to the *refugio* and my ice pack and a long nap.

Later in the evening, Ivar invites me to join him and some of his friends for a beer and a bite to eat. My leg is feeling better after rest and the therapeutic action of Fermín's pill, so I accept and join him, Michel of the stars, and two Belgian girls whom he figures I should meet, one being a native of Leuven itself. After greeting one another, we find a little bar and restaurant a block or two from the *refugio* and go in. Three of the group are ready for a substantial meal, but one of the Belgians and I just want a light snack and a beer. We are shown to an upper deck above the bar where the tables have been set with knives, forks, glasses, and paper napkins. We take our places and begin getting to know one another; the bartender eventually makes his way to us to take our order. The three place their orders for full *menús del día*, while two of us ask for our small dishes. He proceeds to tell the two of us that we'll have to move downstairs since this area of his establishment is reserved for those ordering full meals. I am a bit astonished to find such distinctions in such an ordinary bar and advise him that we are *together* as a group and can we not therefore remain here and enjoy our visit *together*. He insists that the two of us can only remain if we order the full *menú*. I respond a second time, thinking that perhaps he does not understand. His voice rises and he orders us downstairs if we aren't going to eat something substantial. He emphasizes: "The bar is *downstairs*; the restaurant is *upstairs!*" For the first time in the *camino*, I begin to lose control of my patience and argue back that this is the stupidest thing I have ever heard, that since three of our group are ordering full meals, this should be enough to qualify us for a table in the high-rent area of his establishment. He repeats in an even more shrill tone his orders for us to leave, so I finally and angrily retort in my most eloquent Spanish, "Well, then, I'm leaving, and *you*, Sir, are an *IDIOT!*" I get up in a huff and the others follow my lead, leaving behind not only his upper deck with its fine paper napkins but the bar of his ground floor as well. He is not satisfied that we have learned our lesson, for even as we walk out the front door he angrily follows after us yelling to our backs: "The restaurant is *upstairs*; the bar is *downstairs!*" We shake the dust of this ridiculous restaurant from our feet and move to a more normal place just down the block. So far on the *camino*, this has been the only place that I have experienced such idiocy. Everyone else in every other bar *and* restaurant that I and my fellow pilgrims have entered, most often sweaty, dirty, smelly, and with *mochilas* taking up precious floor space, has welcomed us as if we were saints paying an honored visit.

Frómista is deliciously close to the halfway point of my *camino*, and so everything in my soul desires to push on to that midpoint and cross over it: to find myself more than halfway to Compostela is a prospect I've been pondering for days now; that halfway marker is so close that I can almost taste it, and I end the day determined to find myself on the short side of this *camino* by tomorrow noon. Yet as I lie down atop my bunk, adjust my pillow, and curl up for sleep, I can feel it: the tendon is not doing well even with the pills, creams, and icepacks. I will have to see how things feel in the morning, but unless I awake a cripple, I intend to get out that door by hook or by crook. More than once along the way, I have been amazed at how a good night's sleep can heal and restore. Even more importantly, I dread the prospect of being left behind by my present company of pilgrims, friends among whom I have been living since Puente la Reina. These young people are so much fun and so good and so diverse in their personalities, outlooks, and characters, not to mention cultures and languages, that I find it hard to imagine not being with them. I really love

» *July 24: Castrojeriz to Frómista* «

them all now. To start over with whoever is a day behind me, strangers all, is a heavy prospect. As I end the day with visions of sunflowers waiting to adorn my dreams I bravely repeat to myself: "I will walk tomorrow even if I have to crawl my way to Carrión de los Condes!"

» *Girasoles* «

A Good Shepherd

*July 25 and 26: Frómista
to Carrión de los Condes*

Surprisingly, by my five o'clock wake-up, the tendon feels pretty darn good and so without hesitation, I get up, wash, eat my yogurt and banana, and by five forty-five I am out the door and on my way to the next stop: Carrión de los Condes. This is the place (or very close to it) that will be for me the halfway point of the pilgrimage, so I am excited to be reasonably healthy and on my way to that achievement. I am amazed once again at how wonderfully healing is a full night of sleep.

The nineteen kilometers between Frómista and Carrión seem like a snap and I have no real worries as I take them on, one by one. Even better, the road turns out to be mercifully level and so I perk along at a comfortable and, for me, relatively speedy manner. Even at that, I am still being passed by nearly everyone else. For quite a while I lead Alfredo the Argentinean, but he catches up to me just as we hit the first bar along the day's route so together we stop in for our coffee and we enjoy an amiable conversation. The place is a side yard to some local's house where a simple outdoor bar has been set up and Gregorian chant is playing over speakers hidden among the plants and flowers. Alfredo cheerily picks up the tab for both of us and even though we depart together, he quickly leaves me behind, a reminder that this enterprise, at least the walking part of it, is an eminently solitary project in spite of the social life that is shared in bits and pieces along the way.

With about five kilometers remaining before reaching my day's goal, rather suddenly the tightness in my leg returns and becomes increasingly painful. By the time I reach Carrión I am limping badly again and if I step in just the wrong way, a bolt of pain shoots up my leg and into my body. Carrión must be preparing for a festival of some sort, for the place is dressed up in medieval banners streaming high above its streets and colorful bunting adorning its buildings. It seems as if I've limped into another, older century. I stop at the information booth at the entrance to the old city to get my bearings, then head the few blocks more to the *refugio* located just a couple doors down from one of the town's paramount churches, that of Santa María del Camino. I arrive before the *refugio* opens for the day so I limp back to the small, grassy plaza in front of the church and there find my companion from earlier in the day, Alfredo, lying on the grass with his boots off and his feet in the air, letting a slight breeze blowing across the plaza cool them. I join him in the plaza, tug off my own boots and socks, lie down on my back, and, copying his good example, put my feet up on a stone park bench.

It is in this position that I have one of my most curious discussions of the whole *camino*. Alfredo asks me with a bit of caution in his voice: "Kevin, is it true you are an American?" I answer, "Yes," a little incredulously, for I could never think of myself in any other way and find it hard to imagine that others might think of me as anything but an American.

"You speak Spanish very well."

"Thank you, Alfredo. I do my best."

"You know, if I had known you were an American, I would never have spoken to you. I hate America."

This takes me completely by surprise; I have never heard anyone say anything quite so honestly and really quite so bluntly. I wince at his words even as I try not to feel personally offended. I've lived outside my own country long enough that I hope I can now see it with its various faults and its virtues in higher relief than if I had spent my life only within its borders. I therefore ask him:

"You hate America? Really? Why is that?"

As we lay supine in the grass, each of us with our bare feet set high on our particular park bench, Alfredo begins by saying that he has visited the States many times and that with each visit he has found the manner and the attitudes of the American people to be less and less connected to what is important in life. Family relations are eaten away by constant motion incited by children's soccer practices and dance classes. There is no longer any family meal and, perhaps even worse for a Latin American, no ability to celebrate with a good family party. Americans don't know how to dance or sing or just have real fun anymore. Instead they work long hours, make lots of money, worry about increasing their productivity, race about in their SUV's from school to gym to work to school again. Even more, they are people who have become increasingly fearful, isolated, and ignorant of the rest of the world. All this, he notes, is evident in the vapid films produced by Hollywood one after another. He tells me that he works in Argentina as a film critic, among other things, and has followed the cinema for many years. He no longer bothers with most American studio films because they are toilet-paper-thin. There is just nothing to them. He mentions an exception, *Mulholland Drive*, but other than that and a very few others, he now looks elsewhere for films that speak to the mysteries humanity faces in its journey through life. Even more, he says, he never wants to return to America. He has seen enough. And really, he adds with a note in his voice clearly excepting me now, in the end he never wants to have anything more to do with Americans either. Thus it is that if he had known I was an American he would never have spoken to me. Alfredo is clearly happy that he *has* spoken to me, for we have become pretty good friends in the last day or two; but that is beside the point at hand: Alfredo despises America.

What is there to say? A part of me wants to respond that things could not be all that great in Argentina either, a land not so long ago overrun by a vicious military dictatorship and presently in the throes of a devastating economic crisis, but I also realize that this is a lesson for me, not him, and it is not my job at this moment to defend my nation as much as to listen attentively to his critique of it, for seldom in life will I be given an opportunity like this to hear and see how my culture is perceived from the outside with the clarity and feeling that Alfredo is sharing with me as a friend.

Nevertheless, I offer a few insights of my own that I hope might capture at least a bit that which is virtuous in my land and culture. I mention in particular the extraordinary bonding together of the country after the attacks of September 11, 2001, and the generosity and spiritual solidarity with which people responded to that blow. More importantly, I say, there is an optimism in Americans that is a great source of energy and motivation to make the future better. Likewise, we have a sense of not being weighed down by heavy traditions that no longer serve to make humans better. "If it doesn't help, be rid of it." In the end, in spite of our many social ills, we really do want each person to succeed, to have a shot at the prize, to be treated justly.

Alfredo attends to my response with respect and even agrees with it to some extent, but in his mind at least, these things do not outweigh his visceral disgust with what he has experienced of my country. I acknowledge that my culture is far from perfect and offer for his consideration the theory that at the heart of my people's current *dis-ease,* our preoccupation with self-protection, self-defense, and ever-more-isolating security measures is that we are a society fed very high daily doses of fear, fear of ever new diseases, fear of accidents, fear of crime, fear of death, fear of life, fear of anything and everything that might impact what we believe to be our right to a very high quality of life. Other cultures accept that life holds risk and danger and go on living, but we Americans, myself included, live lives mutated by these fears; as we become more and more preoccupied with our own self-defense, both personal and national, we become less generous, less respectful of others, less able to celebrate life and its many joys as human beings must celebrate them. Most of these problems, we both agree, are not exclusive to America and Americans, but they seem most evident in my country, at least at this moment in history, if for no other reason than that its size and extraordinary power make it such a massive player on the world stage. What a contrast between that reality and the reality of life on this *camino* where fear is almost completely absent and people are extraordinarily generous and humble and able to form families and communities based on affection and love.

This has been, all in all, a sad discussion and it comes to an end without the convenience of a conclusion, for the time arrives for us to get up off our backs and make our way to the front door of the now-open *refugio* and get settled for the afternoon. Alfredo and I stuff our socks into our boots and tie them to our *mochilas,* put on our sandals, and together walk up the street to our new home for the night.

» *A Good Shepherd* «

As it turns out, the *refugio* is a rather unsettled place since the bathrooms and showers are presently undergoing a fairly major renovation. Workmen abound, making lots of noise with hammers and trowels throughout the afternoon, and the few facilities available to us to care for our personal hygiene are messy and host increasingly long lines of pilgrims patiently waiting their turns, soap in one hand and clean clothes in the other. Even as I wash myself and my clothes, my throbbing tendon is urging me to take a day off. Kylie and Anne, who after their own "day off" in Burgos have caught up to us again, accept my invitation for lunch and after a short walk further into town we land in a small bar on the main street; we pick a table by an open window looking out on the busy street and place our orders. They choose hamburgers, but after my conversation about the darker side of American culture I choose something more typical of Spain, a sizzling slice of pork. When our dishes are delivered, they receive with enthusiasm huge, homemade hamburgers that I cannot help but admire and wish I had ordered as well. My pork is just fine, though, and we eat with typical pilgrim gusto. Anne and Kylie are nurses in their other life back in Australia and remind me that rest is the best medicine for what I've got. They give me the Spanish brand name of what they consider the best anti-inflammatory cream, Voltarén, which also comes in pill form. After we finish our meal, I go buy the stuff at a pharmacy down the street while they head into town to see the sights.

With evening's arrival I go to dinner with Ivar. After wandering about a bit we find a place just down the street, near the entrance to the old city, with what looks like a decent fixed menu. Inside real tablecloths, cloth napkins, and a waiter dressed in black slacks, white shirt, and black bowtie, make us scruffy hobos feel like we are walking into a place way above our class. We dawdle over our salads, sizeable hunks of lamb, and inconsequential desserts while we talk over issues of our divided Christianity: how would restored unity among our churches happen and what would the whole look like once it did? Why do Catholics store in a gilt box the bread consecrated in the Eucharist? Most importantly, how did each of us discover our vocations to ministry? How did we come to *hear* and *see* and *know* this is what we must do? And so we tell our stories. Night is coming on quickly and so we have to get back before the doors of the *refugio* are locked at ten p.m. We pay our bill and call it a day.

The short walk back to the *refugio* is a difficult one for me. Despite my

» *July 25 and 26: Frómista to Carrión de los Condes* «

heavy dose of Voltarén, the pain from the tendon shoots up my leg and into my groin. I have to run through the wrenching back-and-forth of whether to hold up or go on, hold on to friends or protect the leg, carry on or start over. There are spiritual aspects to my options, of course. To let go as well as to start over are both part and parcel of the pilgrim vocation at least as I am discovering it. Important as it is, the comfort of camaraderie in the end is not the goal; this is, after all, not a permanent city we build here. Holding up, letting go of old friends, the slow and mysterious process of coming to know a new crowd of pilgrims one by one, all of it is an exercise in dying and rising. As before, I leave the final decision in the hands of a good night's sleep, waiting to see what the morning might bring.

With the prospect of once again saying goodbye to good friends, one of the psalms for the evening, the one hundred and forty-fifth, echoes around inside my heart:

> The eyes of all creatures look to you
> And you give them their food in due time.
> You open wide your hand,
> Grant the desires of all who live.

May all of us on this road, under this roof, my pals for these past ten days and more, Fermín, Alfredo, and Ivar, Kylie and Anne, the French cousins, all of us, look to you and may you open wide your hand, giving us the food that will allow us to hear, to see, to know.

I awake at five in the morning and know immediately that the leg must take precedence over friends. Even before I get out of the sack it is aching and I realize there is little choice but to hold back after all. The firmness of the decision to stay put doesn't make it any easier to say goodbye to everyone else as they go out the door one by one or two by two. I know that I will never see most of them again. It is particularly sad to wish Ivar a final *buen camino*; he has been a good companion and has become a spiritual brother over the past few days. He is late getting out the door so he is the last I see off and do so with a clumsy little embrace and a promise to visit him in Oslo some day. With that, they are all gone.

The *hospitalera* graciously allows me to stay a second night, even without presenting a letter from a doctor, the usual protocol. She asks me only to remove my *mochila* from the dormitory and store it in a back garage until the place reopens after cleaning at one in the afternoon. Thus I limp off into the new day very much by myself. My first job is to find an open bar for a little breakfast, but at six in the morning this is not so easy. I am finally directed to a place back near the information booth at the entrance to the old city, and once there I find a number of my pilgrim companions already enjoying their own coffees and tortillas and croissants. This establishment also serves as the local bus stop and all these folks are waiting for the arrival of their various buses to take them from the *camino* and carry them back home; either they are too sick to continue or have run out of vacation time. After a cheery visit and a few additional goodbyes and double-kisses, Spanish style, I walk back into town, finding the Church of Santa María del Camino open and the parish priest standing in its covered porch talking to a young man. I have long felt that confession should be part of my pilgrimage experience and with little else to do on a lonely Saturday morning and a priest now at hand, the moment feels right. I wait for him to finish with the young fellow, then approach him to inquire about going to confession sometime in the day. He responds quickly that I may go anytime I want and why not now. He asks for a few moments more to stamp the *credencial* of the young man and waves me into the church. I enter the cool and dark interior of Santa María and shortly thereafter he follows me in, dips into the sacristy, and comes back vested in surplice and stole; he then hurriedly waves me forward to his small confessional stall. I kneel on the small step in front of him and begin my little confession face-to-face. After the usual formalities that begin the traditional rite I commence by going back several months in my life to relate some things from those days long ago that have been bothering me; the little priest stops me short with the words, "¡*Basta con la historia!* Enough of the history! Tell me what's going on with you now — on the *camino!*" He asks me if I am letting people know I am a priest as I go along and I answer that indeed I am, whenever anyone asks. He asks if I am praying and I tell him, "Yes, *Padre*, out here I am praying like I've never prayed before," but I do not mention the singing or the talking to animals. He asks if I am going to Mass regularly and I respond, "Yes, I am going as much as I can." He then asks me if I concelebrate with the priest at the altar when I go to Mass, and here I have to acknowledge that no, I am not doing that, but assisting rather from the pew with the other pilgrims. This clearly disappoints him and he orders me to concelebrate with him later this afternoon. He next gives me a firm but caring lecture about praying, praying constantly, praying with *rhythm* in my life, and then ends with a flourish: "Be certain not to overlook God in all that you see along the way: in the flowers, in the fields, in the sky, etc! Keep your eyes open! Keep them open to God!" He assigns me a penance that seems like the easiest thing in the world after all the penance I have been doing with my blisters and now a fiery tendon: "Say three Hail Marys." And with that he gives me absolution and dismisses me with the rite's final words: "*Véte in paz.* Go in peace."

I say my three Hail Marys, remaining in the quiet of the church for a good while before wandering out and back down to the bar to see who might still be waiting there.

Lucy is here, sitting at an outdoor table on the sidewalk in front of the bar. She is a Brazilian who speaks Portuguese, Spanish, French, and English. We have been on the road together for days, actually, and have had occasional encounters and the briefest of visits, but have not really become companions along the way. As she waits for her bus after most of the others have left, we finally have ourselves a good talk. She is a calm and soft-spoken lady with a ready smile and kind manner. In the course of our conversation she asks me about my work; I am a little surprised she does not know already, but I tell her I am a priest. She is then the one to be surprised; she smiles and responds: "Ah! Then that is why you are a peaceful man." This is an unexpected and far more moving compliment than the one about being a Mexican.

Surprisingly, Guy is here too. My French-Canadian friend since Puente la Reina looks terrible. He has just walked into town — barely. He has been suffering since the night before with a very bad case of diarrhea and vomiting, probably from consuming bad food or drinking fouled water along the way. He has reached the limit of his endurance and so has decided to quit the *camino*. This morning while on the road he continued to walk in spite of his condition, knowing that Carrión's bus stop would be the nearest place for him to access an exit from the *camino*. From here he will catch the bus to León, then he will take another bus to Madrid, and finally, from the capital city, he will catch a plane back to Montreal. I feel deeply sorry for him, not only for the physical mess he is in at the moment but also for his having to end his pilgrimage long before reaching his goal in Santiago. He is pale and wan and quite disconsolate; all I can do is sit with him as he awaits his coach homeward.

And here too is Antonio, a young Catalán man with a closely shaved head whose path I have crossed in the preceding week at least twice; he has stood out from the rest of the *camino* crowd because he never stays overnight in the *refugios* and this because he is walking with two dogs, one quite large and the other very small. The three of them have been tramping along together since Pamplona. Now, it must be noted that this is an extraordinarily silly thing to do. It is hard enough to walk by yourself with your own mountain of stuff on your back and with your own physical problems to take care of and knowing that you are completely dependent on the open doors of *refugios* every twenty kilometers or so for survival, but to attempt it with two dogs by your side means that you not only have to take care of yourself with all your own issues, but you also have to take care of not one, but two other creatures of God who depend on you for everything: food, water, shelter, care of paws, and so on. It also means that you will not be able to stay overnight in any *refugio* along the way, leaving you and your canine companions to make do along riverbanks and in city parks. It also means you have to carry dog food, which is dense and heavy. And it also means that you have to pull burrs out of their fur and from between the pads of their paws lest they become infected, and they do get infected even with all your best efforts to attend to them several times a day. And finally, if you will be patient for just one more of these "also means," it also means that when these dogs do begin to limp and labor for whatever reason, you have to carry them . . . on top of your *mochila* and over your shoulders, like the Good Shepherd with one of his lost sheep.

I learn all this from Antonio as we sit in front of that bar waiting for the bus to pick up Lucy and Guy. I also learn that he and his dogs disappeared from the road for several days because, in an effort to cut a day or two off the walk, he had taken a train to get a bit ahead, buses not allowing dogs on board. But he slept through his early-morning stop and the train took him at least ninety kilometers afield and there was no way back except to wait for another train going in the return direction, catch it, and start where he had left off, *losing* two days rather than *gaining* them. His bigger dog is named Timba and the little one Tik Tik. He tells me that he spent a good part of the previous day carrying Timba on his shoulders when the dog went lame with an infected paw. Now, Timba must weigh at least fifteen or twenty kilos, just to put this feat into perspective. Why all this sacrifice on behalf of his dogs? There are only two possible explanations: either he loves these creatures or he is just nuts. Antonio gives absolutely no sign of being in any way nuts. He has a gentle smile, pets his dogs with care, and chats with me in a most normal way. This man, I believe, is simply one who loves his dogs for no pragmatic reason and could not imagine being a pilgrim without them being pilgrims with him. The additional burdens they bring him give him more opportunity to care and love them and so he is able to carry them even on his shoulders for hours if he has to. He doesn't mind. Love makes such sacrifices joys. He is the Good Shepherd. He is for me today my best image of God.

The bus to León eventually pulls up only a meter or two from our sidewalk table. I double-kiss Lucy goodbye and shake Guy's weak hand and with a diesel roar off their bus drives down the road carrying them back into the "real world" they left behind weeks ago. Antonio is busy watering Timba and Tik Tik so I amble slowly back into town.

By noon, the new day's wave of arriving pilgrims is already flowing into Carrión. Surprisingly, there are a few familiar faces in the crowd. Catherine, a Flemish lady from Ghent whom I had been introduced to a few days earlier by Robert and Josh, recognizes me and I her. Her arrival is followed by the lumbering image of my old friend from days past, Javier. He had diverted from the *camino* to take a bus up to the famous Monastery of Silos, home of the monks made famous in recent years by their best-selling recordings of Gregorian chant, where he spent a day and a night. Once settled into the *refugio* he shares with me photocopies of the vespers and lauds services he participated in while there; he is positively enthusiastic about the experience and reminds me several times that I have missed something special by not having made the same diversion as he. He also reports on his aching ankles as I share with him the story of my tendonitis. The former tension between us seems now all gone.

Javier, Catherine, and I go to lunch together, then I spend the rest of the afternoon caring for my leg, resting it, massaging it, slathering it with Voltarén and swallowing the pills at the appointed hours. It is a very curious malady, for there are times when it does not hurt at all, even when I walk about, but there are other moments, inexplicably and unexpectedly,

» *A Good Shepherd* «

when it brings me almost to my knees in pain. Later in the afternoon, I go for a little walk through the festive streets of Carrión just to break the monotony of my regime of rest, and on the way back to the *refugio,* I take a slightly wrong step and a bolt of pain shoots from my lower leg into my upper body, almost crippling me in the street and certainly taking a couple breaths away. "Will I be able to walk even tomorrow?" is the question gnawing at the back of my mind through most of the day. I will do my best to move on, but for the moment it does not look good.

On the positive side, the day in Carrión could not be prettier; the heat has diminished and a delightful breeze blows softly through the streets of the colorfully-adorned town. I claim for myself a small corner of the leafy plaza in front of the Santa María del Camino church for my dose of evening psalms, to write in my journal, and to watch the locals promenade about the plaza. Children race about in loose gangs chasing pigeons that they never catch, young mothers push baby carriages and stop and smile when someone asks to look in on the newborn, young men stand in small groups and look cool as they eye the young girls passing to the other side of the plaza. It is life lived on a wonderful scale. It is so different in texture and quality from our mall-based culture back home, where no one looks at another, no one knows anyone else, and the environment is canned, prefabricated, and the air is entirely "conditioned." I suppose this mallhood is at least part of what Alfredo found so disagreeable in his trips to the U.S.

I wander into the church a few minutes before the Saturday evening Mass is to begin and remembering my marching orders from my morning confessor, I also check into the sacristy where the *padre* is preparing himself for the liturgy; I shake his hand and, all business now, he shows me a cabinet fairly bursting with albs, stoles, and cinctures galore, so I find myself an alb that seems like it might fit me, pull it up a bit at the waist with the cincture, and put a stole around my neck. I am ready and so we step into the sanctuary and begin the Sunday liturgy. The *padre* reminds us of something important that I have forgotten: yesterday, the twenty-fifth of July, was the very feast of Santiago, a great day in Spain, of course, and so in his homily he offers us reflections on a long chain of related images: Santiago, Spain, pilgrims, Mary, Jesus, Spain, Jesus, Mary, Spain, and finally back to Santiago. The themes and the very manner of his homily is popular Spanish Catholicism, I suppose, in a nutshell.

» *July 25 and 26: Frómista to Carrión de los Condes* «

Though it is a Catholic piety quite different in seasoning if not in substance from the kind I grew up in, I am glad for the moment to be in the middle of it; it is rich and deep and full of folkloric tones and riffs that I miss in my own more bland religious life.

I can only imagine what must be going on in Compostela on this weekend; the crowds and the festivities inside and outside the cathedral I am still so far from seeing with my own eyes must surely be grand. In my mind's eye I see strolling bands and dancers and crowds beyond counting. It is a sort of Catholic Emerald City for me now, a place at the end of this wonder and adventure-filled road, a place that I know only in my imagination, but which draws me and into which I *will* walk on my own two feet, with my back straight and my head high and one of my incomplete hymns from the way sailing about within my heart. Will I weep or laugh or fall to my knees and kiss the earth? I have no idea. All I know is that I *will* arrive and I will do so singing.

After Mass, I meet Javier and end up at the same bar where I had lunch the day before with Kylie and Anne; this time I order the attractive hamburger they so enjoyed and it is just plain delicious, with ketchup and mustard and juicy fat dripping out the seams and over my fingers. See, Alfredo: America has given *something* good to the world! As we talk about our journeys Javier strikes me as a different person now. He seems his own man. He is no longer dependent on anyone else. There is no suggestion of walking together. It is understood that though we are friends, we are each walking our own *caminos*.

In spite of the cooler weather earlier today, by the time I am ready to crawl into bed, the dormitory is stifling hot. Some among the day's new group of pilgrims obviously have an aversion to fresh air even in the midst of one of the hottest summers in European history, for the window near my bed has been repeatedly closed after my repeated openings. And so accepting the heat as a fact of life and no longer caring a wit about modesty and having left all vanity behind long ago, in the midst of twenty or thirty men and women I lay myself down to sleep atop my mummy bag in nothing more than my briefs.

Slow Moe

July 27: Carrión de los Condes to Ledigos

At four in the morning, I am awakened not only by the familiar sound of the early birds among the pilgrims packing up their *mochilas* and preparing to head out the door, but also by the most unusual sound of a very substantial downpour outside. This rain doesn't just patter on the roof or drip-drop from leafy branches outside, it cascades down upon us in a steady whoosh that fills the air with a delicious dampness. I remain prostrate and almost naked upon my bunk and silently absorb the natural pleasure of it. There is a second thought though that disturbs the tranquility of this waking moment: on the one hand the cool moisture in the air is a grace to breathe in, but on the other I am not so sure I am prepared to walk out into this deluge; after all, I left behind my beautiful red poncho days and days ago in Puente la Reina and have nothing in its place.

As I get up to use the john I pay attention to my leg and it seems that the medicine has done the trick; it doesn't pain me much at all. Javier stirs and I whisper to him that it is pouring rain outside this morning. He doesn't seem concerned by the news but begins to prepare himself for his day's walk. I begin to prepare my own bag, filling the water bladder inside, re-stuffing my mummy bag into its small sack, anointing my feet with Vaseline and my leg with Voltarén, pulling on and tying up my boots. I find a few plastic grocery bags in the garbage bin and salvage them as protective coverings for my *mochila,* copying what I have noticed a few others doing. I ask Javier how he is faring and he nods that all is well. I take another trip to the john and by the time I have returned, there is no sign of Javier upstairs. I go to the ground level with my *mochila* dragging from one hand and my *bastones* in the other but Javier is not there either. Though the rain is still pouring into the street, he has obviously taken off undaunted on his own day's journey. I, however, am daunted, as are a number of other pilgrims who join me in sitting around the *refugio's* lobby, hoping against hope that the rain might let up before it gets very much later. Those who have planned to do the full thirty-eight-kilometer walk all the way to Sahagún have the most to lose as the minutes tick by.

Finally, by seven, the deluge has changed to a drizzle and then just fizzles out altogether. I make my move and head into the heart of Carrión and out of the city again. After I pass a small fountain just beyond the city limits, there is nothing more for the next seventeen kilometers, no village, no bar, no water, nothing at all until the pilgrim route approaches the small town of Calzadilla de la Cueza. I fully expect Calzadilla will be the end point of my trip for the day; seventeen kilometers will be plenty with a gimpy leg like mine.

I am very much alone as I proceed into the damp morning. After only fifteen minutes on the road the tendon is fairly well screaming at me with each footstep. The pain is the worst I have yet felt on the *camino,* far angrier than anything served up by my old blisters. This situation prevails for the next three or four kilometers until something rather remarkable happens: I master the pain. This is a new phenomenon for me and I am amazed by it; by just marching on and gutting my way through it, I lose consciousness of the pain within me. It is almost as if it is a bawling baby that finally realizes it isn't going to have its way with its mother or father so it goes into a corner by itself to sulk, leaving the poor parent in peace and quiet for a while. Every once in that while it stirs from its sulk and sends a jolt up my leg just to remind me that it is still there, ready to interfere with this forced march if it so wills; then it goes back to its corner for more self-preoccupied whimpering. Whatever the psychology or physiology of the experience, I am immensely grateful as I slowly make my way down a well-groomed road and across the expansive countryside towards Calzadilla.

Now here is something else that surprises me in the first hours of my day's walk: perhaps as a result of the extraordinary rain early in the morning I encounter clouds of very funny little bugs at face level. They do not so much fly as *jump* about in the air, up and down, back and forth, side to side, always at right angles. To some degree they make way for me as I pass through their airborne gymnastics class, though occasionally I get a few in my mouth. This is a small price to pay for the enjoyment of watching these creatures' aerobatic antics. Bouncing bugs! I've never heard of such a thing and certainly never seen such a thing. They must be the class clowns of the insect world. They make me smile and I can think of no good reason why the Creator would have put them on this earth except to give pilgrims like me a quiet laugh.

Somewhere further down this well-groomed road, I come across a rather substantial snail slowly, ever so slowly, slithering its way forward toward some unknown destination. The sight grabs my attention. I stop, lean low against my *bastones*, and just watch the snail for quite some time. I take a good look at this poor little fellow and for just a moment I see myself in him. Its huge nautilus seems to tip from side to side as if it were a pilgrim's *mochila*; it certainly appears just as burdensome. His two antennae remind me of my *bastones*. I address him out loud, "*Hola, Señor* Snail. *¿Qué tal?*"

Señor Snail looks up at me and responds: "*Bien.* Just fine. The rain makes everything lovely for us."

"I can see that. You know, you and I are in just about the same fix, aren't we?"

"I don't really know what you mean by a 'fix'; I am what I am."

"Well, I mean that we are both carrying loads and we are both very slow."

"Is that a 'fix'? For me it is life. I know no other way. Can we be bothered by what we are not? I am no hare; I do not care about speed. I am what I am. I do what I can do. That is enough."

"I understand, I think. When I was a kid, all my brothers and sisters called me 'Slow Moe' because I dawdled a lot back then. I was really quite lazy, I suppose, which made me hate the nickname all the more."

"Because it was true."

"Yes, because it was true."

"Laziness is no virtue, but being slow is not always a matter of laziness. It has its good side too. If you weren't slow, after all, you wouldn't be talking to me now, would you?"

"I don't suppose so."

"Then we are in no 'fix' to be slow. I will remember you the rest of the day, pilgrim, as 'Slow Moe.'"

"Thank you, *Señor* Snail. I will be happy the rest of the day being 'Slow Moe.' Anyway, I hope you make it to wherever you are going this day."

"I will. And I trust you will make it to your destination as well. I still have half a road to traverse before day's end, so I really must be moving on, as must you, Slow Moe. Santiago is waiting for you. *Adiós.*"

"*Adiós.*" I stretch upright again, readjust my own *mochila*, take a grip of my *bastones*, and head slowly down my path, leaving the wise snail to his own *camino*.

For the first time in my walking I come upon pilgrims accompanied by a *coche de apoyo*, or "helper car." The concept is simple: why carry your own stuff when you can have someone drive behind you (or ahead of you, for that matter), with your *mochilas*, food, and any luxury you'd otherwise miss happily packed inside the *coche de apoyo*. No muss. No fuss. No hurt. I have been surprised from time to time this morning by a few youthful pilgrims with very light *mochilas* passing me by and sometimes almost running past me. I figure they must be newcomers to the *camino*, fresh and full of energy still. One young fellow with black hair, wire-rim glasses, and an angular face wears a blue Superman t-shirt and actually looks like the young Superman I remember from the comic book days of my boyhood. He flies past me without a greeting or even a nod. I don't like him. Superman indeed. Let's just wait a few days and we'll see if these little superheroes are still running down the road to Santiago! I am then passed by an innocent-looking white van. A little while later, I come over a rise and there along the road is the van with the back doors open, surrounded by a troop of pilgrims, the very ones who have been so efficiently passing me by one by one, including young Superman himself. They are happily hanging about sipping coffee and eating snacks that are being served by two or three very nice ladies who remind me very much of my old Cub Scout den mothers. As I walk by, no one acknowledges me, no offers of coffee come my way, no biscuits are extended to a fellow pilgrim, all of which are grave violations of *camino* etiquette; I soldier on knowing in my heart of hearts that I am stronger than they. *Coche de apoyo!* Really! Not this pilgrim. I am Slow Moe!

The guidebook has promised that a kilometer or two before arriving in Calzadillo, the intrepid pilgrim will notice the tower of the village church appearing suddenly above the rolling fields that he has been steadily traversing. When I see the steeple I can hardly believe that I am so close to my destination for the day; the seventeen kilometers have passed with remarkable speed. Could it be some other village? But there is no other village, or anything else for that matter, between Carrión and Calzadillo, so I cheerily walk to the small village and after rounding a bend or two, sure enough, there it is: Calzadillo. The *refugio* is at the very entrance to the village. I knock at the door and the young *hospitalero* comes out with mop in hand to advise me that I am most welcome but he'll need about another hour to finish cleaning up, then I and the others may come on in. In the meantime, he suggests, I should walk a bit further on to the local bar and have a coffee and a bite to eat. I agree and consider leaving my *mochila* and *bastones* at the door but think better of it and decide to keep them with me. I find the bar easily enough, but it is a bit further than I expected, a couple of blocks beyond the *refugio*.

Catherine from Ghent is finishing up just as I arrive. She informs me that it is just too early to stop for the day and so she is going on another six kilometers to the next village, a place called Ledigos. I wish her well, then leave my *mochila* and *bastones* outside the bar, straighten my back, and walk in for my belated *café con leche* and slice of *tortilla*. It all tastes great, and as always that wonderful mix of caffeine, sugar, cream, egg, potato, and probably more than a little olive oil all hitting an empty stomach at once prove to be a regenerative mix without equal. By the time I pay for my snack, I too am ready to hit the road again. I believe I can manage these six additional kilometers without difficulty. After all, I am Slow Moe! I'm not pretty and I'm not fast, but I get there. I always get there.

The route out of Calzadilla follows the highway to Sahagún and so is far less interesting than the previous kilometers of the day. The mere presence of a highway only a few meters to my right with its roaring traffic seriously diminishes the attractiveness of the journey. Nevertheless, I trek on rather energetically and with the tendon fairly well tamed for the time being.

Being alone on the road, I begin to sing. The first melody that comes

» *July 27: Carrión de los Condes to Ledigos* «

to mind is a lovely hymn we sing often in our seminary for morning prayer, especially in the Lenten season preceding Easter: "Oh Son of Justice, Jesus Christ. . . ." The tune is easy but as always, beyond the first few words, I'm lost, so I just *la-la-la* the rest of it: "Oh Son of Justice, la-la-la . . ." and have a great game of it. When I tire of that tune, I begin with another: "I heard the voice of Jesus say, come unto me and rest . . . la-la-la. . . ." And then this: "Come, my way, my truth, my life . . . la-la-la. . . ." This prayer *qua* entertainment occupies me for quite a while until I am startled by a bicyclist whooshing past my right shoulder; she turns and smiles broadly back at me as if she has been in on my joke for some time. I am embarrassed for just a moment, but there is no room for vanity on a road like this so I pick up where I left off and start inventing my own *camino* words to whatever melody comes to mind: "The King of Glory comes, the nation rejoices; open your gates before him, lift up your voices. The Pilgrim of Leuven comes, the *camino* rejoices; he goes to Compostela, la-la-la-la-la . . . !" So this, of a sort, is my Sunday praise.

On my left I pass a wide-open field that has been tilled and left untended for the time being. It is pure dirt piled up in somewhat disintegrating furrows but out in the middle of the field of black dirt, either having escaped the harvest or having planted itself there as a wandering volunteer, a very hefty sunflower is standing by itself. Its head is very large and its weight is pulling the upper stalk into a substantial hunch. Nevertheless, that head with its aging yellow face remains turned to the sun as best it can. Even in its old age, it still follows nature's orders and slowly, ever so slowly, turns itself to follow the glory of its solar love. Well, I must say that, like *Señor* Snail before it, Old Man *Girasol* reminds me of me right now: tired, alone, aging, and with my head hanging low. I yell over to him, "*¡Hola, Girasolote!*" He cannot turn his head but he smiles to me as best he can under the circumstances, then in his old man's voice calls back to me: "*Sigue fiel*. . . . Be faithful and all will be well." And all will be well.

Just about a kilometer before Ledigos, my humble dirt path is subsumed under the dominating pavement of a highway and thence it begins a steep decline toward the village. For some reason walking downhill is just what this tendon of mine needs to reawaken and start bawling its miserable head off. It becomes very difficult to walk and the sharp pains zinging up my leg put an end to the fun I have been having all morning.

» *Slow Moe* «

To set my right foot down is instant agony and there is no mastering it now. With only a single kilometer left in the day's journey, there is nothing to be done but put one foot in front of another and carry on down the hill no matter the pain. A married couple about my age come up from behind and ask if I am okay. They know immediately that I have a bad case of tendonitis and offer to get help for me. I respond with a wince that it is just a short ways more and that I can certainly make it into Ledigos. They sympathetically wish me well and continue on their way while I slowly, slowly, ever so slowly make my way into the very small *refugio* of the very small village of Ledigos.

The *refugio* of Ledigos is an old farmhouse that has been converted into a couple of dormitories and accompanying baths. It is tranquil, clean, and has a very nice inner yard with a comfortable lawn and a few plastic tables and lawn chairs spread around. Attached is the only bar in the village. Fresh produce, wine, and beer can be purchased from the *hospitalero*, a serious young man who also serves as bartender and store manager. There is really nothing else in this village besides a church and a few old houses. There are about ten of us staying here. After the full house and commotion in Carrión this is a small paradise.

Catherine has already settled in and welcomes me. I rest on my bunk a while, take a shower, wash my soiled clothing, and take another rest. All the morning clouds have passed and the sky is as blue as blue can be. The yard is an oasis of green and shade and wonderful quiet. The hot afternoon passes slowly but very gently. I order a beer from the *hospitalero*. A new acquaintance named María is a physical therapist who gives me an hour's worth of therapy and instructions on how to take care of my tendonitis. She stresses the importance of preventative action: stretch, rotate, and stretch some more, in the morning, in the afternoon, before bed. María and Catherine advise me that they are preparing a *cena* or evening meal, which will feature María's world-famous homemade *tortilla española* and lots of fresh vegetable salads and fruits for dessert. I am expected to provide the wine, which I am delighted to do. We all help in the kitchen as much as our talent allows; in my case, I'm pretty much relegated to slicing tomatoes into wedges.

As we prepare to take our places at table two others gather with us and the two could not be more different from one another. The first is a German pilgrim in his late fifties named Udo. Here is a man who walked out the front door of his home in Bavaria three months ago and has been walking ever since. He walks slowly but surely. This man is a true pilgrim, for he started from home; the rest of us are at best *ersatz* versions for having picked up the trail much further along. He is quiet and unassuming and has a pleasant smile. The *camino* has softened him. He reminds me of my snail friend. The other is a Frenchman. He is a *super-caminante*, or super-walker, the first that I have met. *Supercaminantes* are those who are in this for the sheer sport of it; they are professional trekkers and are superlative at what they do. This guy walks forty kilometers a day — minimum! He is also rather proud and vain and his chatter about himself wears on me. I can detect nothing in him of the pilgrim spirit that I have come to know in so many other, less accomplished travelers down this road. Udo inspires me; this fellow belongs in a comic book for his superhuman feats.

After dinner we clean up the table and small kitchen. I take my leave of the others and lie down on the lawn to practice the new stretches María has taught me. From my prone position with hand pulling my leg tautly up towards my chest, I spy the first star in the darkening sky. It has been there all along, seen or unseen. A medieval aphorism that I was taught on a retreat some years ago comes to mind: *Vocatus atque non vocatus, Deus aderit.* Bidden or unbidden, God is present. That is exactly what I am coming to understand on this road: Like the star above me, seen or unseen, he is here. Felt or unfelt, he is with me. Attended to or not attended to, he is walking with me.

The Children of Bethlehem

July 28: Ledigos to Sahagún

I awake startled in Ledigos, for morning light is pouring in through the small window of my dormitory. I look at my Casio and its numerals report that it is seven A.M. Such a thing has not happened to me before; I have never slept this late on the *camino*. Though I'm a bit irritated with myself for the waste of good walking time, I am also feeling more rested than I have in days. By eight in the morning I have packed my possessions and consumed my yogurt and banana and I am out the door and on my way. The paved highway out of Ledigos leads me on through yet more wheat country; is this what all of Spain looks like? The brown fields surrounding me today have recently been cut, so they hold little of interest for the pilgrim's eye. The great heat of previous days has mercifully diminished today, so the walking is far less difficult. This day's journey will be a measly fifteen kilometers; just about right after yesterday's tendon-burning haul.

As I ramble down this road it dawns on me that something new is happening inside me. I certainly have passed the halfway point of my *camino* by now and with this certainty comes a subtle but clear change in my pilgrim psychology. From an operative mentality of *improbability* (in spite of my bravado in repeatedly saying over the past days: "I will make it! I will get there!"), I have moved to an operative mentality of *inevitability*.

The invisible gravitational pull to Santiago now has a firm hold of me. It is no longer I who push ahead down this road; it is Santiago pulling me forward. That's the psychological side of the change, but there is something more to the transformation happening within me as well. My prayer is changing too. The very walking, with its rhythms and constant movement forward, has become *in itself* my deepest prayer. I now walk without imposing an agenda of my own on the day, that this or that should be happening to me or that I should be doing this or that by way of praying. Just by being out here walking, I am praying. Let what happens happen, let the *camino* teach me with its twists and turns and endless surprises, yes, let God do or not do what he wants to do with me out here. For whatever it is worth, I give him this time and this walking. *That's* enough. He calls the shots. He sets the agenda. He leads me on.

As I walk through the last small village before arriving at the outskirts of Sahagún, a little place called San Nicolás, an elderly gentleman, thin as a rail and dressed in gray work clothes, comes out of his house just as I pass by. I greet him with a polite, *"Buenos días"* and he returns my greeting with a nod. Just at this point, I lose track of the *flechas amarillas* as the road diverges in various vague directions. I have to stop to take a good look for the next *flecha* but I don't spot it. I turn back to the old fellow standing straight as an arrow within the frame of his doorway to ask if I am headed in the right direction. He again nods, *Sí,* then to my surprise, steps off his front porch, joins me at the vague intersection and proceeds to accompany me on my way, guiding me along the right path in lieu of any evident *flecha.* As we walk along side by side, almost like father and son, we carry on an animated conversation about the summer weather and the *camino's* route through this area and the modern exigencies of life on an old farm. He brings me up to where the path becomes clearly marked again just to the left of the highway to Sahagún. We part with a *gracias* and a *buen día* and he heads back from where he came while I move on towards Sahagún. Gestures like this old grandpa's toward an anonymous pilgrim are so insignificant on the grand scale of human history and the great struggle between good and evil that their value to the continued salvation of the race risks being seriously underestimated; in the end, and this is so important to learn, they are where that struggle between good and evil is won or lost. They are what keep human beings worthy of continued hope.

» *The Children of Bethlehem* «

I know that I am supposed to be impressed by Sahagún, for it is a city brimming with history, ancient *camino* stories, and of course many beautiful churches and monasteries worthy of appreciative visits. Perhaps I am becoming increasingly numb to such things at this stage in my journey, but upon arriving in the town, I just cannot work up much enthusiasm for engaging in a fast-paced tour to take it all in. Even more, I have to sadly admit, the city feels congested and charmless to me. The *refugio* is located in a massively renovated monastery in the center of the town, which also serves as a civic exhibition and concert hall, the strangest mixed-use *refugio* I have seen. Its toilets and tin shower stalls are a grade up from porta-potties, but only a grade; their corners and seams are trimmed with black mildew that fills the air I breathe with the smell of must. There is no yard to relax in and only a very small area behind the building to hang damp laundry for drying. But we pilgrims are constantly reminded along the way, *Turistas manden; peregrinos agradecen.* Tourists demand; pilgrims thank. I am a pilgrim so I choose to refrain from further notation of the place's negative aspects and consider instead how good it is to have a place, any place at all, in which to bathe and sleep and sit at a table with friends. What else is necessary in this world?

Antonio, Tik Tik, and Timba show up not long after me and hang around just long enough for Antonio to bathe and wash his clothes before disappearing again, presumably to spend the night in some park or on some nearby riverbank. I almost envy him his choice to live this way out here. He is far closer to the pilgrim spirit than I, with my grumblings about must and mold.

This afternoon I follow my usual routines, have a meal with Catherine, and eventually find an Internet café to send another e-mail report on my pilgrim progress to family and a few friends. One of my correspondents is a friend, Sandra, who lives on the outskirts of Bethlehem, the *real* Bethlehem, in Palestine. Sandra is an United Methodist minister who works for her church among the Palestinian people and is one of the finest people I know anywhere in the world. During the worst of the *intifada* she has faithfully corresponded with people like me, describing the tragic and terrible realities faced by the people she so loves and serves so well. Among the e-mails I receive this late afternoon is one from Sandra, responding to a previous message of mine from days and days ago. She assures me of her prayers in my pilgrimage and writes that my e-mails have made her mindful of the verse from the prophet Isaiah: "How beautiful upon the mountains are the feet of him who brings glad tidings."[1]

Sandra then relates to me a great event in Bethlehem that she and her colleagues organized the previous week. After two years of heavy fighting and months of severe curfews, a relaxation of the latest curfew was announced by the Israeli forces with just enough advance notice that there was time to organize for the children of Bethlehem a footrace through the streets of the ancient city. This would be their first small bit of play together in months. Sandra describes the "fun run" as the most wonderful thing she has beheld in a long time as the children laughed and ran and tumbled and laughed and ran some more. She describes the looks on their faces as they went by her: wide-open smiles and eyes aglitter with joy and little bodies filled to the brim with energy and life. In particular she mentions that what was most touching to her was the children's complete lack of competition one against the other; instead, they shared extraordinary care for one another along their jubilant route. Reaching the finish line first or second or even third was not nearly so important to any child as holding the hand of a little brother, carrying a little sister piggyback, or encouraging a friend to pick himself up from a fall and keep going with yelps of glee.

Reading of this footrace in Bethlehem makes my eyes dampen. I am grateful beyond words for being allowed to be part of these children's extraordinary race through the streets of this beleaguered city so far away from me yet, through Sandra, so close. I write back to Sandra of my gratitude for her story about the children of Bethlehem and I promise that I will dedicate tomorrow's walk, with whatever it might bring by way of joy or pain, to her lovely children of Bethlehem. This Jesus whose feet I have been regularly kissing along my way began his life as a child of Bethlehem and so tomorrow I will imagine his young successors as they cross the finish line and in my mind I will kiss their feet too. That will be my prayer for them.

Out here on the *camino* I have been quite cut off from news of the rest of the world with its many tragedies and injustices. Nevertheless, I feel more immersed in the world and connected to its grave sufferings than ever before. My participation in its pain is, I believe, all the deeper

---

1. Isaiah 52:7.

for being immersed in it not as a blank watcher of TV news, but as a person praying for other persons; though my daily aches and pains are nothing in comparison to those of the homeless, the hungry, or the violated, at least with these physical discomforts I am not numb, I can in a small way unite myself to their pain, cry with them in their great suffering, and even laugh with them in their small joys. I am not doing any great thing for them; it is they who are saving me.

The evening in the great arched monastic hall of Sahagún is not much different from most other *refugio* evenings. As has happened so often along the way, I am treated to another small kindness that alerts me to the fundamental goodness of humanity. A bicycling husband and wife have taken the bunks across from my own. As I am preparing for bed, tending to my tendon by applying, as ever, more Voltarén to it, the gentleman asks if I am sore, and when I acknowledge my problem, he comes over to my bed, identifies himself as a masseur, and asks permission to assist me. I welcome his offer and with that he begins to give my foot and leg a deep massage, the likes of which I have never known. He is a pro and knows exactly where to apply pressure and where to relieve it. The mixture of gentleness and firmness is masterful and the sharing of it is a gift given to me without hesitation or a second thought.

Another feature of the evening is more comical. A very young couple has settled into a bunk just beyond my own, he in the bed below and she above. Bye and bye, he climbs the small ladder up into her bed and the two of them ensconce themselves within her quite substantial sleeping bag where they proceed to nuzzle and smooch and, well, you know. In most corners of Europe such a display of youthful affection would hardly be noticed, but here on the *camino*, it is very rare and curious behavior. First of all, it is very warm in this dormitory, making it nigh on impossible for even one person to remain inside a sleeping bag for long before it becomes intolerably clammy with sweat. How can the two of them stand it in there, even allowing for the power of sexual attraction? However, the real oddity is the romantic activity itself. It is the first and only time so far on the *camino* that I witness such a thing. There has been in fact a surprising lack of romance on the road from the very beginning. I suspect that the energy that goes into the hard daily work of walking twenty or thirty kilometers, up and down mountains and across rolling hills of waving wheat, day after day, just plain reduces to the point of nothing the amount of energy available for other strenuous activities . . . like sex. Add to that the further consideration that we are living night after night in very open and public spaces and the result is that the most intense sexual act I have witnessed before this particular couple's rhythmic embraces has been the gentle kiss of a long-married couple before they parted for the night and retired to separate beds. While washing up before bed at least two other pilgrims quietly comment on the couple's performance with smiles and sighs; says one: "They must be very new to the *camino*."

The Children of Bethlehem:
An Alternate View

July 29: Sahagún to El Burgo Ranero

Perhaps one of the most attractive features of Sahagún to an increasingly weary pilgrim is the geographical fact that it is only sixty kilometers further to León, which means there are only three more days of walking before I achieve that important milestone on this long road. I will have over four hundred kilometers already under my boots by the time I reach León, with only another three hundred kilometers left to go. From there on it will be simply a matter of putting in the daily walking and staying reasonably healthy; I should then be able to finish in good condition. With this thought encouraging me I go out the door of the Sahagún *refugio* and quickly make my way out of town. By the light of the moon I pass a beautiful grove of poplar trees known as the Field of Charlemagne's Lances. The town of Sahagún was supposedly founded by the great Charles himself. I have often visited his palace chapel, now the cathedral of Aachen in Germany, just down the road from us in Leuven; to find his "lances" this far south amazes me. That man did get around! Even apart from the history, this field enchants me: poplar leaves by moonlight are silvery and the trunks are stately and when a slight breeze happens to pass among the leaves they sing a sweet hymn to the passing pilgrim. I sing back the words of the church's morning prayer:

In the tender compassion of our God,
The dawn from on high shall break upon us,
To shine on those who dwell in darkness and the shadow of death,
And to guide our feet in the way of peace.[1]

In spite of the dialogue of hymns, the first two and a half hours on the road are dreadfully painful. The cream and pills and even the massage from the night before are not enough to tame my wild tendon. And something should be said about the road today. Not far outside of Sahagún an extraordinary path for the pilgrims has been built along the highway. It runs for over thirty kilometers and its surface is even and finely graveled. Still-immature plane trees have been planted along its embankment every few meters in an unbroken chain extending to the horizon. The consideration the regional government gave in making this path for us is admirable, but the reality of walking it, hour after hour with a gimpy leg, is another story altogether. It simply runs on endlessly, and the orderly procession of trees offers little in the way of shade nor does it do anything to break the monotony of the road; in fact, it makes it worse. As I progress slowly along, I try to compare that string of trees to something more interesting: A column of green-topped army ants marching off to war? Lime lollipops set on end one after another by some giant child? The leafy beads of a rosary stretching from occident to orient? Sadly, there is nothing to instill the scene with much interest, so I start swinging my *bastones*. Sometimes I swing them back and forth in front of my face as if they were windshield wipers, and other times I swing them front to back and back to front as if I were a cross-country skier and sometimes I just twirl them in the air as if I were a high school baton master. I gain a rhythm in the twirling and pretty soon I am singing along with this rhythm, pure *la-la-la's* and *dum-de-dum's*. And underneath it all, I am rolling in my mind film of giddy children running through Bethlehem's streets, laughing and cheering and having a grand time and as each one passes the finish line, all of us adults joyously kiss his or her perfect little Jesus feet.

I take my morning coffee and slice of *tortilla* in a village called Bercianos del Real Camino, and wonderfully, once I get back on my feet,

1. Luke 1:78-79.

» *The Children of Bethlehem: An Alternate View* «

the caffeine, egg, and potato cure has worked its magic once again: the troublesome tendon has relaxed and my passage onward becomes far more bearable and actually quite pleasant. The final seven kilometers to El Burgo Ranero are still deadly boring, but as far as walking goes, I am strangely free of pain.

As I enter El Burgo Ranero, I am confused at first as to where the *refugio* might be, which is odd since this is a very small village; the building that seems to be the most likely candidate has rock and roll music playing from within but no one answers the door at my knock. No other pilgrims seem to be hanging about, which is a pretty good indicator at this late morning hour that I am not in the right place, so I wander up the street looking for another option. I soon spot a couple of people seated at an outdoor table in front of what looks like a bar about a block further on and so I head in their direction. I am cheerily greeted as I approach. The gathering at the table includes a couple I briefly met on the road earlier in the day as well as a stranger or two. They point out the *refugio* a half-block away, but tell me it will not open for at least another hour; they advise me to drop my *mochila*, go buy myself a beer, and join them in the shade of their red Coca-Cola umbrella. I entrust my bag and *bastones* to their care and wander down the street a short distance to the village store. I pick up a small carton of fruit juice and buy something new to me: an *empanada*, a sort of pie stuffed with tuna fish mixed with tomatoes, onions, and spices. I take a bite and am surprised that I rather enjoy the taste of the thing.

Upon my return to the table and its gathering of pilgrims, a large balding man in his forties seems to be the social center of the group. We begin introducing ourselves to one another in Spanish and as he and I shake hands he tells me his name is Adam. He then asks if by chance I speak English. I respond that I had better since I'm an American. He seems overjoyed. "Well, I'm an American too!" he says. He then adds after a moment of sizing me up, "Are you the American priest I've been hearing about for days?" I answer that I don't know anything about what he might have heard, but that, yes, I am a priest. I pull up a plastic chair to join the amiable group and begin shooting the breeze with them. It surprises me to realize that pilgrims I do not know already know of me. I can only suppose that somehow, inexplicably, I have become something of a *camino* character out here. I don't sense myself as standing out in a pilgrim crowd; except for my age, my nationality, and my profession, I think I pretty much fit in.

As always, once the doors of the *refugio* open, we pay our few euros for the use of the facility, get our *credenciales* stamped, shower, wash clothes, and take a quick nap before lunch. I join Catherine and a couple others for a meal in the village bar, and then we are joined by big Adam, for whom we make room at our table.

As our meal together progresses I find myself increasingly disturbed by the conversation that is developing. The two native Spaniards at the table, a husband and wife, though not Basque themselves, make their home in the Basque territories of Spain. The talk turns to the ongoing violence being perpetrated by members of the radical Basque separatist group known as ETA. This then brings Adam into the conversation, reporting to us that though he is an American, he has recently moved to Israel, a land that knows well the reality of extremist violence. He describes to us the horror of living with suicide bombers infiltrating his new homeland. This is indeed a horror and we all share with him our disgust at this terrorist tactic that spills so much innocent blood.

Adam goes further and adds that the Palestinians have gone crazy and that his people are the innocent victims of this craziness. I am getting uncomfortable now, for I have come to know many Palestinians over the years who are not crazy and who have nothing to do with suicide bombings. To the contrary, I have found them to be very fine people. Their families are warm, their kindness to strangers is unstinting, and, judging by their dedication to prayer, both Christian and Moslem, their relationship to God is probably much deeper than my own.

Yet what comes next from Adam almost takes my breath away. With a cold air of expertise he informs us that the Israeli intelligence services have done studies of the suicide bombers' mentality to see what makes them tick. After extensive questioning of potential bombers captured before they completed their dastardly missions, it is now clear, he informs us, that the cadre of teenage bombers is made up primarily of young homosexual men who have been rejected by their families and disowned by their communities because of their sexual identity. Having suffered the psychological violence and alienation imposed upon them by their own people, they are left desolate and desperate and so with nothing left to live for they choose to end their lives as human bombs. I am stunned.

» *The Children of Bethlehem: An Alternate View* «

And the increasing number of young women who have begun to surface as bombers? He is on a roll so that is confidently explained to us as well. They are girls who have been repeatedly raped by their fathers and uncles and brothers in their own homes and therefore are left desolate and desperate by their repeated violation so with nothing left to live for they choose to end their lives as human bombs. I am doubly stunned.

Whatever one might think about the extremely complex situation in the Middle East, Adam's take on suicide bombers strikes me as grossly simplistic, and his characterization of the Palestinian people as terribly cruel. I am infuriated.

What he is spouting about the young people of Palestine is a calumny that absolves his nation of all blame for the evil on its doorstep by placing all the guilt on someone else's doorstep. Suicide bombers of any kind are formed by many forces. Among these are the desolation and desperation caused by being constantly denied dignity and justice in their own land and by having their homes demolished, their olive orchards bulldozed, their neighbors and their own brothers and children blown up — but having no power to fight any of it except that of a rock thrown at a tank, a hand raised in defiance, or, when all else fails, the horrific evil of choosing to become a human bomb. Yes, it is despair and desolation that makes human bombs out of teenagers, but that despair and desolation comes from many quarters, and the leaders of Adam's Israel have to take their share of the blame for it. I can hardly believe that I am listening to Adam parrot this dark and pathetic propaganda *on the very day* I have devoted to praying for the joyfully running children of Bethlehem.

I have a terrible choice to make at this point: do I respond to this claptrap with the righteous anger it deserves, or do I keep my mouth shut for the sake of some kind of concord on the *camino* — after all, I probably have to live with this Adam and these others for days to come. I choose wrongly. I keep my mouth shut. I say nothing. Adam is a nationalistic blowhard, but I am a spiritual coward. I pay my bill, excuse myself from the table, and go across the street to my bunk for a nap tinged with shame.

In the evening I wander around the town, what there is of it. Its most notable feature is a large pond at the far end of the main street that thousands and thousands of frogs call home. I watch them jump from bank to pond and listen to them burp. As I began the day listening to the delicate

» *July 29: Sahagún to El Burgo Ranero* «

153

hymn of a multitude of birch leaves rustling in the breeze, I now end it with the sad and slow belches of a choir of frogs filling the air. They croak to me a mournful song whose sad bass notes sing to me this day's sin: "Coward. Cowaard. Cowaaard."

To the children of Bethlehem: I am sorry.

Sandals Lost and Family Found

July 30: El Burgo Ranero to Mansilla de las Mulas

Let me say something about the importance of sandals to me as this pilgrimage continues into its third week. Mine are Clarks, a quality English brand that have come to feel very much a part of me over the past weeks. They have formed themselves to my feet. They are as comfortable as anything I have ever worn, and on this *camino* they have become my auxiliary footwear; as soon as the boots come off, the light and airy sandals go on. They give my dear feet respite and refreshment in the afternoons and evenings. They are now my feet's best friends and for that they seem priceless to me.

In the mornings as I prepare to depart the *refugio* I wear my ever-faithful sandals until I am ready to give my feet their daily anointing with Vaseline and anti-inflammatory cream and then dress them in clean socks before putting on my boots. Once my boots are on and laced up, I attach the sandals by their straps to the outside of my *mochila*, where they dangle on either side of the trademark pilgrim shell. This has been my routine every morning since Roncesvalles; it is now a habit that offers me the certainty that I will never make the terrible mistake of leaving these friends of my feet behind.

On this ordinary morning in El Burgo Ranero I do everything as I have always done. Except for one thing: without my being any the wiser a very slight variation in my routine leads to catastrophe. I take my boots and socks out to the small balcony next to my second floor dormitory, sit on a stool there, take my sandals off, anoint my feet, put on my socks and boots, tie the knots, stand up, stretch a little and walk back to my bed to retrieve my *mochila* and *bastones* and happily walk down the stairs and out the front door into the dark. I ramble down the road, pray my rosary, sing a song, enjoy the rising sun, and about forty-five minutes into the walk, I dimly become aware of the absence of something in my hiking life. I stop, cock my head, think of nothing, and begin walking on. I amble down the road another half-kilometer, then stop again. Something still seems missing. On a hunch I give the trunk of my body a little shake back and forth, up and down, and it dawns on me that what I have been feeling the absence of is nothing less than the rhythmic flip-flop of my sandals against the *mochila*. I stretch my arm back to the *mochila* but can't quite reach as far as I need. I drop the *mochila* to see for myself and, sure enough, there are no sandals attached. I just about cry as the realization sinks in. What an idiot am I! My shoulders slump. My frown deepens. I look back down the monotonous path and accompanying line of plane trees. I look at my watch. It is almost seven A.M. I know that I now have a tough decision to make.

There is a sort of unwritten rule among most pilgrims when they in-advertently leave things behind: if the return trip to retrieve the thing is going to take more than thirty minutes, forget about it and just go on (un-less of course it is your money, your credit card, or your *credencial* — those are always worth going back for). The calculation goes like this: You've al-ready spent thirty minutes on the road. To return for your lost item will take another thirty. To get back to the spot where you find yourself now will take yet another thirty minutes. That is ninety minutes of wasted morning. It ain't worth it. And I've been walking for a lot more than thirty minutes. But these are my sandals, my feet's best friends! The content-ment of feet counts for something on this road too! So here I stand in the middle of this gravel path absolutely caught between the two equally dis-agreeable options: just forgetting about the sandals or going back to re-trieve them and thereby losing a big chunk of cool morning hiking. The time calculation finally wins the day: I face west and sadly and angrily walk on. "How could I have been so stupid!" becomes my morning prayer.

In spite of my loss, I have to admit that the morning is far from

» *Sandals Lost and Family Found* «

156

ruined. The sunrise has been beautiful today and the spectacle of night giving way to day always cheers me. Once the sun is up and fiery, though, the boredom of meandering down the monotonous gravel path with its symmetrically placed trees becomes all the greater. This is the second day of this. The land I am passing through is flat and featureless. My mind at some point throws its off-switch and I think of nothing, feel nothing, pray nothing. Well, *almost* pray nothing. At some point in the morning, I become aware that there is a melody way back in the depths of my mind. I listen and try to capture it like one does a dream when coming out of sleep. It slips away. I continue on but the dim awareness of music back there returns. I listen but it fades once again. I relax my efforts to hear it and on its own it rises closer to my consciousness. The dreamy melody shows itself finally: it is the Taizé version of Saint Teresa of Avila's great prayer that I heard days ago in the crypt of San Juan de Ortega: "*Nada te turbe. Nada te espanta . . . Quien a Dios tiene, nada le falta*. Let nothing disturb you. Let nothing frighten you . . . To those who have God, nothing is lacking." The hymn makes its brief appearance, then recedes back into its quiet corner of the heart to do its work on my behalf. This is a discovery: even when we don't know we are praying, prayer is already *in* us, praying *for* us.

The tendon is behaving today; that is good news as well, but a nerve in my back, right across the left shoulder blade, is acting up and sending little shock waves of its own across its field of influence. "*Nada te turbe*; let nothing disturb you." The prospect of spending all afternoon in my boots makes me mourn for my lost sandals. *Quien a Dios tiene, nada le falta*; he who has God, lacks nothing. This road never changes. *Dios no se muda*; God never changes.

When I arrive in Reliegos, more than two thirds of the day's walk has been completed and a sizable crowd of pilgrims is gathered in a small park just across the street from a very busy little bar. It has been a long wait for the morning coffee but everyone is cheery. I find Catherine there ahead of me and we chat a bit. Her knees are bothering her a great deal today; I can see in her face the distant look of those who suffer. I order my *café con leche* and a nice slice of *tortilla* from the bar, then return to the park. A circle of pilgrims whom I do not yet know is crowded around a small picnic table; there is an available plastic chair so I ask if I can be seated with my coffee and food and I am welcomed in.

» *July 30: El Burgo Ranero to Mansilla de las Mulas* «

We make our introductions: a Japanese young man, with a beautiful Canon thirty-five-millimeter camera strung around his neck, greets me; I noticed him for the first time last evening in the Burgo Ranero *refugio*. I have presumed he is from Japan and am fascinated that a Japanese person would be walking the *camino*. I ask him his name and he answers in Spanish, "José." I ask where he is from as a lead up to a further question about how it is a young man from Japan finds himself out here. I am surprised and embarrassed when he tells me that he is actually a Brazilian. A native of São Paolo, José is second-generation Japanese; I quickly realize that despite his Asian physical appearance his mannerisms are mostly Latin. Alessandra, a thin, delicate, gray-haired Italian lady, presents herself in a mix of Spanish, Italian, and English. Lucía María, a Colombian with a delightful sing-song accent, dark eyes, and a great mass of black curly hair that she keeps pulled back in a pony tail, is next to gingerly shake my hand; I have met her before, a long time ago in Estella, but have hardly seen her since. Finally, Marisa says hello; she is a Basque with a husky voice and a great laugh. We finish our refreshments, return our cups and plates to the bar and one by one, take off down the road out of Reliegos and on to Mansilla de las Mulas. I walk out of town beside José and we chat for just a bit before he moves ahead and once again I am alone on the road.

As I enter the outskirts of Mansilla, I happen upon a nun walking in the street towards me. She catches my eye and I hers; I greet her and she in return greets me with the ubiquitous pilgrim greeting, *buen camino*. We both stop in the street and find ourselves introducing ourselves with brief details of our lives. She is from Madrid but is in Mansilla to assist her elderly brother and sister, both of whom are very sick. I tell her I am an American priest, rector of a small seminary in Belgium, and that I am now almost three weeks on the *camino*. She makes mention of my limp and I acknowledge that I have been suffering with a bad tendon but that I am getting along much better today. She promises to pray for my seminarians and me and I promise to pray for her aging brother and sister. We never think to ask one another for each other's name. And that is that: three wonderful minutes of care between perfect strangers and we move on in our lives. The encounter, brief as it has been, quickens my spirit just enough to get me down the road a few blocks more to the *refugio* of Mansilla.

Settling in this afternoon will be more difficult to accomplish without my sandals at hand. I will be relegated to wearing my boots the entire afternoon and evening, a torture I have been dreading all day. I console myself with the hope that I will be able to purchase a new pair of sandals in León, the next big city on my itinerary, and I should be there tomorrow. In the meantime, helpful pilgrims suggest I phone back to the *refugio* in Burgo Ranero and ask if they would look for the sandals and, if they happen to find them, send them on to me in care of some late-leaving bicyclist. One has the phone number handy. I take heart in the suggestion, dig out from the bottom of my *mochila* my almost-abandoned mobile phone, turn it on, wait for a signal, and make the call. I find that the listed number belongs to a neighbor lady who says she will help if she can. The afternoon passes with me parading about in my boots, but despite my repeated inquiries at the *refugio's* front desk, no Clarks show up. They are assuredly down the road themselves by now, proudly being worn by some lucky fellow who discovered them abandoned and alone like waifs tucked under a simple stool on a very small balcony. I hope they are as kind to his feet as they were to mine.

Later in the evening I find my way to the Church of Santa María del Camino for the eight o'clock Mass. The liturgy itself is performed with the rote formalism that I find so disappointing in so many of these churches, but two other things happen that make up for the lack of beauty in the celebration of the Mass itself. The first is that as I turn to offer the sign of peace to the few old folks sitting in pews near me, I also notice behind me José, Lucía María, Alessandra, and Marisa, the pilgrims I enjoyed coffee with in Reliegos. We smile a "peace" across the several pews separating us. I am rather thrilled that among the hundreds of pilgrims slowly making their way to Santiago these new acquaintances share this place with me as a home. I sense a new commonality with them, a sort of intimacy that is unexpected and touching.

The second event is just as important to me: as I leave the church, I run into the very nun whom I met on the street earlier in the day. She spots me just as I spot her and so we greet each other as warmly as if we were old and dear friends. She tells me that she has been praying for me all day and that even before she noticed me in church this evening she had offered this Mass for me, the limping pilgrim priest. What a fine surprise to see me now. I heartily thank her and promise that when I reach

» *July 30: El Burgo Ranero to Mansilla de las Mulas* «

Compostela I will return the favor by praying for her before the relics of the apostle. Again, we don't think to ask one another for names but it does not matter, for she and I have found ourselves bound together by a road and a prayer, which are, I am discovering, pretty much the same thing.

This age-old practice of praying for one another runs deep in the Christian tradition; it is an expression of the profound sense that in this life with all its difficulties and troubles, we need one another and we have to support one another. When someone is sick the healthy take care of him; when that person returns to health, he in turn takes care of another who is sick. We imagine the faces of the people we love or even of the ones we hate and we ask God's blessings on them. We pray for them in their need whatever their need. May she be healed. May he be strong. May he avoid this evil. May she grow in wisdom. We trust that others are doing the same for us. For Catholics in particular, there is a deep sense that this community of mutual aid founded in a common faith is not just for the living; we count on the support in prayer of those who have gone before us, our deceased parents and friends and holy ones. We presume that we are all of us a family, a real family, one family whose blood bonds are not cut by geography, race, time, or death itself. This sense of presence with one another has a doctrinal name: it is called simply "the communion of saints." Both in unexpectedly meeting the sister from Madrid twice in the same day and in unexpectedly finding my *camino* acquaintances sitting behind me in evening Mass, I experience in a particularly personal way this doctrine which makes so much sense for me. "May the Peace of Christ be with you!" we say to one another before we go to communion; thus our communion with God cannot be separated from communion with that good sister, with José, Lucía María, Alessandra, and Marisa, with these old ladies sitting next to me with their black shawls draped over their shoulders and rosary beads rattling in their arthritic fingers, and with the whole bunch of us, all of us, living and dead.

"May the Peace of Christ be with you. And also with you." In other words: I have a family and this family has me. Moreover, binding our family together is something much greater and deeper than any of us or all of us. That "something greater" has a name. I kiss his feet before I leave this Church of Santa María del Camino and then I return "home" to our *refugio* and get ready for bed, for tomorrow I march on León.

» *Sandals Lost and Family Found* «

El Santísimo

July 31: Mansilla de las Mulas to León

I have been hearing warnings about the entry into the big city of León. It is hazardous because of the major highways that must be crossed; a number of pilgrims, including Catherine, have decided to take a bus from Mansilla into the center of Leon so as to avoid these dangers. I personally don't feel so moved; since surviving the wild streets of Pamplona in full fiesta I have promised myself that I will walk every step of the way or not at all. I will take the chance of getting myself squashed like a backpacking bug on some four-lane highway if that is what it takes to earn my "every step of the way" merit badge.

With the arrival of a new morning in Mansilla, I find my back aching even before I begin the day. I decide that I am still packing just too much weight as I lumber down the *camino* from day to day. The only thing I can think of ditching is the usual candidate: my stainless steel Coleman thermos. I have resisted the thought of leaving it behind on any number of occasions over the previous weeks, for I am fond of the possession in spite of its weight and well-proven uselessness. Imagine: falling in love with a thermos! This is a silliness my back can no longer afford. I decide definitively that it is time to throw off this final vestige of my old-world materialism, so I set the thermos by the door of the *hospitalera's* room before I walk into the streets of Mansilla. Finally, I am free. Strangely, my *mochila* feels just as heavy as it ever did and the nerve in my back just as fiery.

I believe that for the very first time as a pilgrim I am the first out the door of the *refugio*, and I enjoy the five-thirty walk down the empty main street of the town; the place is still very much asleep and the sound of my footsteps on stone echoing off the close buildings pleases me. This pleasure is a feeling akin to being the first to walk through fresh-fallen snow or the first to dip a knife into a jar of peanut butter. As far as I know, no one is ahead of me and this is new and delightful. My leg is almost completely pain-free and that too is new and delightful. I am well into the second decade of my morning rosary by the time I cross the medieval bridge that marks the edge of the city and sets me on the path to León.

After four easy kilometers, I am the first to arrive at a crossroad where there is a bar that has just opened for the morning, so I order my coffee, use the john, and watch as the place gradually fills up with those pilgrims following close behind me. I am proud that I stayed ahead of them, a most unusual situation since almost always on the *camino* I am passed by the young and the healthy. I brag to some about how well my leg is doing and what a great morning I am having. My bragging words turn to ashes in my mouth, however, for as soon as I heave my *mochila* up over my right shoulder, cinch up its various straps, grab my *bastones*, and head back to the road, the old tendon begins to rebel again. This is discouraging beyond words but there is nothing to be done but walk to León.

Now León is a very substantial city, and well before I come close to its outer limits signs of its looming presence are seen and felt. From a height near the village of Valdelafuente a panoramic view of the city is displayed below me. Traffic on the major highway to the left of the *camino* path becomes heavier and faster. The *camino* route has to detour around and between an increasing numbers of factories, automobile dealerships, and cheap hotels. Finally the path's *flechas amarillas* direct the pilgrim to the bank of the dreaded highway crossing of which he has been duly warned. It is an extraordinary sight to behold: First, there are the four lanes of speeding traffic, two lanes in each direction, all four carrying freight-laden semi-trucks roaring by in both directions at blazing speeds. Second, there is an access road on the other side of the expressway bringing fresh trucks and cars onto the highway; it too must be calculated into the poor pilgrim's plan for crossing to safety on the other side. This same road is equipped with a white crash rail running its length, presenting an additional obstacle to be overcome by the heavy-burdened pilgrim. Third, there is the very road the pilgrim has followed to the intersection, which also feeds traffic into the highway stream; it holds several vehicles awaiting the same break in cross-traffic to make their turns left or right. Those turning right will directly cross over the hapless pilgrim's own path across the expressway and this with the drivers' eyes turned to the left away from the pilgrim so as to attend to the oncoming traffic. Fourth, the walker notices that there are no zebra-stripe crosswalks, no red-yellow-green traffic lights, no center island, no blinking yellow caution lights, no overhead passages, and no tunnels underneath to facilitate his passage. As he faces this fearsome scene, the hapless pilgrim must also calculate the weight of his *mochila* (luckily my own is now a half-kilo lighter, having just left behind my once-precious thermos), and the state of his legs and feet (never very good after fourteen kilometers of steady walking), and of course the speed of all those trucks and cars as they approach from both the left and the right. Like schoolyard kids ready to insert themselves into the counter-twirling cords of double jump-rope, the pilgrim stands watching and waiting and wavering for just the right moment to make his move. When that moment comes, he makes a break for it, hoping for dear life that he has calculated well, for if he has not he will surely die a miserable death on the radiator grill of a massive Volvo semi.

I breathlessly report to you that I survive the dash and so does everyone else today as far as I know, but all of us come out of the experience dazed and aghast at the risk to life and limb we have just taken. Ironically, just a half-kilometer further on, a beautiful pedestrian overpass and paved walkway is provided us as the *flechas* of the *camino* direct us over yet another highway and then lead us past the grassy campus of a bank headquarters and down into the city.

The humble painted yellow arrows that have been leading us on all these weeks are now accompanied in León by shiny brass *conchas* embedded into the city's sidewalks. Beautiful as they are, they accomplish nothing more than do our familiar old *flechas amarillas*. Both lead me to the *refugio* of the Benedictine sisters not far from the ancient center of León.

The sisters make a segment of their school available as dormitories for pilgrims. A couple of the sisters are near the entrance to supervise the volunteer *hospitaleras* and to extend a warm welcome to the arriving pilgrims. Perhaps to avoid embarrassing moral indiscretions like that which we experienced back in Sahagún, the nuns direct the men to one dormitory while the women are sent further on to their own. Curiously, men and women end up sharing the same toilets and baths. The sisters' efforts, though frustrated by the common architecture of the schoolroom, seem rather endearing. What delights me most about the Benedictine nuns of León is that they are very direct in inviting us to join them for their community prayers and daily Mass. I am already feeling at home in this big city, which has almost cost me my life to get to.

After washing I invite José to lunch and together we wander into a plaza surrounded by restaurants and bars. I feel very odd walking about in my old boots; after eating I will begin my search for a new pair of sandals. We arbitrarily choose a restaurant and seat ourselves at an outdoor table shaded by the inevitable large red Coca-Cola umbrella. We order for ourselves the usual three-course *menú del día* and over a cool salad, a sizzling slice of pork, and a Dixie cup of ice cream, José and I get to know one another. He tells me about his life as a banker in São Paolo and I share a story or two from my life back in Belgium. When we finish, he is ready for a nap while I am determined to find a shoe store; so he returns to the Benedictines while I head into the maze of small streets surrounding the plaza to search for my new pair of sandals. I bounce from shoe store to shoe store, not finding what I want. Finally I pass by a sporting goods store and in the display window, amidst fishing poles, pots and pans for camping, and high-tech binoculars, I spot what look like suitable replacements for my long-lost Clarks. They are tagged at forty euros: not bad. I try them on, my feet approve, and so I make my purchase and carry these new pals for my feet off in a plastic bag.

Coming out of the sporting goods store, I take a right and within a block I happen upon the open plaza surrounding León's famous cathedral; I walk up to it with hopes of spending some time inside, but its iron gates have already closed for the afternoon *siesta* so I return to the Benedictine sisters' place and have myself a good nap on this increasingly warm afternoon.

I stir from a deep sleep not being able to hold on for even a moment to whatever filled my dream world a second before. I sit up on my bunk, unwrap my new sandals, strap them on, and after a stretch or two I determine to return to the cathedral. The sandals are stiff and not broken in, but my feet are willing to give them some time. The doors of the cathedral are open when I arrive so I leave behind the heat of the outdoors and step into the church's cool interior. The stained glass stuns me with its beauty; as the cathedral in Burgos was magnificent in its light and grace, this one is extraordinary for the rich colors that cut like prismatic knives through its otherwise dark Gothic spaces. I walk about slowly with my eyes cast upward toward the rank of windows high above me; my gaze descends as it follows the ethereal shafts of light emanating from the windows to the floor below, where they speckle the stone with impressionistic splashes of color. It is a special treat to plant myself in the middle of one of those shafts of light so that the colors wash my face and fill my eyes with their beauty. I take in as much of this otherworldly atmosphere as I can hold. I breathe deeply, then sigh with awe.

I wander by an inviting archway that is labeled *Capilla del Santísimo*; I enter, grab hold of the back support of a bench, make a stiff half-genuflection, slide myself into the pew, then sink into a heap before the altar, ambo, tabernacle, and flickering red candle that is the universal Catholic sign that the Lord is present. In the utter silence and refreshing cool of this place, for the second time in this pilgrimage, I inexplicably begin to cry. I have no words to attach to these tears, nothing with which I might identify their source or purpose. The tears just come and so I let them be and simply enjoy their return visit.

Perhaps the meaning of these tears can be sensed if I pause in my story for a moment to explain as best I am able what manner of place this is that has opened so wide my tear ducts. I have entered into, as I mentioned, a special precinct of many Catholic churches, the *Capilla del Santísimo*. In the Catholic tradition, the bread that is consecrated in the Eucharist and which, along with many other Christians, we believe to be the true Body of Christ, is commonly called in Spanish *el Santísimo*, and in English the Blessed Sacrament. It is held in reserve within an ornate safe-like box called the "tabernacle," which itself is often placed in a special chapel like this one. Reserving the *Santísimo* has two purposes: first, so that it can be carried to the sick and homebound, allowing them to participate in the Eucharist from afar; and second, as a focus for personal prayer. To pray before the Eucharistic bread, still very much "the Body of Christ" for us, is about as intimate a personal conversation with Christ as we can imagine. It is physical and spiritual at the same time. It is something akin to sitting quietly with a person you love, gently leaning against one another, perhaps hand held in hand, sharing in soft voices an occasional word or two, and simply enjoying as deeply as possible the solidity of this love. This is how we experience our relationship with Christ when we find ourselves with him in a chapel like this. For me, then, to find my way into this out-of-the-way precinct of the cathedral is very much like coming home and being welcomed through the door and into the living room of the person I love most deeply in life, and just sitting there together in humble communion with one another. Sitting here in this cool, quiet place, with my imagination engaged, is to sit beside Jesus himself, with his strong arm over my shoulder in brotherly support. I feel him not only beside me but also behind me and ahead of me, around me and within me, in the light above me and in the stone beneath me. I know this fellow pilgrim and he knows me. I behold him and he beholds me. This small piece of bread blessed and broken is like a window between heaven and earth through which Christ's friendship streams out to me and washes my face in colors that no artist can imagine. I suppose that is why I find myself crying.

After returning to the hot streets of León, I walk down a wide avenue in the commercial center of the city on my way to another great church closely identified with the *camino*. After taking a turn or two, I come upon the Basilica of San Isidro, which is a great Romanesque pile, very different in style and feel from the Gothic cathedral I have just visited. This basilica dates back to the eleventh century and holds the bones of its patron, San Isidro, to whom plenty of miracles were attributed in the Middle Ages, thus making him and his church destinations for pilgrims in their own right. I enter this womb of stone and dark and once again I disappear into a pew, close my eyes, and breathe something more than air. There are no tears this time, but tranquility abounds all the same. The peace, I now know, is not something *outside* me, for a troop of high-school-age kids has just arrived. The kids are causing a commotion while their adult guides try to corral them into a corner for a talk, but they do not bother me in the least. This moment's peace is *within* me. The troubles and worries and preoccupations from my other life wane in significance as to become nothing before the wide knowledge that, to borrow the words of Julian of Norwich, the medieval mystic: all shall be well and all shall be well and all manner of things shall be well.

» *El Santísimo* «

Finally I leave this haven too and find my way back to the Benedictine sisters' *refugio* for their seven P.M. vespers service and Mass, stopping to buy myself an *empanada* along the way, half of which will be my *cena* tonight and the other half my *desayuno*, or breakfast, in the morning. The celebration of both vespers and Mass with the sisters is probably the best liturgy I have experienced since coming to Spain: tranquil, devout, simple, prayerful, and beautifully chanted. It serves to deepen my sense of being welcomed, being home, being fed. A quiet peace with my God, my world, my fellow *caminantes*, my own self, upholds me this evening. After Mass I sit in the plaza near the Benedictines' place, eat a good portion of my *empanada*, watch a young couple across the square woo one another, then go inside to prepare for the night and the next morning.

Unfortunately, a good night's sleep is interrupted several times by some poor young man vomiting his poor young guts out. Several nearby pilgrims jump to his aid, help him to the bathroom, clean up, go back to bed, only to be awakened an hour later by the same poor young man vomiting his poor young guts out. Is he suffering from the flu or food poisoning or the effects of bad water? No, I overhear one of the helping pilgrims say to another: "This boy is so drunk he can't even stand up." I don't expect he will have a good day tomorrow on the road. Perhaps, if he is open to it, the road will teach him that it provides the highs here. I fall back to sleep only to awaken a couple hours later: it is five A.M. and time to begin a new day.

» *July 31: Mansilla de las Mulas to León* «

Matamoros or Peregino?

August 1: León to Villadangos del Páramo

Out the door and onto the silent streets of León before six A.M., I am safely led through the heart of the city by the brass *conchas* and an occasional yellow *flecha*. Traffic on the streets is thin for the first half hour but picks up quickly as morning comes on. At some unnoticed point the traffic lights stop flashing yellow and return to their day-job of cycling through green-amber-red. Sunshine doesn't break over the tops of the city's buildings until much later than it does in open country, making the light of dawn diffuse and gray rather than the brilliant pink and orange I have become used to. My leg is feeling pretty darn good. My *mochila*, even without the weight of my once-prized thermos, is still killing me.

A Spanish man, well into his sixties, catches up to me and accompanies me for several blocks, chatting away about his progress on this *camino*, his third or fourth time to do it. He is a fast walker, his back as straight as an arrow, and he seems as fresh as a daisy. He tells me he expects to make it to Astorga before nightfall, a journey of about forty-five kilometers, then says he has to move on, so he moves on, leaving me behind, which I actually appreciate. I untangle my rosary beads and take care of my morning prayer.

The route out of the city takes a turn to the left that is not well marked; I continue straight. A couple of young girls a block behind me yell and whistle so I turn back to see what the ruckus is about and they wildly wave their hands and indicate that I am going astray. "Come back and then to the left!" I have to backtrack just a bit to right my mistake and with that the new road begins a steep climb up through an altogether unendearing industrial area, followed by some newly developed suburbs, equally unendearing, and finally, after four or five kilometers and an hour's walk, I am above and beyond León. I can feel already that it will be a very hot day very soon. The troublesome nerve over my left shoulder blade is blazing mad.

Though out of the city, the route stays close to the major highway towards Astorga, crossing it at several points; blessedly, none of these crossings is as frightening as the one we ran across yesterday coming into León. Nevertheless, the constant rumble of the traffic and the ever-present mishmash of stores, hotels, and automobile dealerships lining the highway make for one of the least engaging stretches of *camino* I have thus far passed.

I pass by the Sanctuary of the Virgin del Camino, a very contemporary church that I would like to see from the inside if for no other reason than that contemporary churches are such a rarity on the *camino*; this one has some very interesting artwork on its exterior: the twelve apostles and Mary in relief against a wall of dark stained glass. The images seem to beckon to the passing pilgrim to come and see, but the doors are still locked at this hour of the morning and so I continue on my way. It is very dry country here, so dry and stark and wide and flat, in fact, that it has its own word in Spanish to describe it: *páramo*.

For not being a large town, Villadangos del Páramo certainly has a long lead-up to it. Well before I find myself welcomed into its heart, I must pass over the blazing hot parking lot pavement of a string of hotels, fuel stations, restaurants, and still more fuel stations for two or three kilometers. My body and mind move into automaton mode for the remainder of the morning and I just walk this commercial gauntlet without thought or sentiment.

Finally, the roadway passes through a verdant area and rises back to the highway where it opens onto a vista of the Villadangos *refugio* set on a slight hill with a manicured green lawn before it and tired pilgrims already relaxing in the shade of its trees. One final crossing of the highway and I am home for the day.

» *August 1: León to Villadangos del Páramo* «

The *refugio* is not yet open, but the young lady and her husband cleaning within welcome us in anyway and with a smile stamp our *credenciales*, accept a donation for the night, then direct us to the dormitories. I choose a mattress on the floor, at the far end of the building; it is cool and quiet and there is plenty of room to spread out. Among the guests for the day is a young Catalán man, Toni, whom I briefly met a few days back in El Burgo Ranero. Then he was the very image of health and energy. Today his feet are wrapped in gauze and he is barely able to get around, a victim of poorly tended blisters for which he now suffers the consequences; infections have laid him about as low as a pilgrim can be laid. He has, in fact, been here already for a night; he explains to me sadly that he made a big push forward, walking over forty kilometers the previous day, but by the time he got to Villadangos, his feet were a mess, requiring a visit to the doctor. Remembering my own early attempts at blister surgery, I can only sympathize with him; there but for the grace of God go I.

Also staying the night are José, Alessandra, Marisa, and Lucía María. The French gentleman in the jogging shorts, Michel, whom I finally meet, and Catherine are here as well. The crowd is small enough that I get to know a number of others for the first time: two energetic and bright-eyed teenage kids from Granada, Julio and Manuel; and a foursome of Spaniards walking together, David and Marina (very young husband and wife), Rafa, and a cheery young lady named Cristina. João, an auto executive from Brazil, rounds out the list of new *caminantes* in my life. The newest pilgrims among the group, having been on the road only since León, lack the road-wise look of the rest of us.

After showering, doing the day's laundry, and having a meal with Toni at a bar down the street (he can walk that far after all), I take a nap, write some postcards, and rest some more out on the green lawn. I catch up on two days' worth of jottings in my journal. I am invited to join Alessandra and Marisa for a light *cena* later in the evening; they ask me to bring a couple tomatoes for the salad. So I head into the village to make my purchases and if possible to gain entry into the local parish dedicated to the apostle Santiago. While making my way toward the church, I run into the Spanish foursome and we continue together; when we arrive we find its main door is open and from within singing and guitar music emanate. Today is Saturday afternoon and, as it turns out, preparations are underway for a wedding. A small choir is in the loft of the church rehearsing hymns for the celebration; they are the same hymns we used to sing in the Mexican parish communities I pastored back in the United States. "*Vienen con alegría, Señor, cantando, vienen con alegría, Señor. . . .*" The young members even have the same disagreements about the proper tempos and melodies of these hymns, which are usually passed on from person to person and from generation to generation without musical notations. I feel at home listening to them strum and sing and argue and strum and sing again: "*Vienen con alegría, Señor, cantando, vienen con alegría, Señor. . . .*" A large kneeler wrapped in red velvet has been placed in front of the sanctuary and large baskets of artificial flowers have been set on either side of the altar, again just like home.

The church is dedicated to our Santiago, yes, but with a difference. He is not represented in the church as the paradigmatic pilgrim with heavy cape, wide-brimmed hat, seashell, walking staff, and water gourd. Instead, here he is Santiago *Matamoros*, the Moor Slayer. This is not the Santiago I have grown to love over the previous twenty days, the one who calls me forward, the one who consoles me when I am sore and tired and my back is aching, the one whose pilgrim feet I have often kissed along the way. This is the *soldier* Santiago, who appeared on a great white steed in the midst of a terrible battle between Catholic troops and the Islamic Moors they were pushing into the sea with fearsome force and violence. The Catholics were losing the battle, so goes the tale, until Santiago famously rode to their rescue, slashing at the Moors with a vengeance, lopping off their heads and running his sword through their gullets. The Moors lost. All this is pictured in these images of the apostle: he is on his great horse, he is dressed in metal armor, and under the heels of his steed is a writhing Moor about to take Santiago's sword in his undefended throat.

Such is the Santiago presiding over the altar of this little church, and I detest him. I say as much to my new Spanish friends and they respond kindly but a bit patronizingly that I should try to understand the mentality of the times, dismissing my objection without further bother. Of course, one has to understand the mentality of any period of history, but does that also mean that one has to *accept* or *excuse* the mentality of those times? Does it mean by necessity that in *our times* we cannot be disgusted by this symbolism and the message it proclaims: that the apostle James, and through him Christ, and through *him* all of us who gather under Christ's name, possess the right to wage such violence as that depicted in this statue of Santiago Matamoros against fellow human beings so as to defend the truth of our doctrines? The blood of those who fall by our swords is not doctrinally purified blood but real blood, and their bodies lie not in doctrinally cleansed graves but graves cut deep in the cold earth. Those Moorish soldiers would never again make love to their wives, never again enjoy the voices of their children and grandchildren laughing at play in the yards of their own homes, never grow into the precious wisdom of old age. I for one don't accept this vision of Santiago. The truth of our doctrines is evidenced in mercy, not in murder. I'll take Santiago the Pilgrim any day and I reserve my right in conscience to reject Santiago the Moor Slayer and all that he stands for whenever and wherever I find him.

Well, of course, all this brave talk comes from the coward of El Burgo Ranero, so I guess I should just keep my mouth shut. Unless, of course, I've learned something from that cowardly moment just a few days back in this *camino*. I hope that such is the case. I truly hope I am learning lessons such as this on the pilgrimage.

Perhaps graciously, I am brought back to the reality at hand: not a statue set in a niche but a marriage about to take place that will unite two people in love and respect for the rest of their lives. The priest arrives and is very busy setting things in order. Young women dressed in satin and carrying bouquets and sporting lots of makeup on their beautiful faces gather in the vestibule. Young men in uncomfortable suits do the same. Old ladies with shawls and old farmers who look like their own suits have been fitted over their overalls are walking towards the church. A limo pulls up, a bride gets out, and a ripple of "ahs" greets her appearance. I watch for a while with my friends; we jokingly ask a passerby if we are invited and we are told that of course we are. "And to the *fiesta* too?" Light laughter is the response. I wish this bride and groom a full life through thick and thin and I hope that someday they will walk all the way from this Church of Santiago *Matamoros* to that of Compostela, where together they might embrace Santiago *Peregrino*.

I remember that I've got tomatoes to deliver, so I leave the scene and walk against the flow of wedding traffic to my *refugio* and my new friends and the grand salad they are happily throwing together in the grassy front

» *Matamoros or Peregino?* «

yard. I am put to work slicing my tomatoes for the salad being concocted on the picnic table. It is not long before Toni and João are invited in as well and we are all buzzing about, improvising our evening picnic as best we can with the limited utensils available to us. When all is ready, we squeeze together around the table, and with ample wine and plenty of salad and bread we jabber about things we've seen and places we've been and we all become great friends. There is a pattern here, of course: bread plus wine plus plenty of food shared around a common table creates family. There is power in the table. I pray that this evening's newlyweds come to understand the importance of a bottle of wine, a loaf of bread, and plenty of shared food for the new family they are creating this night in Villadangos del Páramo.

My Own Damn Fault

August 2: Villadangos del Páramo to Astorga

The twenty-six kilometers between Villadangos and the sizable city of Astorga mark a transition from the wheat country upon which my eyes have subsisted for so long now to a land that is becoming increasingly more varied in texture and tone. By the time I arrive at the town of Puente de Órbigo, ten kilometers from Villadangos, all the shades of green that nature has to offer have returned to refresh me with a vision of a brighter world than that which I have known in the almost interminable wheat country. The new scenery allows me to focus my attention outside myself rather than on my sore leg, which doubles its value to me as I walk this morning.

I cross the massive stone bridge that leads into Puente de Órbigo, a structure famous for its graceful arches and its rich history, which includes a number of battles fought over its access. Yet what once must have been a wide and deep river is now only a small stream passing beneath its great arches. It is impossible not to be struck by the contrast between what must have been and what is now and how all the work that went into building this edifice and all the blood that went into defending it now seem for naught. The river is gone.

Once over the bridge I turn onto a side street in search of a place to enjoy my morning *café con leche* and spot a number of my fellow walkers already enjoying their coffees and *tortillas*. We greet one another. I drop my *mochila* and *bastones*, stretch my back, then stiffly walk into the dark interior of the bar to place my order. I return to the fresh air outside and take my place with the others at their tables. The jolt of caffeine, the eggy *tortilla*, and the grace of aimless conversation with friends is so restorative that after twenty minutes or so I am feeling like a new man and am ready to get going one more time. I steal a line from John Wayne and declare in English: "We're burning daylight here!" but no one understands the expression. Nevertheless they are ready too and are already hoisting *mochilas* up on their backs like I am. I am delayed a bit as I adjust the straps of my own *mochila*. The others move on. I am happy for the prospect of walking by myself for a while longer.

The route out of Órbigo promptly diverges from the noisy highway and leads me instead through a further village or two and then up a steep hill that I conquer in spite of my leg: once again I discover that climbing uphill actually offers relief to my tendon, but once the path returns to flat terrain the leg resumes its sharp yelping in spite of all the bombings of Voltarén I have been giving it in both pill and handy cream form. I now move down the road slowly and I am passed by nearly everyone. There is humility in this and I do my best to accept my lot. In a way, I cannot complain too much about the trouble my leg is causing me because I've been pushing this poor tendon to its limit day after day when by all rights it should be given at least forty-eight hours of rest. It's a tradeoff: walk and hurt or don't hurt and don't walk. I choose to walk and accept the consequences as best I am able.

Since León the number of pilgrims on the road has increased substantially and I notice in particular today that it is more and more difficult to find space and time alone during the day's walk. Fresh pilgrims are not only passing me by, they are beginning to feel like a stream passing me by. At one point in today's walk I come over the crest of a hill and am able to view a lengthy stretch of the road ahead; as it winds across the plain below, it carries a continuous column of anonymous pilgrims in an irregular file, some alone, others side by side, still others in large packs like scout troops, all moving in the same direction. *All moving in the same direction*: that is the thing that strikes me and inspires me. I miss the solitude of earlier days but on the other hand, I feel now that I am part of something much bigger than myself as I walk

» *August 2: Villadangos del Páramo to Astorga* «

175

to Santiago. I am not only a lone pilgrim out here; I am one part of a grand pilgrimage extending beyond the horizon and back into time. My efforts take on a feeling of momentousness that soothes me as I limp on down the road.

The entrance to Astorga follows a secondary highway that eventually leads me to a railroad crossing where a very long and slow freight train holds me up for at least ten minutes under the hot sun. The endlessly rolling steel wheels on their rails, the passing freight cars, and the flashing red lights and clanging bells hypnotize me into an angry state that I cannot shake even when I am finally free to pass. I determinedly follow the *flechas amarillas* across yet another Roman bridge that leads me to the traditional pilgrim entrance into the walled city, the Puertasol. I have walked some twenty-six kilometers already and believe I must surely have arrived, only to discover that the route into the heart of the city now winds up and around for at least another kilometer before I am actually in the city's heart. Then the *flechas* disappear from my view in a mishmash of streets coming and going at a multitude of angles, so that I am left to guess the way to the *refugio*. This really irks me, but luckily the inhabitants of Astorga are kind to lost pilgrims and so an inquiry made of a stray man on the street resolves the issue. "Follow the wall!" is the simple direction given to me. On the far side of Astorga a manmade escarpment holds the city from falling precipitously into a deep valley below. Following its upper rampart leads me to an aging school building that has been transformed into the civic *refugio*. It is very large and must have beds for a couple hundred of us. It is charmless, but the beds are firm and the showers are clean. That's enough for today.

I greet José and then Marisa, who have arrived well ahead of me, and then Alessandra and Lucía María turn a corner and welcome me warmly. After showering, I gather up my dirty clothes and take them downstairs to wash. At the basins I find myself next to a very old man with a sun-toughened face framed by long gray hair and a straggly beard. In Spanish he asks me where I am from and when I tell him that I am an American, he switches to the English of the Irish.

"There aren't many of you Yanks out here, are there?"

"No, not many at all. And you, sir, where might you be from?"

"I'm from everywhere . . . and nowhere. I am from wherever I began today and tomorrow I'll be from here. That's the way of the pilgrim."

I chew over his answer for a moment but before I can think of anything more to ask him, he asks me if I read.

"Some." I answer.

"And what do you think of Hemingway?"

"I like Hemingway. He changed the way Americans write. He marked the end of the florid style common up to his time, and by keeping his writing basic he showed that there is power in his kind of simplicity of expression." I believe this to be a pretty good answer.

"I don't like the man. What about Faulkner? Do you think he compares to Joyce?"

I am quickly getting out of my literary league and shouldn't have been such a know-it-all in my Hemingway answer. "I find Faulkner difficult: 'My mother is a fish.' and all that. Joyce swamps me, the little I've read of him, except for 'The Dead.' I love that story."

"Hmmm. And what do you think of Bush?"

"He's not my favorite."

"Dangerous. He's going to get us all killed."

"I hope not."

"It is people like him who make me walk."

And with that there is a moment of silence as we rinse our soapy clothes under the cold-water faucets. I excuse myself and take my clean laundry out to the basketball court for drying on the chain-link fence surrounding the schoolyard while the old man from nowhere and everywhere continues his work at the basins.

I accept an invitation from the foursome I met yesterday, David, Marina, Rafa, and Cristina to go to lunch. João joins us as well. We walk down the street in a loose pack, keeping an eye out for some typical little restaurant to settle into, and finally choosing a homey little bar several blocks from the *refugio*. The keepers of the place are a family of loud and happy people and they tend to us as though we were regular customers. We get started with some cold beers and a simple salad and before long the family and us and the few other locals standing around the bar are all having a fine old time. The son who serves as easy-going waiter to us asks if we want our *credenciales* stamped; it is hard to refuse the offer, for he is clearly anxious to have his family seal take its place in our *credenciales* and in fact we *want* the *sello* imprinted forever in our *camino* passports as a memento of all the fun we're having here. He retrieves his stamp and

» *August 2: Villadangos del Páramo to Astorga* «

inkpad, sets the pad on the edge of the table, and we each pass our document to him for its official sealing. The boy's intense face shows that he relishes the triple-action of hitting the inkpad with the stamp, lifting it high, then crashing it down on our *credenciales* with authority and self-confidence. We are now branded forever as members of the household. The two teenagers from Granada, Julio and Manuel, come in and take seats at the next table over from us and before long they too are part of the grand family within the bar. Now this is an extraordinary thing that I can't imagine happening back home: the instant camaraderie and welcome into the circle that is so much a part of life in this pilgrim world is lost to the fast and fear-laden society that I ordinarily live within. I feel myself less a human being for not having grown up in a world where anyone who walks in the door is presumed to be a friend and *is* a friend. The loss of this gift is as great as any that our wholesale dive into modernity has caused. I mourn the fact that keys and locks and walls rule my life, except here, here on the *camino*.

The others order big, heavy blood sausages, while I settle for my *camino* favorite, a grilled slice of pork. We all share more beers as we consume our dinners with gusto, and after making our goodbyes to our hosts we head outside and into the increasingly suffocating heat of the street.

The beer and meat settling in my gut have made me sleepy, so I leave the others as they go to see the city's sights. I return to the *refugio* for a nap and the hope of whiling away the remainder of the hot afternoon enjoying a breeze from somewhere and writing a few lines in my journal.

After a few hours of hanging around the *refugio* I grow tired of resting, so I wander up to the Astorga cathedral. Upon entering I can see immediately that it is no match for those of León and Burgos. A young pilgrim priest at the main altar is finishing Mass in French for his group of teenage girls. Even as he says the final prayer an old man carrying a large key ring that rattles with ancient authority makes his way through the nave of the church announcing to us few stragglers still within that it is closing time. He works us like a good sheepdog, herding us to the outside through a large door that closes behind us with a solemn thud. The sound of keys turning tumblers to lock the great portal is the last word of the cathedral to the last of its visitors this day.

I wander to the building next door and have a look. It was designed, at least in part, by the wild and deeply religious Catalán architect of the nineteenth century, Gaudí; but though it has a touch of the master about it, I find this building to be only a shadow of its much grander sisters in Barcelona, especially the mysterious Basilica de la Sagrada Família which appears from the outside to be melting but from the inside to be growing. This building appears to me to be just a building, pretty as it is.

To get at least a dose of mystery before the day is over, I walk down a street or two looking for a Saturday evening Mass and find one just beginning at a convent of Benedictine sisters a short way from the cathedral. The interior of the chapel is colorful and the sisters and priest pray the Eucharist with care and in relationship to the rest of us. This priest looks at us. I leave feeling fed. Coming out of the chapel, I bump into my lunchtime companions again and we take a pleasant walk through the commercial center of Astorga, arriving at the *Plaza Mayor* just in time to see the town's great clock chime, with two mechanical figures dressed in traditional folk-wear doing the bell-striking honors. We examine the Roman ruins in the heart of the city, then begin the easy walk back to the *refugio*.

Along the way, Cristina asks me what I do for a living. I tell her that I am a Catholic priest and currently oversee an American seminary in Belgium. She is pleased and tells me she suspected as much but was too timid to ask until she knew me better. She is something of a rarity now in much of Europe: a practicing and devoted *young* Catholic, and I enjoy chatting with her as we amble down the street together. She shares with me a few details of her life, all the while looking anxiously for a pay phone so that she might call home, for it is Saturday evening and her parents always expect a call from their daughter on Saturday evening. She is a teacher of the Spanish language to foreigners, mostly retirees, who congregate during the winter months in southern Spain, the European iteration of Florida's "snowbirds." She also shares that she has a difficult question that has been troubling her and asks if I would be willing to talk with her about it. I assure her that I'd be happy to do so whereupon she tells me she'd prefer to wait until another occasion. This is odd but agreeable to me: less work for now.

Back at the *refugio*, Alessandra, José, Marisa, and Lucía María are sitting on the front stoop, shooting the breeze and enjoying the evening's cool. Lucía María asks me if I have a thread and needle, something a little tougher than the usual, as she is repairing a seam on her *mochila*. "I have just the thing!" I respond, and retrieve from my own bag a small roll of dental floss. "This should hold that seam forever!" I feel pleased to be generous, helpful, and clever all at the same time even in such a small thing.

Alessandra asks me how my leg is faring after today's lengthy trek, and I tell her honestly that it remains quite sore. Almost as bad, I tell her, is my back, which now carries within it a chronic ache that neither disables nor disappears. Alessandra scolds me in her inimitable mixture of Spanish, Italian, and English: "Kevin, the back problem is *in* you. You have very bad posture. Even on the road, when I see you walking, you are slouching. Stand up straight!" She is absolutely right, but I wince at the criticism, for it is something I have heard over and over again throughout my childhood from my father. I resist hearing it now as an adult, but the truth of the matter is clear: I *am* a sloucher. As her words soak in, I realize something even more important: I have figured out the mystery of the *mochila* that never lightens no matter what I dispose of along the way. It is not the *mochila* that is too heavy, it is my faulty posture that makes it heavy no matter how much or how little it weighs. I've been blaming the *mochila outside* me, while the true culprit is *within* me. I go to bed pondering this fact: I do it all the time; I'm always blaming circumstances and others for my unhappiness when it is really I who am to blame and it is I who hold the secret to resolving that unhappiness. As a wise old priest counseled me years ago, "Young man, if you are unhappy, it is your own damn fault." His advice remains absolutely correct: it *is* my own damn fault. I take consolation in the fact that even with my damn fault, I am moving ahead. I am still moving ahead with all these others. Even with all our damn faults, we, this grand gaggle of pilgrims, we are, still and all, moving ahead.

» *My Own Damn Fault* «

Shock and Awe

August 3: Astorga to Rabanal

At five fifty I am out the door and on the street, *mochila* feeling comfortable, *bastones* in one hand, and the other already twiddling my rosary beads. I am no longer alone on these early morning departures; I am led and followed by a long string of pilgrims every morning and today's fellow walkers include the same group of ebullient teenage girls I saw in the cathedral last night at Mass. Their priest is with them and all are wearing the same t-shirt announcing their parish affiliation. They are very chatty and their laughter as they walk along does not bother me, as I would have expected; to the contrary, this morning their teenage talk is like musical accompaniment to my morning prayer.

Once I leave behind the halogen streetlights illuminating the city of Astorga the darkness of the open road seems particularly heavy this morning. There is no moon and not a hint of dawn. I feel a strangeness in the air that I have not known before. Off to my left, far away, almost at horizon's edge, I notice out of the side of my eye a momentary flash that is diffused through a very low cloud. With a second dim flash to the right a moment later I realize that what I am seeing is lightning and that the morning's weird darkness is that of a massive cloud blocking the light of moon and stars. For the moment it is perfectly still everywhere; there is no thunder, no wind, not even a breeze. Silence reigns except for our footsteps on the pavement and the happy chatter of the girls before, beside, and behind me. Another flash lights up the landscape; this one is dead ahead of us. And yet another from the right. "This is just great," I think to myself. "We're walking straight into a lightning storm." But we all keep walking. I consider turning back to Astorga, but since everyone else continues forward, I continue forward as well.

With the coming of daylight, it is clearer than ever that something very ominous indeed is developing here and is doing so very quickly. The cloud cover is dense and dark and in the distance I see those vertical downslides of cloud and mist that indicate the fall of rain. And here I am walking into this without a poncho or even a plastic grocery bag to cover either me or my *mochila*. The storm is getting closer. *Flash!* from the left. *Flash!* from the right. *Flash!* dead ahead. A roll of thunder passes over us maybe ten seconds after each of these flashes. A single drop of rain lands on the end of my nose. The terrain around us has become flat and featureless, except for a long string of colossal power-line towers to our right. The first hint of a breeze stirs the brim of my hat. We are sitting ducks. Another drop, then another, and then ten more. *Flash! Rumble! Drop-drip-drop! Boom!* Once again I consider turning back, but no one else seems at all concerned and we all just keep trooping on. Some are stopping just long enough to pull cheap plastic ponchos out of their *mochilas* and throw them over themselves, making them look like frosted gingerbread men. Others have more sophisticated canvas gear to protect their *mochilas*. I wonder how any of this is going to keep them from getting sizzled once the heart of the storm hits us. We keep walking. I ask one pilgrim as he passes me by if he's concerned about the lightning and he answers, "Why?" and pushes ahead with a happy *buen camino* greeting. *Buen camino*, indeed. We're all going to get ourselves killed out here. *FLASH!* Count to seven. *BOOM!*

I keep my eye open for a culvert or a shed or anything that might serve as cover from the bolts of high-tension energy racing our way, but there is absolutely nothing. I spot a town off to my right and think to detour there but it is actually quite a long ways off, probably about as far as Astorga is behind me. It is now raining with a fury and the thunder is no longer a distant rumble but follows the flashes of lightning with only five-second delays. Yet everyone seems inexplicably content walking across this field of death. I feel as though we are a bunch of dumb sheep being led to the slaughter. I am becoming very afraid now and can only

» *Shock and Awe* «

182

imagine the worst. Is it this fear that is raising the hair on the back of my neck, or is it the electric charge in the air all around me? The rays of lightning are clearly visible as they zigzag to earth. I'm getting very wet; the better to be electrocuted. *FLASH! CRASH!* The thunder delay is now only a few seconds. With this latest clap sending shock waves through my head I suddenly remember that Saint James, Santiago himself, was known in the Gospels as one of the "Sons of Thunder," and so I address him: "Okay, Santiago, *Boanerges*, James the Great, show us your greatness: Give us safe passage for God's sake! Divide this storm in two and let us walk through dry-shod!" I repeat the prayer each time a bolt of lightning zigzags down to the earth and the thunder shakes our bodies. "*Boanerges, SANTIAGUITO:* HELP US!"

I don't suppose many will believe this, but it is the absolute, factual, meteorological truth: at this very moment, the massive storm begins ever so slowly to divide into two cells, one drifting to the south and the other sliding ever so slowly away to the north. I watch this phenomenon with deep attention, measuring the increasing distance between the dividing clouds. Am I imagining this? No! The clouds continue to part their ways. "*Boanerges:* you are doing it! You are saving us!" By the time I get to the little road sign announcing the village of Santa Catalina de Somoza, I am still being rained upon, but the sky directly above me is no longer the ash-gray of death. There is lightning to the north and lightning to the south, but I and the others are walking *between* those strikes, far from dry-shod, but we are safely walking *between* those strikes. "*Santiaguito*, Son of Thunder, what can I say but *¡Gracias! ¡Gracias! ¡Muchísimas gracias!*"

My relief as I enter a very small bar in Santa Catalina for rest and coffee is palpable. The place is filled with soggy pilgrims all yakking up a storm about the storm. Now this bar is nothing more really than some enterprising villager's living room set up with a few tables and straight-back chairs. Lacking one of those classy Italian espresso machines, the busy barkeeper keeps us plied with all the coffee two overworked Mr. Coffee percolators can produce. When not pouring coffee, he is handing out packs and packs of cookies and biscuits for us to share among ourselves as we drink our coffees. When we offer to pay for the treats he responds with a flick of his hand, "*¡Gratis!* No charge today, my friends!"

I'm at table with José, Alessandra, Marisa, and Lucía María, the Colombian. I ask if anyone was afraid of the lightning and they as one say with bravura: "Not at all!" I admit that I was very afraid and that I am glad none of them now have the onerous task of calling my family to tell them that their brother has been fried alive while walking to Santiago de Compostela. Lucía María with her singsong tones and droll humor answers: "*Ni modo, un Gringo menos.* No problem, one Gringo less." I am stunned for half a second, not knowing how personally to take the joke. Everyone sees the look on my face, I'm sure. I break the moment of tension by turning the slur back at her with a twist: "And if it were you who were fried out there, *ni modo, una traficante menos.* No problem, one trafficker less."

"*¿Traficante? ¿Yo?* Me? A drug-trafficker?"

"*Traficante de drogas, no. Tu eres nuestra traficante de sonrisas.* Drug trafficker, no. You, you are our trafficker in smiles." And with that double-dose of sugary revenge all have a laugh and the dark cloud of a national slur is divided in two.

The barkeeper speaks some English and when he learns I'm an American, he tells me that he used to live in Los Angeles and loves America. So there.

As I leave the small bar along with a group of others it is still raining, but only slightly, and the skies are getting brighter all the time. On my way down the main street of Santa Catalina, I spend two euros on a cheap plastic poncho, so that I too look like a glazed gingerbread man along with all the rest. Within fifteen minutes the rain has stopped completely and the sun is shining and life under the poncho has begun to feel like a tropical swamp, so I stop, take it off, stuff it into my *mochila* and continue on whistling like Moses on the far side of the Red Sea with all his troubles behind him.

As I amble on, I am certain that this morning's meteorological event was a miracle, that my plaintive plea to Santiago was directly heard, heavenly intervention was accomplished, and God, through his powers as Master of all Nature, deliberately split that storm in two just for me. Even if it was not a class-A miracle, I do know that what happened is part of a much grander miracle. I am coming to understand out here that all nature is a miracle even when its built-in rules are not suspended in response to a poor human being's plea. Creation is in itself the miracle. Something from nothing: that awes me as miracle-*plus*. Every little thing in this created world of ours is miracle: the gossamer wings of a fly, the yellow of a canary feather, the tender flesh of a newborn baby. Rain and lightning and thunder are miracles. The movement of storm cells, combining and dividing and moving on, is a miracle. The fact that I, that we, exist and think and love, this is an extraordinary miracle too. The trick is to see it, to recognize it, to know in my heart that in and around and beneath and above all the marvels of this world created from nothing, there is *someone*. Someone whom I can know and who knows me. Someone to whom I can ask for support and help and mercy. Someone who hears me and perhaps even someone who might suspend a small law of nature for my benefit from time to time. Maybe he did; maybe he didn't. This is the bottom line: I prayed and the storm split in two and I did not die. Whatever the explanation, I remain in awe.

The road from Santa Catalina rises gently and leads us into rich and rolling country dappled with pine and oak. Eventually, it leads us into the quaint village of Rabanal del Camino. I meet José at a bar at the entrance to the town and he indicates that the *refugios* are a bit farther on, in the center of the village. Though this is a small place, it has two *refugios* and so our company for the day will be divided between the two. The one preferred by Alessandra, Marisa, Lucía María, and José is operated by the Benedictine fathers who also tend the ancient church at the center of town. I join them there even though we have to wait an hour or so for its opening. We sit on the flagstone porch, drink, nibble, and release our feet from their booted captivity. Among the others waiting about is the very group of young girls I started the morning with as we left Astorga. Accompanying them is their leader and guide, the same priest I saw finishing Mass last evening in the Astorga cathedral. In Spanish I introduce myself to him and let him know of our shared vocation. *Père* Nicolas explains that he is the parish priest from a small town in France and is leading his gang of parish youth, all girls, on pilgrimage. They've been on the road since León. I admire his courage in the matter. He lets me know that a little later in the afternoon Mass will be celebrated in the Benedictines' church here and that we pilgrim priests have been welcomed to vest and concelebrate at the altar. It is Sunday so I eagerly agree to join him for the liturgy after a bath and a little laundry.

When we arrive at the church we are met in the sacristy by one of the Benedictine fathers, who warmly welcomes us and has us write our names in the parish guest book, and then a third priest comes in as well; *Padre* Javier, also a pilgrim priest, is leading a parish youth group, girls and boys, from Sevilla. The twelfth-century Romanesque church is not in great condition, and though some repairs have been done there is clearly much more yet to be accomplished. Nevertheless, it is beautiful in its own way and its acoustics give full resonance to the human voice. Mass is lovely, especially as I look out across the altar at the faces of my pilgrim companions. They are beautiful to behold. There is light in their eyes. The flesh is clean and free of make-up and tinted from the inside in so many ethnic shades. Some mouths are held in slight smiles; others dip at either end in solemn seriousness. They are alive, these flesh-and-blood creatures; there is spirit within them. "The Body of Christ," I say to them and they say, "Amen."

After the great prayer is completed, I join the loose crowd of pilgrims on the porch of the church. João expresses his surprise at seeing me on the altar and tells me he had no idea over the past days that I was a priest. Lucía María also wasn't aware of my vocation and asks how she should address me now that she knows my identity. Does she have to call me "Padre"? I answer, "Of course not, just 'Kevin,' as always." She responds, "How about 'el Gringo'; may I call you that?" She adds then in her beautiful Colombian singsong tones: "Even better, how about 'Mi querido Gringo!' My beloved Gringo." And I say, "Sure!" I am more than happy to be anyone's querido Gringo. I suppose her new title for me is her way of making up for the close-to-the-edge joke she made earlier in the day.

The presence of the Benedictine fathers in this isolated outpost of the camino is of immense importance, for they provide a high-quality refugio for pilgrims; their ancient commitment to hospitality makes itself felt in the very stones of the place. They have a way of making a transient crowd like us feel at home even as they care for the life of their own small community. More importantly, they share their common prayer with those passing through and make a point of making it accessible with printed fliers in a variety of languages and by offering a brief spoken explanation before each service so that the visitors can easily follow the chanting of the psalms and prayers.

In the afternoon, word begins to spread among the pilgrims that the Benedictines will be doing their prayers in Gregorian chant later in the evening. The excitement at this news is very high, and at seven P.M., the appointed hour, the church is packed. There are only two monks in the sanctuary, sitting face to face across from one another; despite their small number, they chant the entire liturgy from beginning to end. The pilgrim visitors seem intensely interested and pay rapt attention. It is one of the most beautiful moments of common prayer I have yet had along the *camino*, and it refreshes me and, I believe, the others. It also gives the lie to the common belief that this generation of young people has no thirst for the beautiful and the holy. I have repeated this lie too many times myself. This evening prayer makes it clear that they do thirst for something transcendent in their lives, but to our shame don't find it often enough in those of us who are supposed to be mediators of the holy in this world. To the extent that they are empty and thirsty it is to an uncomfortable degree our fault, not theirs.

I have dinner with João and we have a long talk about the humility that comes from walking the *camino*. He reflects on his experience of the road: with all its twists and turns, ups and downs, it finds your weak spots and takes advantage of them. No matter how strong you believe you are, both in body and in mind, it brings you down to dirt level sooner or later. Failure and weakness are always part of the *camino*. There is little room for vanity or arrogance out here. He then lets me know how tired he is of walking. This is his second time to walk the *camino* and it is very different this time, he says; it lacks the sense of excitement and mission it had the first time. It is more like work than an adventure. He just wants to get to Santiago and then go home. He's going to push hard to finish up quickly and just be done with it. He'll never do it again, he says sadly.

After dinner, I go to night prayer with the monks in the church; again there is a crowd, but there is no buzz in the air this time; everyone is quietly sitting, gazing, breathing. A warm tranquility fills the church interior. The simple prayers are chanted and the final blessing for the night is given. "Into your hands, O Lord, I commend my spirit." As others leave to prepare for bed, I stay behind a few moments, light a candle before Santiago's statue, kiss his feet, and thank him for getting us all through the storm. I ask him to restore my leg while I sleep, for we have an imposing mountain to climb on the morrow and I am very tired of this pain and I don't want to end up feeling like João about the whole *camino*. A brother invites me to leave and the church is closed and locked for the night. Before falling asleep I wonder in awe at the mystery of it all: the storm divided and we passed through unharmed. Extraordinary.

» *August 3: Astorga to Rabanal* «

Cross and a Conscience

August 4: Rabanal to Molinaseca

Upon waking in Rabanal, I immediately know that my leg is better. Even as I do my morning stretches atop my bed, then head to the john, then return to pack the last of my things, that tendon feels as good as new. I am suspicious, for I have been tricked before like this; just when I think all is well, all goes to hell. However, for the moment, anointing my feet with Vaseline and my leg with another dose of Voltarén, I am pretty sure that this is different. Is it my prayer to Santiago from the night before being answered or is the Voltarén finally kicking in? I don't know and leave the question open. Anyway, I stretch again and whisper: *"Santiaguito,* my brother, you are being very good to me of late."

Last evening one of the monks mentioned that it was an ancient tradition for the pilgrims holding up in Rabanal to take a rock from this place and as a penance haul it up the steep mountain road that begins just outside of town; once at the foot of the *Cruz de Ferro* which towers over the high point of the day's walk, the rock is let go. It is a symbol of letting go of our sin. I disregard the tradition, figuring I have had enough penance over the previous days and weeks, and so at six thirty begin my walk feeling mighty chipper, with absolutely no pain in my leg or body anywhere.

The first hour of the morning, the most precious one of any day, is made less so by a squawking family of pseudo-pilgrims who walk along at my pace so that I cannot escape their annoying company. They yak and yammer and laugh bawdily and generally disturb the peace without let-up. Only one or two of the bunch wears a *mochila*, which makes me suspicious of their authenticity as pilgrims. As we climb up the highway and round a bend, a white car, the despicable *coche de apoyo*, is waiting for them, ready to take even more off their backs. There is a loud man standing off to the side yelling at full voice and with an obnoxious laugh: "What kind of *pinche pereginos* are you, anyway! Ha-ha-ha-h-ha!" I don't know how to translate the word *pinche* into English, but perhaps the closest in crudity would be our "f-word." As they drop their minor-league loads, gather round the car cackling like old crows and take their unearned rest, I would like to be enough of a Superman to tip their *coche de apoyo* over the bank of the road and have it tumble into the gully below, forcing them to walk as true pilgrims; lacking for the moment the superpowers required for the accomplishment of such a feat, I merely pass by silently and unnoticed and move far enough ahead of them to never have to encounter their big mouths and lazy butts again.

The rise to the top of *Monte Irago* is as steep as advertised, but I tackle it with energy and a fair amount of speed for me. In fact, I hardly stop for a breath all the way up the eight or nine kilometers of roadway to the top. I do pause momentarily to gaze out over the plains of Castile far below me and now behind me. I have walked as far as the eye can see and much more; it is with a sense of having accomplished something grand that a pilgrim like me beholds this vista over the lands he has already journeyed. I feel as grand as the view. Even when I pass through the village of Foncebadón, largely abandoned except for a large restaurant that has recently been placed there for dogged pilgrims with little left in them to finish off the climb to the top of *Monte Irago*, I walk right on by, for I am not weary in the least today.

I arrive at the peak of the mountain to find a wide-open space populated by small groups of pilgrims sitting or standing around with their *mochilas* off and their snacks and water bottles being generously shared about. In the center of it all is a massive pile of stones with a large wooden pole sticking out of it, and attached to that, shooting high up into the blue sky of morning, a great cross of iron. Numerous pilgrims are adding rocks to the heap from their own pockets as others post notes and photographs to the wooden base of the cross. I lay down my *mochila* as well, take from a pocket a handful of almonds and raisins to snack on, then sit on the worn mountain grass just to take it all in. Seated next to me are two Italian girls I have seen on the road but have not yet met. We all take a deep breath together and laugh and so I introduce myself to them and Elena and Nicoletta present themselves to me. They ask me to take a couple pictures of them in front of the cross, which I happily do. José, Alessandra, Lucía María, and all the others are here as well. José pulls out his fancy camera from deep in his *mochila* and takes some shots; I offer to take some of him at the foot of the cross, and then he takes one or two of me in the same stance. I climb the mound of penitential stones to look over the notes and photographs posted to the base of the cross and am touched by the simple notes left behind. "María: today is Monday, I'll wait for you in Ponferrada on Wednesday. Call me. Love Juan." "Pray for me." "My brother has cancer. Pray for him to be healed. He has three children." "Help me, Jesus, to be patient with my husband."

As I stand atop the heap of rocks beneath this great cross, I deeply regret my cold, practical decision not to bring a rock up in my own pocket. Enough penance already? Who am I kidding? There is great significance in this place and in these rocks and it extends from this very moment back to times even before the Romans trooped through these parts. Piles of stones like this one, and including this one, had some kind of significance for the ancient populations that lived here, but no one knows what exactly that might have been. The Romans took them over and dedicated them to their own god, Mercury. Eventually the Christians came along, stuck a cross in this one, and transformed it into a sign of penance and renewal. Since the pilgrim streams first began crossing this mountain top on their way to Compostela well over a millennium ago, to lay a stone atop this heap has been a poignant symbol of leaving behind that which is hard in our hearts, that which is cold in our lives, and turning those lives over to the warm embrace symbolized in the open arms of the cross of Christ. Stupid me for not understanding this *before* I climbed the mountain!

Just a few kilometers down from the *Cruz de Ferro*, I pass the entrance to the most unusual *refugio* of the entire *camino*, at least so far. Its entrance from the highway is filled with pilgrims standing about, enjoying coffee and cookies, amiably conversing with one another. The spirit in the air is remarkably upbeat for this far into the day. I wander in myself and am greeted both by pilgrims I now know well and *hospitaleros* for whom I seem to be a long-awaited guest. They offer to stamp my *credencial* even as they hand me a cup of coffee and a few cookies to snack on. Don is my host, the only American *hospitalero* I have come across on the *camino* thus far. He is a Texan and explains that he's been here for about a month and loves this place. Even more importantly, he explains to me the story of this oddly placed *refugio*, which offers the pilgrim no electricity, no running water, no beds, just hospitality and, for those who stay over, the privilege of passing a night in utter poverty with Tomás. Tomás, it turns out, founded this mountain refuge in the abandoned village of Manjarín after he found himself caught on this mountain in the midst of a storm, unable to find any place to take refuge from nature's torments. He has been here ever since. He has declared himself a Knight Templar, because he believes that in a "previous life" he was a member of this medieval order of knights dedicated to protecting the defenseless pilgrims walking to the Holy Land. The spirit of the Templars is something he attempts to live out in modern times through the work of his intentionally primitive *refugio*. He has been written about in magazines and newspapers throughout Spain and his persona has taken on almost mythic proportions; word has spread wide and far among pilgrims that "sleeping with Tomás" is a singular experience not to be missed on the way to Santiago. Unfortunately for me, Don tells me, Tomás is out herding his sheep on a hillside somewhere and won't be back until the evening, so neither I nor the other pilgrims milling about this morning will have the opportunity to meet this strange and extraordinary person. We do meet his spirit though, living in the hospitality and warmth of those who tend to us in his stead this morning. I leave grateful enough for this.

As I follow the highway down from Tomás's *refugio*, I find myself curiously alone on the road. It is all the more odd then to see my solitude interrupted by a figure coming towards me; a woman with staff in hand and *mochila* weighing her down is climbing up the very road I am descending. As we come closer, our eyes meet and she smiles at me in unassuming greeting; we both stop and on the edge of the paved road we begin a simple conversation.

"*¿Qué tal?*" I ask.

» *August 4: Rabanal to Molinaseca* «

She responds, *"Bien,"* but upon hearing my accent switches to English. "I'm doing okay, but it is much harder now."

"Have you already been to Santiago?" I inquire. "Yes. I started in Bavaria. I've been on the road for three months. Going back is much more difficult; I am much more alone now. Everyone else is going *to* Santiago. I just feel tremendous fatigue all the time. No matter how many things I have left behind along the way, my rucksack never gets lighter."

"Nor mine. How long before you are home?"

"I don't know. I'm not going home soon. I will walk back over the Pyrenees, then take a train up into the Italian Alps, then walk to Rome to visit the apostles Peter and Paul, then I'll walk to the coast and catch a boat to Haifa and from there I will walk to Jerusalem. *Then,* once I've been to the Lord's tomb, then I will be done. Then I will go home."

I have never met a pilgrim like her before. The breadth of her mission astounds me, but instead of asking why she does it I lose the opportunity to hear a life story and stupidly ask instead: "And how long will this take?" She has no idea but gives no sign that time is an issue for her; her mission is set. I finally say, "Well, God bless you on your way. You inspire me." She responds, "And God bless *you.* You are doing a very good thing." With that we part company, she to climb back over Monte Irago and on to Jerusalem and I to head west only as far as Santiago. Small as it is in comparison to her mission, I believe in what she has said to me: what I am doing *is* a very good thing.

The trail down the mountain gradually becomes more and more wild, with switchbacks and huge stones and a wonderful variety of plant life and trees on all sides. I am loving it, as I agilely continue on my best trek of the whole *camino.* Along the way down, I come upon an old man settled into a small gully who has set up a makeshift station of canvas stretched among three trees, a few pieces of cardboard, and a sign hung from a tree trunk advertising massages for pilgrims. José is already with the fellow chatting away when I come along and so I join them for a moment. The geezer asks if I want an excellent massage and at first I decline, then I think twice about it and say, "Sure; why not?" So I drop my load, take off my shirt, lie down on the flattened cardboard box and entrust my body to the old man's powerful hands. He works on my back, legs, and shoulders and then after he finishes he shows me a few stretches of the upper body to keep this back of mine in better shape. I feel like a new

» *Cross and a Conscience* «

man, of course. I give the fellow a few euros in gratitude, then José takes off his shirt and enjoys the same blessing after me.

The rest of the way into Molinaseca is a breeze except that the day is getting very hot and the smell of smoke and the sound of helicopters begin to fill the air. This being the hottest summer in over a hundred years in Europe, it has been only a matter of time before wildfires should begin to break out somewhere; today seems to be that time. The fires are far enough away that they do not trouble us, but the sky loses its brilliance and the smelly air makes a number of us sneeze, cough, and wheeze.

The town of Molinaseca has the appearance of a pleasant enough place as I climb down a steep hillside toward the highway that leads into it. A sparkling river guards its flank, toward which I now approach. At this entry point to the town there is a bridge, and below it a verdant park along the riverbank where people by the hundreds have gathered for swimming and sunning themselves. The tranquility of the scene is disturbed by the heavy chop-chop of an immense helicopter hovering over the river. It drops a massive bucket into the water then lifts it up by its wire umbilicus and swings it over the town to take the load to dump on some conflagration somewhere. The helicopter causes a great stir as the population runs to any good vantage point to see it do its work. I carry on down the town's main street keeping my eye open for any sign of the local *refugio* but see none. Perplexed, I ask a storekeeper about the location of the *refugio* but she is much more interested in the helicopter than in her store or me at the moment so she simply waves me further down the street. Before long I am leaving the town and still have not found the place and my perplexity only increases as my enthusiasm for Molinaseca flags. I am just about to turn around presuming I have somehow missed the place when I spot Manuel and Julio, my two teenage friends from Granada, coming toward me. They are heading back to the river for a swim after having checked in at the *refugio*. They too wave me on and tell me it is just a couple blocks further on, ". . . just look for the tents and you'll be there." So on I go, now feeling really tired for the first time in the day.

The Molinaseca *refugio* is completely inadequate to the task of housing several hundred pilgrims a night. The central building had once been a chapel dedicated to Saint Roque, one of Europe's favorite saints and a pilgrim himself; the small place has been converted into a *refugio* with a small kitchen and a few beds. More bunks are stacked outside under an awning, while the ample yard is covered with blue and yellow pup tents. I pay my dues, receive my *sello*, and settle for one of the two-man tents in the yard. A little while later, José comes into camp and joins me in the tent as my partner for the night.

The tent might as well be an oven; it is intolerably hot within its thin canvas walls. Even worse, the dirt from outside is impossible to keep outside, and small ants crawl over everything. I realize how lucky I have been to have had such relatively comfortable *refugios* all along the way since Roncesvalles. Nevertheless, even with the deficiencies here, there are at least toilets, showers, and washbasins, the only things that are really necessary. I wash and do my laundry, then check my feet, only to find a blister developing over a callus on my heel. It is a small one and not so painful, but a reminder on a good walking day that it would not take much to yet fell me along this way.

Alessandra, Marisa, and the others invite me to join them for dinner; Alessandra will prepare her specialty: homemade spaghetti Bolognese. Meanwhile, the camp fills up with all our friends and we begin to have a very good time. After dinner a musician comes into camp with a small amplifier and microphone, a harmonica, and a didgeridoo. He sets up under an awning and we gather around him, some sitting on the grass and others in plastic lawn chairs. Bottles of wine are passed about as everyone delights in the unknown musician's diverse selection of music, everything from aboriginal Australian to American blues.

The Granada boys have become great pals and sit near me as we listen. They ask me about my favorite music, what I do for a living, what life is like in the U.S. ("Is it like in the movies where everyone has money but their lives are meaningless?"). Then someone spots a terrific sight: the sun is setting in the west, and with the smoke in the air the solar disk appears immense and apocalyptically red as it sinks ever so slowly towards the horizon. Almost as a body, everyone gets up, walks up to a spot in the yard beyond the buildings and in utter silence gazes upon the spectacle of our great sun ever-so-slowly lowering itself into its galactic bed for the night.

And now Cristina and her question come back into my story. After the sunset, several of us sit in a loose circle on the lawn shooting the breeze: the Granada boys, Rafa, a mother and her two twenty-something sons whom I met a few times on the road earlier in the day, and, of course, Cristina herself. As we are chatting, Cristina asks if she may put to me

» *Cross and a Conscience* «

now her troubling question. I am surprised because I thought the matter must surely have been something personal and not something to be discussed with a circle of strangers listening in. Nevertheless, I agree: "If it's okay with you, it is okay with me."

And so she begins: "Kevin, sometimes when I go to confession I confess things that I don't think are really sins but I know that the Church thinks they are sins, so is it a sin to confess them even if I don't believe they are sins, or is it a sin not to confess them because the Church believes they are sins?"

Oh my God.

Rafa interjects incredulously: "Kevin, are *you* a priest?"

"I am."

"I didn't know."

"You never asked." We both laugh and then I must begin: "Cristina, the answer is both simple and not-so-simple, but I'll do my best to answer it well for you, both ways. The simple answer is that it is never correct for you to confess something that you don't believe is a sin, and the Church *never* asks any of us to do that. Why? Because of a simple and beautiful principle that many people do not know or understand: the human conscience is inviolable, it always rules. We must never act against our conscience and we must always act in accord with our conscience. That has been the teaching of the Church for as long as we've taught anything about morality.

"That is the simple answer. Now for the complicated part. It is our responsibility as human beings and especially for us as believers to form our consciences as well as we possibly can. That is, to come to know as fully as possible what hurts us and what helps us as individuals, as a society, as a church family, as a world. That which hurts us, diminishes us, or in any way makes us less human, less than what God has created us to be, that is evil. That which makes us our best selves, that which promotes us, heals us, strengthens us, makes us love and trust one another, that which leads us to God, that is good. To learn how to know the difference between the two and to have the strength to choose the good and reject the evil, this is a life skill we must learn with help from others, our parents, our teachers, our church family, the scriptures, the wisest traditions handed on to us by our cultures. What happens to so many of us is that we stop learning any of this when we are six or seven years old and so we make moral decisions as if we were children, not adults. Some choose to make all their decisions as if no one else could ever teach them anything, while others want a parent or authority to tell them what to do rather than to take upon themselves the responsibility to learn, prepare, study, grow, and in the end make a choice in freedom based on a well-formed and responsible conscience. A person with a well-formed conscience is one who has learned from others how to make decisions that make her free to love and serve others with joy. In the end, it is always our responsibility to form our conscience as well as possible and to act in freedom according to that conscience but it is also our responsibility to do so as members of a body, a family, a community who have claims on us in love and who will always be affected by our decisions."

As I end my monologue on the first principles of conscience formation, I look up at the crowd of perhaps fifteen people listening to me and realize they are hanging on my every word. I can almost hear them saying incredulously, "This is what the Catholic Church teaches? We've never heard anything like this before!" And I find myself feeling slightly frightened for some reason; I suppose I feel a touch of fear because on this night in this campground with these good people surrounding me I have been unexpectedly entrusted with the responsibility to teach them a catechism lesson they should have received twenty years before. To have them looking to me as if they were baby birds with their beaks stretched wide open waiting to be fed by their mother makes me suddenly feel the responsibility of having their lives in my hands. To care for these people, to teach them in a way I didn't expect, this has taken me aback. It is my job to do precisely this in my ordinary life, but out here, on this road without the usual role expectations controlling and guiding the process, the raw power of the responsibility is so much more deeply felt. I suppose it is this clarity of vision into my own vocation that stuns me tonight. After a few more far less significant questions about why does the Church think this or why does the Church do that, the discussion peters out as night deepens and the stars begin to appear one by one above our heads.

Sleep is terribly difficult to come by during this long night in the pup tent. The noise of tractors and trucks and motorcycles racing up and down the highway just beyond the camp fence is unending. Ants chew at my back, leaving it full of small, itchy welts. Just as bad, it doesn't cool off inside this tent until it is almost time to get up for the next day's walk. José tosses and turns almost as much as I. Five A.M. comes way too early.

Visitations

August 5: Molinaseca to Villafranca del Bierzo

As soon as the small alarm built into my plastic Casio watch chirps its five A.M. wake-up call, I know it is going to be a difficult day. I can feel the lack of sleep in my very bones. Nothing in my body wants to move and everything in my mind desires to slip back into dreamland. My back itches with ant bites. I force myself up and in the confined space of the pup tent begin to prepare myself and my things for the day ahead. José wakes up a few minutes later and, like me, complains of a terrible night's sleep. I wander off to the toilet, return, and finish packing. I consume a yogurt and two small bananas and join the procession of pilgrims heading down the main highway away from Molinaseca. My *mochila* has seldom felt worse: out of balance, tipping me sideways, and ruining my gait enough to demand corrective action, but no matter what I do to adjust, re-cinch, or even stop, open, and push things around inside, it continues to irritate me greatly. Every footstep seems a burden and there is nothing I can do to make myself happy this morning. Though my feet and legs do not really hurt they have little fight in them; there is nothing to be done except to force them to keep walking through sheer exertion of my will. What has happened to the joy on the road I knew only yesterday? It has vanished in a sleepless night filled with the sound of diesel engines, roaring motorcycles, and rumbling semi-trucks, that's what.

Lucía María has become quite sick and has to stay back. We will miss her. Will we see her again further on? No one knows. Perhaps in Santiago itself.

After an hour on the road, Cristina and a young man I have not seen before catch up to me and begin walking with me in the dawning light. She is in an altogether cheery mood. He, on the other hand, though quite animated for this hour of the morning, has an edge of brashness about him; he loudly proposes his opinions on any variety of topics and themes, including his utter disdain for that old Catholic nonsense of confession. "I can go directly to God with my problems. I don't need any priest to put himself between God and me! Why should I reveal my sins to another man; most priests are just as much sinners as I am, if not more! They drink, they go to discos, and everyone knows they have their women on the side!" And so on and on he asserts his point of view. Neither Cristina nor I tell him that I am a priest. I feel that this will just egg him on to engage me in that most typical of Spanish diversions: the shouting match. I want no part of it, at least not on this grim morning. Cristina, on the other hand, perhaps with some need to defend the Church on my behalf, attempts to offer a contrary view of the matter, but anything she says is roundly rebuffed with a reiteration of his position made with ever greater force and volume. I dislike this young man and I am in no mood to spend an entire morning with his bluster so I excuse myself from their company with the pretext that I must stop to adjust my uncomfortable *mochila*, which, in fact, is no lie. I gratefully lose them as they move on down the road leaving me behind.

After once again re-stuffing my *mochila* and working on its various straps and cinches I walk on, now a considerable distance behind them. The young man's broadside against the Catholic sacrament of confession in general and against priests in particular rolls around in my mind, giving me something to gnaw on as I walk alone. I suppose it is not altogether his fault that his view of the matter is so bitter; perhaps he was forced as a child to undergo this treatment for the soul as something akin to swallowing a tablespoon of castor oil. If his childhood was like that of many Catholic children, he may well have been taught to tally up his boyish sins, making sure not to overlook the slightest offense, then ordered to step into a dark closet where he would be met by a disembodied voice from behind a screen, a voice fearsome enough to make him wet his pants. His list of sins spoken aloud, though insignificant on the grand scale of life, would be the source of further interrogation by the priest, forcing the boy into a panicky making up of details to please his invisible inquisitor, but there would be no pleasing him. Finally, he is told to make "a firm act of contrition," forcing him to recite a complicated prayer from memory, but the stress is so high he cannot get through it all without forgetting the words and so he has to begin again . . . and perhaps again . . . until finally, the priest with disgust in his voice, says the prayer of absolution and dismisses the poor fellow, who then must face those waiting in lines on either side of the closet with the shame of his wet pants on display for all to see. If this is what Cristina's young friend is rejecting, who can blame him?

But this is a such a long way from what I have experienced as both a confessee and confessor in my adult life that I feel a great sadness that some, perhaps many, have never in their lives experienced this sacrament as the healing balm that it can be when ministered by a caring and wise pastor. The symbolic gesture of those stones being left behind on that pile under the *Cruz de Ferro* is an image of what this sacrament is meant to be: a letting go of the garbage, the contamination, the poison, all those bags of *merde* that we carry in our spiritual pockets. To put into words the evil we have done and the good we have not done, to share those words with another, and to actually hear the simple affirmation, "You are forgiven. Go in peace." This is an experience that lets loose the spirit, frees the soul, and opens the heart anew. Though small and private in itself, confession such as this is powerful on the grand scale of life because it breaks cycles of vengeance upon vengeance, it restores broken relationships, it lifts up the poor and humbles the rich, it stops wars. Can I confess on my own, without a priest, just God and me? Sure. But since it pertains to the order of love, a reality like forgiveness needs to be symbolized, ritualized, and, yes, spoken aloud. Husbands and wives know this: spoken words give substance to forgiveness. It is seldom enough to *think* words of apology or forgiveness; spouses who love one another also have to *say* those words and often enough seal them with a gift, a touch, an embrace. So do we all.

And what of our young man's accusation that we priests are sinners too, and probably bigger sinners than everyone else? That we are sinners? Absolutely, and no one knows that better than we. That we are *bigger* sinners than everyone else? Well, we are bigger sinners than many, that's for sure. Certainly we are greater sinners than many of the people we are asked to pastor. My own experience is that this humbling reality does not disqualify us from the work of reconciliation; to the contrary, it is an essential prerequisite for a confessor to do his work well. A man humbled daily by the knowledge of his own failings will treat another sinner with a care that heals rather than with a heavy-handed arrogance and superiority that intimidates and shames. For me, there is nothing in my life as a priest that has been more moving than to say God's best words to humanity: "You are forgiven."

I meet up with Cristina and her friend in the city of Ponferrada and once again the blabber begins. I can tell that Cristina very much wants me to engage this fellow in debate, but I again refuse to be drawn into his argumentative web, and so I tell Cristina that I am having a very difficult morning and just need some time alone on the road, which is the certain truth. The two of them disappear into a small store and I trudge wearily on by myself.

The succeeding hours drag by in slow motion and even though I pass through a couple of small villages, I don't stop for my usual morning refreshment but keep walking on, interested in neither company nor coffee nor debates over religion. After perhaps three more hours I come into the village of Camponaraya and here finally relent of my dogged determination to keep marching on in spite of myself. I find a small plaza with a lovely fountain at its center and a bar to one side where a few pilgrims unknown to me have gathered for their own coffees. I drop my bag and *bastones* outside the bar, cross the street to take a good draught of the fresh water pouring from each of the four sides of the stone fountain in the center of the plaza, then return to the bar for the usual *café con leche* and a bite to eat. I politely greet the other pilgrims but they are their own group and though polite in returning my greeting, have no great interest in welcoming me into their own jovial conversation. I am just as happy to remain alone for the moment. I take a seat at an outside table and slowly sip at my coffee and nibble at my mid-morning snack, a piece of utterly uninteresting *empanada* left over from the day before. I dawdle for a while, though not having any of my usual companions with me makes the experience far less refreshing than usual. I don't know that I have ever been this cheerless on the *camino* before.

By this point in this pilgrim's story it is surely clear that one of the recurring mysteries of the experience is the fascinating manner in which relationships come about. Somewhere back in the early days of this adventure, I mentioned how from out of the crowd one first *notices* others, then one *meets* those others, then one *gets to know* the others, then one has friends for life. It is all a matter of happenstance at one level, but at another level one feels that there is a sort of plan or destiny at work, especially *after* the first meeting has turned into a prized friendship. How could it be otherwise? The set of random circumstances that collude to bring two or three people together at the same time at the same place, the odd glance, a moment of eye contact here and a simple greeting there, a meeting of one person's bad morning with another's freshness on the road, well, it all seems, after the fact, to be too much to be blind coincidence. It seems like a mystery, like God at play. And so it is at this fountain in the plaza of Camponaraya; here I meet Toni.

While sitting with my coffee and my day-old slice of tuna *empanada*, I have little more to do than watch the pilgrims come and go, all of them stopping at the fountain, some of them dropping their *mochilas* and holding up for a coffee as I have done. So into the plaza comes a sole pilgrim wearing a canary yellow t-shirt, a beige backpack, and a canvas hat with a broad rim all the way around. He drops his *mochila*, bends down to take a drink from the fountain; for the moment that is as much as I notice about him, for my eye moves to someone else passing through. I finish my coffee and return my cup and saucer to the bar, heave my *mochila* up over my shoulders once again, adjust it as best I am able, grab my *bastones*, and, before walking out of town, stiffly wander back to the fountain for one last swig of fresh water before trudging on. As I take my own last drink from the fountain, the fellow in the bright yellow t-shirt comes around the corner of the fountain, takes one last sip himself, looks at me and says quietly, "*Hola. ¿Qué tal?* Hello. How's it going?"

"*Bien. Más o menos.* Okay. Not great."

"*¿Te vas?* Are you going on?"

"*Sí, me voy adelante. Tengo que continuar.* Yes, I'm going on. I have to go on."

"*Pues, vámanos.* Well then, let's go . . ."

With that we begin to walk together down the street and out of town. He introduces himself as Toni, from Galicia, the province in

» *August 5: Molinaseca to Villafranca del Bierzo* «

Spain wherein Santiago de Compostela is located. He has some time on his hands between jobs so he has decided to do at least part of the *camino*, having begun his own journey in Astorga. He's lived close to Santiago and been there many times over in his twenty-nine years of life, but he has never walked to it, never done the *camino*. It is time he did it, if only a part. I tell him of my own beginning in Saint-Jean-Pied-de-Port and of some of the places I have passed through and a little about my life. Thus we slowly come to know one another as we amble down the road together.

I am now breaking a personal rule I have enforced upon myself since my first problematic experience having taken up with Javier and Manuel back in Zubiri so long ago: enjoy people in the afternoon, but in the morning walk alone. But this is a different time now, and after so many, many days on the road and so much time alone already and feeling so absolutely knackered this particular morning, Toni's company feels right and I find myself welcoming it with all my heart. He is the first person since my very first day on the road when I was accompanied for a while by the French boy, Jean Luc, who walks *with* me. The thing is that I walk slowly. Almost everyone passes me by every day. They greet me, perhaps chat a while on the road, then they move ahead. I have no problem with this; it is the way of the road and I am used to it and actually like it for it helps me protect the experience as a pilgrimage of the spirit as much as of the body. Though he is fresh, energetic, and young, Toni slows himself down to walk at my poky pace and continues to do so for hours. *He walks at my pace.* Now this is something.

As we walk along we share bits and pieces of our lives. He is very involved in the Scouting movement in Galicia. I am a priest. He is a practicing Catholic and has grown up in a very Catholic family. I have ten brothers and sisters; he has one sister; both my mom and dad have died. His mother died when he was a teen; now he lives with his father in Ourense. He compliments me on my Spanish and says I speak it almost perfectly. I am rector of a seminary in Belgium. He says that he should take this rare opportunity of walking with an American to talk about America and so we do. He wonders about our political and military domination of the world, but of a world we don't seem to understand or belong to. Why do we separate ourselves from Europe? Why are we so isolated and seemingly uncaring about the needs of anyone else? He admits these questions may be prejudices garnered from the media in Europe, but still and all, they are important questions; maybe I can give him a better view of America. I do my best to answer and to explain myself and my country to him. And as we traverse the countryside together, I find that I have forgotten my earlier weariness. Yesterday's spring is back in my step. My shoulders straighten and my mood is no longer dark. It is almost as if by walking with me he is allowing me to absorb some of his freshness, his energy, and indeed his very youth. I feel like God is back in my life.

What I experience this morning with Toni must be something akin to the manner in which angels visit important personages in the Scriptures. I imagine that the angel slips into a life through a side door, waits quietly to be noticed, shares a fleeting moment of eye-contact. Eventually there is a friendly greeting back and forth, a walk (at the other's pace!), and finally the speaking of a word that opens the person's life to God. Then the angel disappears, leaving behind the memory of a visitation and a life changed forever by the brief encounter. Toni's walking with me today feels exactly like this. I think the down and up of this day is making me a little bit nuts: I tell Toni too many times how grateful I am for his walking with me, walking at my pace, and after the tenth or fifteenth time he cuts me off with a smile: "*¡Ya basta con las gracias!* Enough already with the thank you's!"

As we arrive in the bustling town of Cacabelos, almost immediately I come upon Marisa, Alessandra, and José having beers and sharing a *bocadillo*, a sandwich of ham or cheese on a long stretch of French bread, and I am very glad to see them. I introduce Toni to my friends and ask him if he'd like a beer or a sandwich. He turns down my offer and says that he intends to spend the night here in Cacabelos; and so we make our goodbyes and he disappears down the street in search of the town's *refugio*. And so with a simple *adios* Toni walks out of my *camino* as suddenly as he walked into it.

After I have quaffed my beer, the others tell me that they are going on another eight kilometers to spend the night in the rather isolated village of Villafranca del Bierzo, which boasts much *camino* history, some interesting old churches, and a river with a beach. I am feeling fairly strong again in spite of having already covered twenty-four kilometers this day and I agree to join them in the march onwards. This will be my longest walk yet.

» *August 5: Molinaseca to Villafranca del Bierzo* «

We leave town together, but as always it is not long before we string out along the way as we move at different paces and I, slowpoke that I am, take up my position at the rear. Soon I am alone again. The day is getting hotter by the minute, shade is spare, and the road is an uphill pull; these are all the conditions needed for me to slip into low gear and find myself in automaton mode, walking without thought, feeling, and only with the barest of consciousness.

When I finally arrive in Villafranca, worn out from the thirty-two kilometers under my shoe leather this day, I cautiously work my way down a steep hill to the public *refugio* of the town, which itself seems to be built on nothing but steep hills. José, Marisa, and the others are waiting in line at the entrance and I drop my bag and fall in behind them. For some reason the check-in process here is very complicated and time-consuming. I and those arriving behind me have to wait fifteen, twenty, then thirty minutes in the hot sun while those ahead of us are "processed." When it is my turn at the *hospitalera's* table, she looks at me and says in a most commanding voice: "*Completa.* Full." *¿Completa?* You've got to be kidding! She advises me and the others that there is no room in the inn, there is nothing to be done about it, and if we want to stay in Villafranca tonight there is another *refugio*, a private one, up the hill and down the street, next to the Church of Santiago. And that is that.

Deeply annoyed at having been left to wait outside in the sun when the lady should have known there would be no room for us and should have advised us of the fact as soon as we arrived, I and the other poor rejects reload our *mochilas* and head up the steep hill a hundred and fifty meters further to the other place. In comparison to what we saw of the civic *refugio*, this new place is at first sight a dump, and as we check in, it becomes apparent that it will cost us a few euros more for the night than the other would have. Even worse, a large part of the rather ramshackle place is under repair. I pay my euros, get my *credencial* duly stamped, and am just lifting my *bastones* and pack to haul them to the upper level when my companion from the morning reappears. "Toni," I call to him before he sees me. He turns around, smiles, and we shake hands again. He is already showered and in his clean clothes for the afternoon; I ask him how it is that he is here, of all places. Wasn't he going to stay the night in Cacabelos? Well, it seems the *refugio* down there was almost full and he figured he could do the eight additional kilometers with no problem, so up he came. "Well, it is good to see you again." We smile and I head up to the bunks while he goes out for a walk.

Without noticing the sign on the door of the small dormitory I choose for the night, I unknowingly claim a bunk in the room reserved "for snorers or the deaf." By the time I discover my error, there is no other bunk open in the place so I am stuck. Hopefully I will be tired enough tonight to sleep; I will certainly take full advantage of my foam earplugs. I take a quick tour of our home for the night. A peek into the toilets reveals the worst of all possibilities for the tired pilgrim: the johns are porcelain holes in the floor with the corresponding mess of amateurish targeting evident all about. There is no toilet paper, only hoses with small showerheads with which to wash oneself before leaving the stall. This should be fun in the morning. I take my shower, wash my clothes, hang them out to dry out back, lie down for half an hour, then walk back to the first *refugio* to see if I can find anyone interested in a meal. Surprisingly, João is there and once again we share a lunch together. I later run into José, Marisa, and Alessandra and we walk into town, spend a few minutes in one of its beautiful churches, then make our way to the river, where a huge crowd of locals and pilgrims are either sunning themselves on the lawn or rollicking about in the cool waters of a rolling little river, the Rio Burbia.

Surprisingly, I am the only one of our group to dip into the river; the others sit on rocks and dangle their feet in the fresh water. I have a ball swimming and floating and splashing about in the midst of a great crowd of kids. The simple joy of water tumbling about me, lifting me, embracing me with its cool charm makes me laugh and smile like I haven't for days. It restores me; it is liquid grace.

With dripping shorts and damp sandals, I head back with the others up the hilly streets of this town, stopping on the way to purchase a few groceries for an evening snack and for the road the next day. Even before I get a few blocks from the river, my clothes are almost completely dry; it is that hot a day out here.

After getting back to the *refugio* I wander over to the church next door for a visit. The Church of Santiago is yet another Romanesque marvel. I look around its deep interior, enjoy its cool, then walk into the sanctuary, behind the altar, and sit upon one of the acolyte's chairs there. I am absolutely alone. I look up into the face of the medieval Christ hanging

» *August 5: Molinaseca to Villafranca del Bierzo* «

on the cross that is set in the soft round of the apse. It is a face of un-rivaled tranquility. Agony is portrayed in the simply carved lines of Jesus' body, but the cruelty of that agony does not overcome the ineffable peace in this face. This death is brutal and bloody and completely unjust; this is absolutely self-evident in this carving. But the face says more: "No one is taking this life from me. I give it up. It is my gift. This life is now yours, take it, learn its lessons. Forgive your enemy. Wash the feet of your lesser. In your good God trust. Love is greater than death." I have never seen a more beautiful crucifix anywhere, so I sit quietly below it for a long while. Finally, I rise, walk over to his centuries-old feet, nailed still to centuries-old wood, and I kiss them. I have been visited . . . again.

I cannot know what is going on at the other *refugio* in Villafranca, but I do know what is going on in our rough little place this night. It is as good as any human being might hope for from a one-night visit to an iso-lated town on the way to Santiago de Compostela. A spirit of camarade-rie seeps through the walls of this place to infect us all with its gracious geniality. The various pilgrims, so diverse in cultures, tongues, and states of mind, come together in this old building as if they are all long-lost brothers and sisters finding themselves together again. People tend to one another, share with one another, and in the end enjoy an evening of quiet peace together as if they were family. A number of the pilgrims from the other *refugio* below, including my own pals, make their way up to our humble lodge, and join Toni, Michel, the elderly Frenchman in the running shorts, and the rest of us as we sit on stone steps and chunks of wood, passing around bottles of wine, sharing olives and cheese, splitting bananas and sharing stories from life and the *camino* until dark comes deep upon us all. There are no arguments over religion and no arrogance and no yelling. These are very good people, every one of them, and I am about as happy as I've ever been.

By nine thirty, I am feeling very tired after this long day of walking and a sleepless night before, so I go to bed not to the sound of snoring but to the pleasing sound of pilgrims at the end of the day laughing at some tall tale being told by the *hospitalero*, an old fellow named Jesús.

Our Camino

August 6: Villafranco del Bierzo to Ruitelán

I survive my night with the snorers and have actually had a very good sleep thanks to my ever-faithful set of foam earplugs. As I perform the usual Vaseline unction of my feet Toni passes by and asks if he can walk with me again today. "Sure," I say, and offer him a surplus yogurt with granola mixed in to seal the deal. Then, without much more ado, I pull my socks and boots on, we secure our *mochilas* to our backs, and before we know it the two of us are following the *Calle del Agua* through Villafranca. We choose a route that zigzags its way up a steep escarpment just outside town and has the advantage of avoiding the modern highway, the tarry pavement of which now covers the ancient pilgrim route in this area. The climb is a serious one and takes the wind out of even Toni. After our scramble up the steepest segment of the route, the path continues winding upwards, though far more gradually now, eventually taking us over the top of a high mountain pass.

As yesterday, he again slows his pace to accommodate me. As we walk along together, we talk over many things. Since he is a young person and a Catholic, I ask him how his generation of Europeans, Spaniards, Galicians, see the Church. His response is thoughtful and well expressed; he tells me that the Church seems quite irrelevant to most young people's lives. In his words Toni exhibits a broad and deep understanding of the church, the issues it faces in the wake of the Second Vatican Council, and its particular problems in Spain. I wonder to myself if he has been a seminarian at one time. I finally ask him and he responds that no, he has never been in the seminary. He pauses for a few moments as if to think over whether he really wants to reveal something to me, then goes ahead and tells me that in fact his uncle is a bishop. He knows the Church well because its concerns are very much a part of his family life.

At one point along the rising road as we pass through beautiful chestnut groves filled with massive trees that must be several hundred years old, he asks if we might speak in English so that he can take advantage of his time in my company to improve his skills in the language. This is a great idea and so we amble our way through the great stands of chestnut trees chattering on in rudimentary English with me serving as tutor, correcting his occasional errors in grammar or suggesting a better word here or there. His conversational skills are not high but they are good enough for us to come to know one another better and better as the kilometers pass under our feet.

As we walk along I notice that our relationship seems to change depending on the language we use. When Toni speaks in Spanish he exudes self-confidence and an eloquence that is like that of a good teacher. When he speaks to me in English both eloquence and self-confidence disappear, replaced by an economy of expression and a dependence on me for a proper word or phrase that puts him in the role of the humble learner, making his manner almost childlike. It is endearing, really. I enjoy both Tonis and the variety that comes from alternating between the two makes the hours of walking pass without notice.

By the time we have crested the mountain and have picked our way down the other side we have returned to the same highway we had previously avoided. We stop to buy some fruit at a truck stop and after a few more kilometers along a secondary road through verdant countryside we reach the small village of Ruitelán, where Marisa and all the others are waiting for us with smiles and greetings of welcome. It has been a relatively short walk today, only about twenty kilometers; after the previous two days' long journeys, this seems almost like a day off.

The *refugio* of Ruitelán is a small country home whose bedrooms have been turned into dormitories with four or five bunk beds in each one. The *hospitaleros* welcome us in, again, as if we were family, and ask if we'd like to pay an extra couple of euros each to have dinner with them. They will prepare a soup, a great salad, have plenty of bread, and a home-made dessert for us, and they will happily share it all, "home-style." We all buy in to the familial extra being offered to us and proceed to clean up.

Ruitelán is surrounded by green fields of hay alternating with stands of oak and chestnut. Best of all, there is a cool creek running through the town. After cleaning up, Toni and I walk down to a grassy clearing along the far bank of the creek with our journals in hand and with the intention of doing our day's writing. We find a shady spot where we can easily drop our feet into the rushing water. The dampness of the grass beneath us, the cool of the emerald shade above us, the sound of the water flowing around slippery rocks and over shiny pebbles, the numbing feel of the icy water on our feet, all of it conspire to make us forget every ache and worry and we simply lie back, each of us in his own world, and rest in the bosom of this grand earth with a peace that is as sweet as any pilgrim could hope to know. No writing gets done. I eventually wade cautiously into the creek itself and walk around in a rather tame pool; the gravel under my feet provides a massage, further relieving me of my various stresses and strains. Perhaps after an hour and a half of living within this leafy and rocky and altogether watery world we slip on our sandals and walk back to the house, where we tell the others of our find and give them directions to this spot that they surely do not want to bypass.

The meal prepared by our hosts features a massive salad bowl filled to the brim with a wondrous variety of ingredients from this earth's grand store: tomatoes and tuna and lettuce and broccoli and olives and little cubes of goat cheese fill the dish. Plenty of bread and wine and home-made flan are passed about generously, and spirits rise with every mouthful and sip. It is a wonderful dinner, and it is at this point that I realize that lithe Alessandra, peaceful José, laughing Marisa, Toni the newest, and I have become something of a family. We are now walking together even if we don't actually *walk* together. Perhaps it is because the number of new pilgrims on the *camino* is growing each day, which in turn makes the road not only more crowded but also diminishes the opportunity for solitude, that the time has arrived to let go of *my camino* and allow it to become from this point on *our camino*. From here on, the pilgrimage becomes something new for me. I am no longer alone on this strange road across Iberia; we are in this together, to the end.

» *August 6: Villafranco del Bierzo to Ruitelán* «

Also at the table this evening is a married couple that arrived in the *refugio* a short time after we did. Puri and Manuel are perhaps in their late fifties. They engage in the family fun around the big table with us all, and though they are not that much older than I, they seem like parents to us children. While Manuel observes, Puri directs the progress of bowls and bread and wine bottles from one side of the table to the other.

As we sit in the garden of the Ruitelán *refugio*, waiting for the first star to adorn the darkening sky, it dawns on us that we are less than a week from Compostela.

Ai-la-la-le-lo

August 7: Ruitelán to Alto del Poio

The proof, if proof were needed, that something has changed among us since the day before is that on this morning, we prepare our *mochilas*, tend our feet, put on our socks and shoes, enjoy a cup of coffee and a few small cakes "on the house," thank our salad-making hosts as deeply as we are able, and all head down the road *together*. There is no discussion or decision made in this regard; it just happens because it seems the most natural thing for a family to do. The morning walk leads us through countryside lushly populated with oak and chestnut trees; these first hours on the road involve mostly uphill climbs. Though we walk as a group there is little talk. The silence binds us together more deeply than conversation could, at least in this mystical hour separating the tail end of night and the leading edge of day.

Our quiet procession upward, with me following behind the others, gives me the opportunity to appreciatively observe them with the perspective offered by slight distance and with the appreciation that comes from increasing intimacy.

Alessandra is an Italian woman, slight of build, her thin olive face crowned with silver-gray hair, strands of which are often rustled by the breeze as she walks. Though small of stature, she hikes energetically with a large wooden staff carved from a tree branch in her right hand. She also carries a diaphanous white scarf over her head and across her shoulders to protect her from the sun; it too flies in the breeze, making her seem like a gossamer-winged angel when seen on the road from behind. Her *mochila* never seems to burden her. Her posture is always perfect. As she glides down the road ahead of me, I can only look on with admiration; she makes this work look so easy. Her language is a tossed salad of Spanish, Italian, and English. She picks and chooses her vocabulary and grammar from whatever tongue comes first and whichever is most handy at any given moment or in the midst of any given thought. It is up to the listener to put it together; if you try too hard, you'll miss the point; it's better to relax, listen, and pick up her meaning intuitively. She speaks softly; each word is formed with care as if it were the only word in the world worth speaking. But even at that, the words themselves are less important than the other forms of communication of which she is a master: the subtle lift of an eyebrow, a hand flowing in the air like a sparrow, or a slight smile or frown forming for just a moment on one end or other of the slim lips of her mouth. She is a woman of faith. Sometimes she calls me one of her sons, which is odd in a way since I am fifty and she is less than sixty, I suspect. Nevertheless, the sentiment is appreciated and I am glad to be considered a "son" of someone of her beauty and grace. She is a noble and lovely person. I am aware that she has a family back in Italy, but I know nothing more about her life beyond the *camino* than this.

José is next in the morning procession. His first language is Portuguese, the Brazilian variety, but his English is quite good, as is his Spanish. When he and I visit alone, we speak English; when we are together with the group, we slip into Spanish. When he is with Toni, they speak both Portuguese and Galician, since the two tongues are very close to each other. His Brazilian accent makes the English words come out of his mouth in a slow staccato that gives those words a round Latin bounce. It continues to upset my ethnic presuppositions to see so much Latin culture come from someone so physically Japanese; his almond eyes reveal his genetic heritage but his open personality shows forth his Brazilian roots. José often wears a bright yellow and green Brazilian soccer shirt that rather clashes with his equally bright red *mochila*, but the two make him always very visible from a long way off. He is always kind and friendly to me and in the past days has never failed to greet me as we pass on the road: "Hey Kevin! *¡Buen camino!*" "Hey José, see you at the *refugio*."

» *Ai-la-la-le-lo* «

Marisa is the Basque in the group. She sports hair that has been cut fairly short and dyed a russet red that is popular among European women these days. It only adds to the impression she gives of being fiery, brimming with energy, and not someone with whom I'd want to pick an unnecessary fight. She is also full of fun and a person to whom laughter comes easily. When I am most weighed down by the burdens of this road she can lift my spirits with a smile or a buoyant *"Qué tal, Kevin?"* Her voice is husky and loud and her only visible fault is that our walking with her is often interrupted by the ring of her mobile phone even on the most remote stretches of the route; we are patient with the interruption because she is taking time to visit with her real family back home and that is to be honored. Marisa also walks with a staff in one hand, but hers is the modern kind, like mine, sophisticated and technical with height adjustments and a spring-loaded shock absorber in the handle. She, too, is a great walker and often teams up with Alessandra as they leave me behind until the next fountain or village. Sometimes, too, she strikes out on her own at a very substantial clip. At these times she really leaves the rest of us in her dust. This is not a bad thing, since it is a pleasure to see the determination and enjoyment she displays as she marches onward; it is tonic for me when I am most unenthusiastic about the road ahead. Often enough when I come around a bend in the road, there she is, taking a pause, waiting up for us slowpokes with a smile and a laugh and a word of encouragement and often enough a biscuit or two to share.

And Toni is just ahead of me for now. He is a man of medium build, lean and fit, has a dark complexion and closely cropped curly black hair. I learn much from him in these days about his life and about his heritage as a son of Galicia. Before walking with Toni, I did not know that this part of the Iberian Peninsula has a very distinct culture going back to the Celts, and that his people proudly speak their own language, again closer to Portuguese than to Castilian Spanish. His Galician pride extends to much more than just his mother tongue; he lets me know that in the self-understanding of his people, they are *Galegos* before they are Spaniards. To speak at length with him is to do far more than simply talk; it is to enter into his world, his mind, his heart, even as he respectfully and carefully enters into mine.

The older couple whom we met last night, Puri and Manuel, is way ahead of us, which is all to the good. Manuel is quiet and timid, while

Puri is a nonstop talker and quite bossy. Though nothing is said one way or another among the rest of us, it is not clear yet whether they are part of our small band of pilgrimage brothers and sisters or not. Time will tell, I can only suppose.

As we move forward this day, Toni teaches us a Galician folk song, *Catro Vellos Mariñeiros*, "Four Old Sailors," which features a simple but very engaging melody, and even better for us non-*Galegos*, a good portion of the song is pure "la-la-la-la," or more accurately *ai-la-la-le-lo*, which even I can remember. I can only vaguely understand the words but the *life* of the song captivates me and everyone else. We sing it going down the road together so many times that all those *ai-la-la-le-lo's* take their place in the depths of my brain where music lives and breathes even when I am not aware of it.

> *Ai-la-le-lo, ai-la-la-le-lo,*
> *ai-la-le-lo, ai-la-la-la!*

By and by we pass a tall stone marker advising us that we have just entered Galicia, the homeland of Santiago. I stop and with my *mochila* still on my back, drop to my knees in the very middle of the road, and kiss the soil of Galicia. I love this country even as I enter it. Those with cameras take snapshots of us gathered around the grand milestone. From here forward every half-kilometer of the route is marked with a much smaller stone announcing the distance yet remaining to the plaza in front of the Santiago cathedral.

The road continues to climb for some distance and to our surprise Marisa begins to show signs of distress. She slows down and complains of stomach pains. After a pause she continues on, only to stop again a half-kilometer further down the road. Again after a short rest, she continues. Finally, with only a few kilometers remaining before entering O Cebreiro, she collapses on the road moaning in deep pain and wrapping her arms around her abdomen. Tears flow down her cheeks. The road at this point is a dusty one so we help her off to one side where a grassy field extends downhill towards a deep valley below. Alessandra and José take responsibility for tending to Marisa. They speak to her gently and hold her. Toni and I can do nothing but stand by and wait. She is in agony. Alessandra and José help her to relax. She closes her

» *Ai-la-la-le-lo* «

eyes, stretches out in the tall grass, and their quiet ministrations continue with a solemnity, gentleness, and prayerfulness that I can only join in from a distance. None of us have a clue what is wrong with Marisa, which makes the situation all the more frightening. Did she eat bad food or drink bad water? Is it something more serious like appendicitis? Can we get her the last few kilometers to O Cebreiro? There is almost perfect silence as we all pray intensely for Marisa. Passing pilgrims ask if she is okay and offer to help but it seems nothing more can be done for the moment. Minutes pass, then a half-hour. The sky is as blue as a robin's egg, the field as green as an emerald, the sun a bright disk high above us already at this hour in the morning. Finally, Marisa quietly tells us all that she is feeling better and thinks she can go. She is helped to her feet and much more slowly than before but with the same determination as always, she and all of us with her walk the last brief stretch to O Cebreiro. There she will see a doctor.

O Cebreiro is a unique stop along the *camino*. It is a very old village that in recent years has turned itself into something of a tourist destination. It boasts houses built as they were in past times — round, with stone walls and thatched roofs — and at least some of the natives of the village are dressed in medieval costume. Shops sell the usual tourist-oriented bric-a-brac. It is a beautiful spot. Situated at an elevation of well over 1,200 meters, it remains cool even on a summer day. There is a very homey feel to the place. Pilgrims sit on stone benches beside their *mochilas* taking nourishment and drinking from town fountains. This place has been tending to pilgrims for over a millennium and the people here know their business well. Kindness and hospitality blow through this village like a late-afternoon breeze.

The central feature of the village is the parish church. It is a pre-Romanesque edifice, built in the ancient local style. Within its dark interior, two important treasures await the tired pilgrim who comes inside to visit and pray. The first is a twelfth-century polychrome statue of a seated Mary and the Child Jesus seated in turn on her lap. His hand is raised in blessing while she is clearly presenting him to the onlooker and to the world. Their faces are remarkably similar and it is easy to see that they are, both "genetically" and spiritually, mother and son. The statue lacks the realism of later Western art, but its solid, plain, upright, almost Byzantine manner has its own beauty and manner of expressing spiritual truths important to the early medieval Christians: Jesus' blood relationship to Mary so eloquently expressed in their common facial "look" affirms his humanity. His sign of blessing with one hand proclaims his divinity, while the small orb he holds in the other announces this child's lordship over the created world. Both faces convey solemnity, responsibility, and wisdom. These are serious personages and are to be taken seriously. "Attend to us, visitor! Behold us carefully, pilgrim! Take on our wisdom as your own, priest!"

The second treasure of the church comes with a story. In a protective glass case a twelfth-century chalice and paten, the cup and small plate used for the bread and wine consecrated in the Mass, are exposed to view. The story goes that sometime in about the fourteenth century a peasant from a neighboring village struggled through a terrible winter storm to O Cebreiro, risking his life to do so, for the sole reason that he desired to attend Mass and receive communion. The priest presiding at the Mass, a man of little faith, found this altogether too much, for he did not value the Eucharist nearly as much as did the peasant. As the peasant approached to receive communion, the priest cynically looked down on him for the faith and devotion that led him to risk his life just to participate in the Mass. At that very moment, the moment when he said, "This is my body . . . this is my blood . . ." and before the doubting priest's own eyes and in his own hands, the consecrated wine held in the priest's chalice turned into physical blood and the consecrated host on his paten became physical flesh, the very body and blood of Christ. This was clearly a divine rebuke of his cynicism, his lack of faith, and his arrogance toward a humble peasant who in fact was far richer in faith than was he. The priest repented of his spiritual callousness, and according to tradition both men are now buried together in the small side chapel where the chalice and paten are held. Their common tomb endures as a reminder not only to believe but also to walk away from the cold cynicism and haughty arrogance that are the handmaids of a desiccated faith.

Though I would like to consider myself on the side of the peasant, as I look up to this chalice and paten I know that I am much more likely to share spiritual kinship with the priest in the story. I find a pew in the nave of the church in which to sit and slump. I pray that I might take to heart the story's lesson. I close my eyes for a long time and once again, for the third time on this voyage of the soul, these eyes well with tears.

» *Ai-la-la-le-lo* «

On this third run of tears, I finally have a couple of words to locate whence they come. The first is sorrow, sorrow for my faithlessness, my lukewarmness, my lack of enthusiasm for the work of my life, my compromises in living my deepest promises, my disregard for so many. The second is gratitude. As I sit here with my eyes running, I feel the deepest thanksgiving for everything in general and for everything in particular: this heartbeat, this life, this church, these friends, mother and father, brothers and sisters, the road, the earth under my feet, my feet, my aches and weariness, wooden Mary and son, faith, the Eucharist, my imperfect yet graced priesthood, all of it. I am grateful. I am just enormously grateful over it all. Yes, for everything in general and everything in particular, I am grateful to tears.

I meet José as I leave the church and his eyes are as damp as mine.

While José and I have been in church, Marisa has been to the doctor. All seems well, but to be on the safe side, she hires a taxi to take her to the next town where we will meet up for the evening. It is only about seven or eight kilometers further down the road, a place called Alto de Poio, which is another hundred meters higher in elevation even than O Cebreiro. With *mochila* restored to its privileged position on my back and *bastones* in hand, I join Alessandra, José, and Toni in the cobblestone street outside the church, and there to my own surprise as much as theirs, I dance a jig. Alessandra joins in and with laughter and song off the four of us go down the road to Alto de Poio, singing Toni's song with all its *ai-la-le-lo's*.

Alto de Poio turns out to be a very small place, little more than a wide spot in the road, with a hotel-restaurant on one side of the pavement and our *refugio* on the other. Both are equipped with bars. When we arrive, we find that Marisa has signed herself in and has also done something very unusual on the *camino*: she has reserved four additional beds for us even before we have arrived, by making the case that she has been ill, that we are her companions, and that she needs us with her. The never-smiling *hospitalera* agrees to break the usually absolute rule of "first come, first served," and so though others are already being turned away for the night we have a place to hang our hats. Those unfortunate others have either to go across the highway to the hotel for a thirty-euro room or keep moving down the road another eight kilometers to the next village.

Puri and Manuel have arrived ahead of us and, as always, she is talk-

ing up a storm while he goes about his life as an attentive and polite listener to his spouse. Cristina is here already as well, and happily without
her opinionated companion from two mornings before. I learn that she
too fell ill on the road, becoming violently sick to her stomach. She lost a
day but then took a taxi ahead and is now back in our "wave." We all share
some cool beers, nibble on dry almonds and raisins, and talk over the day's
adventures. Marisa is clearly feeling better and has her chipper spirit back
as she phones home to share with her family in detail the great story of her
camino malady and her healing at the hands of Alessandra and José.

After our showers and laundry duties have been accomplished, Toni,
Marisa, José, and I traipse across the highway for our big meal of the day.
It costs us ten euros each for the *menú del día*, a price that approaches
highway robbery, but there are few options this far from anywhere, so we
pay up and enjoy our three-course *menú* all the same. After the meal,
there is nothing to see and nothing to do for the rest of the afternoon,
which is quickly becoming one of the hottest on the *camino* so far; the radio news is reporting temperatures well over forty degrees centigrade.
We nap, write in our journals, go to the bar for another round of beer,
play a little foosball, talk, have another beer, sing another round of *ai-la-
le-lo's*. What could be more pleasant in all of life than sitting out a hot
summer afternoon with friends singing *ai-la-la-le-lo* after *ai-la-la-le-lo?*

As the afternoon wears into evening, I wander to the back yard of the
refugio to collect my dry laundry. Though it is now mercilessly hot outside, I am taken by the view out over the end of the yard and down a substantial precipice, the bottom of which extends out into great fields of
green bordered on the far horizon by blue hills and purple mountains.
With the golden sun casting its late-afternoon rays across the landscape
and the shadows of an occasional building or tree growing long towards
the east, it is a vista to be beheld with the purest of awe. While I stand
looking out, Toni comes to retrieve his own laundry and joins me. In a
serious tone, he asks, "Kevin, *¿qué tal estás?* How are you doing?" I answer
simply, "*Bien,*" and that is the truth. I feel fine. Very fine. I feel extraordinarily fine. There are no words full enough for how fine I feel. He too
spends some time gazing out over the panorama spreading forth from
our very feet. Finally, he says, "*Está bien.*" Nothing more can be said. We
haul our laundry back to our bunks for folding and repacking and the
spell is broken.

» *Ai-la-la-le-lo* «

Always ebullient and faithful, Cristina has another request for me. She asks me if in the morning I wouldn't lead the pilgrims in a prayer before we leave for the day. I am hesitant to impose a structure on other people's way of living the *camino*, but respond that I would be happy to do so if she will get the people together for it. She frowns at my answer but proceeds anyway to ask others if they would like to have a prayer together in the morning — "after all, we *are* pilgrims!" There is not much enthusiasm expressed for the notion from anyone else. I leave it in her hands to make it happen.

Cumulus clouds roll in after the heat of the day and I wonder if we will be subjected to another Astorga-style electrical storm in the morning. We buy ourselves some final snacks for tomorrow from the bar, visit a little more, then before long, blessed sleep comes to hold our poor bodies in its healing hands so that they might be restored to us for the day to come.

» *August 7: Ruitelán to Alto del Poio* «

Planning Our Attack

August 8: Alto del Poio to Calvor

Cristina's group prayer doesn't happen, though she brings it up again several times as we are preparing for our morning departure. I continue to invite her to organize it, but I sense that she is upset with me for not taking the bull by the horns myself and corralling the others into a prayer circle; I offer to pray with her, but by now she seems to have written me off as useless and she heads out the door and down the dark highway on her own.

As José, Marisa, Alessandra, Toni, and I depart together the orange flames of a forest fire can be seen in the dark somewhere ahead of us and this sends small shivers of fear through the stream of morning pilgrims that we have joined. As dawn gradually illuminates the scene before us, we see nothing more and we move on without incident. The heavy smell of smoke nevertheless lingers in the morning air.

All of us are mightily impressed with what we are seeing of Galicia thus far. For those of us who have crossed Castile and León with their endless fields of wheat and stubble, this place is a feast for our eyes and a paradise for our hearts. The verdant countryside spreads out in all directions and the forests of oak and chestnut and eucalyptus seem like scenery borrowed from a fable, populated by fairies and gnomes.

As we walk, Toni offers me an ongoing commentary on the many details of Galician farming and culture. He describes to me the flat slate stone that is used for house building here, and tells me that in his part of Galicia, to the south of Compostela, the houses are also made of stone, but in the form of massive boulders of granite that have to be carved into usable shapes and sizes. He tells me about the small chapel-like buildings set atop pylons of stone that increasingly dot the rural scene; they are *ahorros* and are typical of Galician culture: "Notice the way the main part of the structure is made of wood slats; that's so the air can get in to dry out and preserve the farmer's stocks of corn or other grains he might have inside. Just as important is the fact that the building is set high off the ground on two vertical pedestals of slate. And between the pedestals and *ahorro* you see that horizontal slab of slate with a substantial ledge protruding on all four sides? That's to keep the mice and rats out of whatever is inside. You see, vermin can't crawl upside down, so even if they get up the pillars they can't get around that ledge, they always fall to the ground." It is a pretty clever, if elegantly simple, trick developed, of course, by farmers who never saw the inside of an engineering school. At the top of each *ahorro* there is a stone cross on the gable at one end and a round ball on the other. "Why do you think that is so, Kevin?"

"I suppose to make it look like a church?"

"Exactly. In a way, it *is* a church: the *other* church in the farmer's life: the land, the rain, the fruit of the field, all that comes from the earth is not separate from God and religion; it's really all part of the same thing. So the *ahorros* look like chapels because in a way they *are* chapels." This I understand.

At Triacastela, the *camino* divides and the pilgrim must make a choice between two possible paths, though both end in the next large town on the route, Sarria. The left-hand road is less direct but passes the Monastery of Samos, which dates back to the sixth century and is a great spiritual and historical landmark of Galicia and all of Spain, but from there on into Sarria there are no further villages or facilities, a twelve-kilometer stretch to manage at the end of what is becoming the hottest day of the century. The other route, to the right, passes through any number of villages, some of them with small *refugios*, making it possible to stop if the heat becomes too much before making it to Sarria. We, together with Puri and Manuel, choose the right-hand route, losing our chance to visit Samos but gaining the important advantage of safety in the increasingly oppressive heat. We are, after all, over seventeen kilome-

» *August 8: Alto del Poio to Calvor* «

ters from Sarria. If we must stop before arriving at Sarria, we decide, we will set our provisional sights on the village of Calvor, which has a *refugio.*

We take some time in Triacastela to buy provisions for dinner, since someone's guidebook says to expect no food or bar service in Calvor. I am assigned to buy the wine, so I stock up on two-liter boxes of Rioja, not the most elegant selection, but the extra weight that glass bottles would bring leaves me little choice. I also buy a tube of sunscreen and hit a cash machine for a new stash of euros to get me through my final days on the road. By the time I throw in two cups of yogurt and a banana, a nectarine, and an orange, the increased weight of my *mochila* is felt the moment I slip myself back into its straps. Others buy spaghetti, tomatoes, salad fixings, sauce for the spaghetti, and fruit for dessert; thus with dinner safely loaded onto our backs we bear to the right and on to Calvor.

I am proud this day to be able to keep up with my companions on the road, and not because they are slowing down for me; I am walking like a healthy man for a change.

By the time we encounter the crossroads that is Calvor, the heat of the day is intense and we all contentedly decide to call it quits. The stifling air everywhere is just too much to bear without taking huge risks to our health; we are told that the latest report from Sarria is that the temperature in the shade is already well above the forty centigrade mark and it is still only midday. As reported in someone's guidebook, there is indeed a small *refugio* here in Calvor and our group is among the first to decide to hold up in it. We sign ourselves in and stamp our own *credenciales*, then choose our bunks and make ourselves at home. Later, with the arrival of the *hospitalera*, we pay up for our night's stay. Before long, the place is packed, with every available centimeter of floor space taken up by later arrivals who, like us, cannot endure any more hours in the suffocating heat of the afternoon.

After showering and doing laundry, Toni reveals that he has discovered a bad rash around his ankles and lower legs. Indeed, when he shows us the trouble it looks grim. The skin is raw and inflamed and sensitive to the touch. After some discussion, he decides he should call a taxi, go into Sarria, and have it checked out at the hospital there. I offer to go along, and so a taxi from Sarria is called to carry us into the city. Meanwhile, the ladies have put all the pieces for dinner into place. Alessandra is supposed to be in charge since she is the master of pasta. Puri, as always, places herself in charge even when she isn't; without consulting Alessandra she advises Toni that he and I should be back for dinner by seven. So out the door we go with the sure belief that we have three good hours before we need to be back for our bowls of spaghetti Bolognese and plates of green salad laced with tuna, tomatoes, and eggs.

Toni and I are rushed into the city at a speed I have not experienced in weeks. While Toni sits up front with the driver, I am seated in the rear seat of the taxi. As they talk in Galician, I quietly watch the scenery whiz by my open window. It seems very strange to see the whole world become a blur as we are carried forth within one of these shiny conveyances I have only seen from the outside for so long. The breakneck ride seems alien to me and I feel as if I am betraying my ever-faithful feet. I recognize the great gift of their slowness now, for they have allowed me to see the world and myself and my race as I have never before seen them: slowly, attentively, caringly. From within this vehicle the world outside becomes just scenery and I feel guilty seeing it thus, as if it were naked before prurient eyes.

In just a few minutes' time we arrive at the hospital emergency room and we are both ushered into the doctor's office where, after suitable consultation, Toni is told that his kind of rash is common for pilgrims who have in the past suffered with eczema as he has. The condition is exacerbated by sweat and dust from the road. The doctor writes Toni a couple prescriptions and shows him how to bandage the affected area with a special gauze wrapping, then out the door we go to find a pharmacy and get the prescriptions filled. With the extra time we have on our hands, we enjoy a beer in a cool bar he knows down the street. It is only six thirty as we finish our beers; our timing could not be better: we will be back in Calvor at exactly seven o'clock as directed. Yet Toni's mobile phone rings even as we are paying our bill; the ladies, it seems, are furious with us for not being back at six for dinner; the spaghetti is getting cold and mushy and there is no sign of the two of us. *"Where are you?"* Toni gently protests that in fact we were told to be back at seven by Puri and with that he gives me a look that indicates that even as the spaghetti has boiled big trouble has brewed, and so we briskly hail our taxi for the six or seven kilometers' drive back up the hill to Calvor.

What Puri has done is not just a little mistake in Alessandra's eyes; this is an insult to her spaghetti and by extension to her very soul. To a person from a land where *al dente* is almost a religion, to have a lovely spaghetti Bolognese turn into something only a shade better than Chef Boyardee is a sin against humanity and God; at least that is the feeling in the air when we walk into the *refugio* kitchen with apologies all around. Marisa whispers to us that it is not our fault and with a sidelong glance indicates the culprit: a strangely silent Puri. The air only thickens. At my first bite of the pasty pasta I jokingly say to no one in particular: "Hmmm. Some of the best I've ever eaten!" To which Marisa says, "Kevin, *¡cállate!* Shut up." Alessandra steams. We eat and clean up and that is that; Puri's bossy ways have led her to the commission of an unforgivable sin: the ruination of a beautiful dinner. From this point on, it is clear that in the eyes of the majority she has lost whatever chance she had to be a real member of this little pilgrim household.

After the calamitous *cena*, José brightens things up by organizing a plan-of-attack party. With only five or six days of walking left, it is time to size up the task, divide up the days, and come up with a game plan for our march on Santiago. This brings new excitement back into the air as we realize just how close we now are, no more than spitting distance, really, when you consider that I, at least, have almost seven hundred *camino* kilometers already notched into the leather of my boots. José suggests that the primary considerations in making our plans should be two: first, to avoid the big and probably full *refugios*, for as we all can see, there are more and more pilgrims on the road, but the quantity of bunks does not increase with them. Second, we need to keep the daily *etapas* relatively short so that we arrive at our chosen *refugios* early and beat the crowds of latecomers — after all, is any of our group in a rush to get to Compostela? "No," we all agree and then with our various maps and guidebooks spread out on the table, we come up with our scheme, revisable at any time as circumstances might require:

Tomorrow, that is, Saturday: Calvor to Ferreiros, passing through Sarria.
Sunday: Ferreiros to Hospital de la Cruz.
Monday: Hospital to Casa Nuevo.
Tuesday: Casa Nuevo to Ribadiso.
Wednesday: Ribadiso to Santa Irene.
Thursday: We arrive in Santiago de Compostela in time for the noon pilgrims' Mass.

» *Planning Our Attack* «

We look at each other with a sudden awareness gripping us all: by this time next week, it will all be over, we'll be done, and what then will become of us? We cannot imagine a life other than this and sadness touches us all. José is the first to say it aloud: "I want to get to Santiago but I don't want the *camino* to end." We all feel the same, but what can be done? We talk until finally the sun slips behind the western hills, dark descends, and we go to bed. There are precious few nights on this road left to us.

» *August 8: Alto del Poio to Calvor* «

Under the Oak Trees

August 9: Calvor to Ferreiros

I am one of the first to leave the Calvor *refugio*, taking off on my own as the others are dawdling about. After last night's spaghetti fiasco, I feel the need for some quiet time for myself. I have to follow the road to Sarria carefully, because the leafy canopy overhead makes the early morning dark seem all the more dense along this road. I pick my way along, pray my rosary, and within twenty minutes or so Marisa and Toni overtake me, then Puri and Manuel, then José and Alessandra. They all pass me by, wishing me a good morning as they go. Once again I am trailing everyone else, but even worse, I am having another gutless morning and for some reason feel great discouragement as the growing light of the new day makes the path clear to view.

As I walk into Sarria, it is easy to find the others, and there we regroup and wander our way through the sleepy city, taking time to look at the ancient castle at its center and have a coffee. It seems like a very long walk out of the city as we follow the *flechas* through a park lining one side of the Celeiro River, across a bridge, over some railway tracks, and finally into the heart of an oak grove. No one misses city life as these woods envelop us with a life that is not mechanical or petroleum-based or supervised by a digital clock. Knowing we have so few days left on this road makes these earthy environs we pass through now all the more dear to us.

I trail behind once again and find myself alone on the *camino*, having my wish for solitude granted perhaps a bit more than I might have liked. We decided over coffee in Sarria that we would call it a day in Ferreiros, only about a twenty-kilometer walk from Calvor, a snap for me now. However, somewhere along the trail between Sarria and Ferreiros, I begin to feel the tendon in my left leg tighten up, exactly the same feeling I had when the other began to give me trouble two weeks before. I stop, stretch, and twist the leg and foot, using all the best physical therapy techniques I have learned along the way. I hope for the best, but the tendon continues to make its unhappy mood felt even as my own mood sinks. I so hoped and even believed just yesterday that my physical problems were all behind me; to start a whole new case of tendonitis at this late stage in the game is just too much. Why not just give me two new blisters as well? Why not infect them for good measure? And could I order up a little food poisoning while we are at the bar? I hate being grumpy like this, but I cannot turn it off, at least for the moment.

I stop, drop my *bastones*, take off my *mochila*, dig deep into its cache for my toiletry bag, pop a leftover Voltarén pill into my mouth, chase it with a big swig of water, and top it off with a small tub of yogurt to protect my stomach from the pill's ulcer-inducing side effects. I reconstitute myself as a pilgrim as best I am able and continue slowly and disconsolately to Ferreiros.

Though I mentioned being alone just a moment ago, I am actually alone only in the sense that I am not presently walking with my own *camino* comrades. The *camino* route is becoming increasingly congested with fresh pilgrims, many of whom walk without *mochilas* and presumably with *coches de apoyo* somewhere in the background. On a good day their presence is insignificant to me, but on a bad day, their lack of *camino* manners irritates to no end a veteran pilgrim, as I now consider myself. These gangs of pseudo-pilgrims are frisky and loud and they hog the road as they wander along, strung out not in single file but horizontally across the roadway, forcing me to push my way through them. Some are pretty good walkers, while others are huffing and puffing and taking rest every few meters. I have no desire to meet any of them, though I continue the courtesy of wishing them a *buen camino*, a point of pilgrim protocol many of these newcomers are not familiar with. My companions and I have coined a word for these characters: *los sinmochilas*, those without backpacks. When we say it, it is not generally with kindness. I try with varying degrees of success to control my irritation with the *sinmochilas* and their ilk and tend to my own pilgrimage and its exigencies, especially the interior ones, but it is just not so easy.

I come to a small but steep hill as the road passes through yet another gnomish wood of oak and chestnut. As I rise over the crest of the hill, I find myself at an expansive fountain built into the side of a further hill. It has the conch emblem of Santiago carved into it, and the water makes an irregular clapping sound as it splashes out of the fountain's many spigots and echoes to and fro about the woods. What is best is that I am reunited here with my pals and am welcomed back into the fold with warm greetings and questions about my well-being. I keep my tendon problem to myself for the moment but do complain a bit about having a slow day. As we sit, nibble on snacks, and drink up as much of the fresh mountain water as we can hold, we commiserate about *los sinmochilas* and what a nuisance they are.

As we move on, I take up with Toni and Marisa and we begin a lengthy discussion about the ongoing effects being experienced along the Galician coastline after the accidental sinking of an oil tanker, the *Prestige*, in November of 2002. Its store of polluting petroleum has washed up on shorelines all along the coast and caused a century's worth of ecological damage to the sensitive marine environments found there. The response of Spain's politicians has been abysmal and deceitful, according to Toni and Marisa, and they merit being thrown out of office for it. On some days Toni wears a black t-shirt with bright blue letters that declare in Galician: ¡*Nunca Mais!* Never Again! The same image appears on balconies and overhead bridges in almost every Galician town and city we walk through. The tragedy feels all the greater out here, so attached to the earth as we have become on this *camino*.

Like a road the conversation winds on from Spain's president to my own and the still-fresh wounds caused by the invasion of Iraq. The subject of Iraq leads us finally to that most personal of questions that Europeans want explained to them: Why has the American character become so distorted? Why are we so small-minded, so culturally insensitive, so Hollywoodish, such big bullies on the world stage? One more time, I want to tell them, even yell at them, that we Americans are not who you imagine us to be! We are not the oafs, the bullies, the rich and spoiled kids of this world. Well, maybe in a way we are, but we don't *mean* to be that way. We *believe* we are honorable and good people, and we too care deeply about the great values that serve humanity's search for freedom, justice, and peace in this world of ours.

I want to explain this but I fail; I can't quite find the words I need in Spanish to express the truth that, like all societies, ours is very complex, a mixture of both good and bad. I try to explain our character to them as something that springs out of a unique national myth: We are, or at least we aspire to be, a "land of the free," but this freedom envelops many different and sometimes conflicting traits. We are a confederation of individualists, a community of people who care about one another to some degree but who also want to be left alone and only minimally bothered by others. We are the big boy on the international block, for sure, and we spend most of our economy maintaining the military power to enforce our unrivaled position on the world stage, but we are also fundamentally a very reluctant player on that stage; we care about the world generally, but we really don't want the world bothering us, either. We are nesters now, not adventurers; threaten our nest and we will fight like hell against all comers to protect all that we have collected for ourselves. We are a people who pride ourselves on having integrated wave after wave of immigrants into our society, but who also remain deeply fearful and suspicious of new immigrants' effect on our society; we don't want their cultures infecting ours with strange smells and different notions of personal space. We'll adopt the immigrant's food, but we'll only adopt the immigrant if he quickly loses his accent. We jealously guard the separation of church and state, but we actually mean it when we say "God bless America" even if we haven't been inside a church in years. America is big and diverse and complicated and chock-full of contradictions, so how can it ever be adequately explained to an outsider? Though it is mine, I don't even understand it fully myself! What is most important, in the end, is that even with all our faults and failures, we are, still and all, good people, people who are honest and true, people who love and care, people who want to do right and care about justice.

But then, I wonder if I protest perhaps too much. Perhaps Toni and Marisa see something I can't see or don't want to see. Is it possible that America's military and economic power in the world has corrupted it irretrievably? Is this war in Iraq a sign that our national nobility has been bullied into submission by our fear and arrogance and petroleum-based greed? In the end, I don't believe it. I don't think we are so far gone. I think of my brothers and sisters and so many of my old parishioners from small places like Twisp and Tonasket and Walla Walla. They are so good, and *they* are Americans. America cannot be a kingdom of darkness with people like these inhabiting its many precincts and counties. Yet there is so much that *is* wrong, and I know it and regret it. We have to be so careful now not to fall so deeply into fear and greed that we cannot get out. The world counts on our better side. I suppose that is what frightens Europeans about us these days. If we go down, everyone goes down.

Well, what more can I say and think on the topic? No matter my assessment of the American national character, the simple fact is that this just isn't a very good summer to be an American in Europe. And with that thought, we arrive in little Ferreiros.

We have arrived so early that the girl serving us our beers and coffee in the village's only bar suggests strongly that we should just keep moving on down the road and leave the *refugio's* beds to those who will come late in the day. Marisa loudly begs to differ and in very clear terms explains to the young lady that we've been on the road for weeks and have just had some very long days of walking and we need a short day today or we are not going to make it to Santiago. The girl backs off, but serves us truculently. We take our *mochilas* and queue them up like overstuffed dominos in front of the *refugio's* front door as a first-come-first-serve claim on the limited number of beds within. Puri and Manuel are among the other early arrivers. Eventually the doors open and we move inside, claim our beds, take our showers, wash our clothes, and go back to the bar for lunch.

The heat of this afternoon is as bad as yesterday's, so most everyone settles in an expansive oak grove that might as well be the front yard of the *refugio*. Once the beds and floor space of the *refugio* have all been claimed, the grove fills up with latecomers setting up camp under the trees, some with pup tents, others with simple plastic canvases, but many without anything except their sleeping bags to protect them during the night. There is a particular moment described in the Christian Gospels when the crowds who have been listening to the teaching of Jesus grow hungry. The disciples are asked to seat them, and with that a few small loaves and fish are multiplied many times over to feed the thousands of men, women, and children. The people are described as sitting in the grass in small groups as the miracle takes place.[1] Such is exactly my impression of this oak grove now as I watch it slowly fill up with pilgrims. These folks are settling in under trees or on soft spots of grass. Some are alone, stretched out, napping. Others are writing in their journals. Still others sit in small circles talking quietly among themselves, sharing a bottle of wine, breaking bread, nibbling on olives or almonds. For quite a while, I am myself in the middle of this Gospel scene, under a tree, writing in my own journal. Then I am joined by Toni and we talk for a while, then Alessandra, then José, then Marisa, and our little family is all here under the boughs of this great oak and once again we are home. I mention to the others that I have been having leg troubles again, this time the left leg, so Alessandra spreads me flat on my back, tells me to close my eyes, and with her thin, holy hands, and with the help of those of José, they massage my tendon. I drift into a deep, sleep-like peace.

Some time later I look up and recognize a young couple that I have met on the road from time to time over the preceding days, Lorenzo and his wife Elena; they come into camp looking exhausted and move laconically as they set up their open camp under the boughs of a wide oak just a few meters from us. I get up, walk over, and ask them how they are faring; they almost break into tears, they are so troubled. The previous night they had to sleep outside and it was cold and miserable. Today they have walked over thirty kilometers, only to arrive here and find that they have to sleep outside yet again. The worst, they tell me, is the dew; without the covering afforded by a tent the early morning damp soaks them to the bone and they have to begin their day's walk wet and cold and shivering until the sun rises high enough to warm them again. I hesitatingly make them an offer: "Look, I've never had to sleep outside yet and I had a good night's sleep last night, I only have one bed but I'd be happy to give it to one of you for the night." I am surprised when they reject my proposal immediately and forcefully. In my selfishness, I am also secretly relieved.

Later in the afternoon, I go back to the bar for a beer. Alessandra, José, and Marisa are already there and call me over to their table. They have been discussing something serious. They are tired of Puri. They

1. Mark 6:35-44.

» *August 9: Calvor to Ferreiros* «

231

don't want to continue being with her and having her ordering us around and making our plans for us. Alessandra says with determination, "I want to walk into Santiago with my friends, with the people I love." Having been through this sort of thing already once on this *camino* with Javier, I try to be both understanding of their frustration but also cautious in the matter. I share their irritation with the lady, but I suggest that it is likely that Puri and Manuel will move ahead on their own; we are just moving too slowly for them. The matter will take care of itself, I suggest. As we weigh our options, Toni joins us; he seems uncomfortable with this discussion. In the end, we decide to let things go as they may but won't do anything to encourage Puri to consider herself a part of our family. I realize that even out here after all these days and with so much good all around us, we human beings can't escape our darker sides. In this we are not so unlike our world's nations. We are both weak and strong and from moment to moment we pilgrims never quite know which one is on top. Just when we think we are strong we fall, and when we feel most weak we later realize it was right then that we were at our best.

Seventy-Five Verses
for Seventy-Five Kilometers

August 10: Ferreiros to Ligonde

Things both inside and outside the *refugio* of Ferreiros are stirring at an early hour. For those of us inside, it is a morning like most others; we go about our quiet business of using the toilet, preparing our *mochilas*, tending to our feet, eating a bit of breakfast, and heading for the door. Outside it must surely be a different story, for a thick blanket of fog has settled overnight. Looking through the window, I can only feel for the young Italian couple, Elena and Lorenzo, who once again must be waking up to dew-drenched sleeping bags and wet clothes after little, if any, sleep. Through the fog, I can see the dim beams of small flashlights twisting and turning this way and that out among the oaks as the newly awake begin to pull their things together, look for a place to relieve themselves, or just search for a separated sock, a mislaid toothbrush, or a missing hat.

Puri and Manuel are out the door long before the rest of us; I was right about them moving ahead. Alessandra, José, Marisa, Toni, and I leave as one and walk the first few kilometers in silence. All is dark and fog. It is as if the mists and the night bring forth from us an instinctive respect for imminent dawn. Solemnity is called for here. The mysteries of life and death and new life are about to be played out on the scale of a new day. Keep an eye open and your mouth shut: God may be rising.

After a couple hours we reach a sleek bridge that carries us over a river to the outskirts of a very modern town set on a hill. This is Portomarín, once one of the ancient cities of the *camino*, but now its buildings and streets are an orderly shadow of their helter-skelter medieval selves. The movement of humanity to a brighter future has overrun the past once again. With the construction of a large dam further down the river in 1962, the old Portomarín was drowned, and so an altogether new city was built at this higher elevation, well above the reservoir created behind the dam. Almost nothing in this place is more than forty years old — a mere tick of the clock considering that the old city had been here since Roman times. I wonder what stories and treasures now lie under the waters we are walking over on this slick new bridge.

We climb a steep street that takes us around the mount that the new city sits atop and before we know it we are in the modern *Plaza Mayor*. At least one treasure of the old city was saved: the ancient Church of San Nicolás was carefully taken down stone by stone and reconstructed at the very center of this modern plaza. My companions and I gather at a plastic table in front of a bar nestled within the archway surrounding the plaza. As we sip our coffees and nibble on our fresh croissants I report happily to my friends that my legs are pain-free today and I profusely thank Alessandra and José for the massage they offered me under the oak trees yesterday.

Having restored ourselves with coffee, cream, and sugar we cross town, drop back down to the level of the bridge, traverse a much older footbridge over a deep gully, and then we are on the day's path again as it passes through brambles and bushes that rise well above our heads on either side; everything is dappled by sunlight passing through the lush leaves that form an expansive canopy above our heads. What a painting a Manet or Monet could make of this! I break the silence just to say to Toni, "I have fallen in love with Galicia." He smiles and we walk on.

Keeping to our plan of avoiding the big cities and trying to arrive early at the small places, we pass through Hospital de la Cruz, one of our planned stops, and go on instead to Ligonde, only about four kilometers further down the road.

For a time, Toni and I walk with each other as the others move ahead at a sprightlier clip. At one point he stops in the road and motions me to do the same, as if he has just spotted something extraordinary; he drops his *mochila* and asks me if I know what *moras* are. I respond that I believe so; they are what we English-speakers call blackberries. He then points to the brambles to the left side of the road and says, "Look! They're ripe." He begins picking the dark berries off the thorny branches and enthusiastically popping them in his mouth. I drop my *mochila* and *bastones* and take a good look at one of the berries: a bit dusty, but not bad. I pull it off and pop it in my mouth just as he has done; its juicy sweetness explodes there. It becomes a joyful game, examining these branches, choosing the best berry, pulling it off its stubby stem, feeling its dark juice squirt onto my fingertips, popping it into my mouth, letting the charge of flavor zing my taste buds with sweet delight, then starting all over again. I can hardly get enough of them — and to think I would have walked by this bounty of joy wrapped in such a small purple package if I had not had a wiser man than I to slow me down and teach me to take time to taste the *moras*. This earth is so good to us and gives us so much; she gives us so much more than we ever stop long enough to know. We contentedly walk on with our tongues colored black and an enduring sweetness in our bellies. It is not long before we attain the day's destination: little Ligonde.

For several kilometers before arriving we have been seeing occasional signs announcing the *Fuente del Peregrino* straight ahead. Why exactly this *fuente* might be so special as to merit all the advance notice is unclear until we arrive in the village of Ligonde. Here we find that the *fuente* in itself is nothing much, just a small stone fountain built into the exterior wall of the village *refugio*. As with so many others, fresh water tumbles from its spigot into a wide basin below giving passing pilgrims like us the opportunity for a drink of cool water. More noteworthy is the *refugio's* garage, with its big door pulled open to reveal a large table covered with cassette tapes, booklets, and other small pieces of printed material. A young American lady tends the table and offers us bits and pieces of free literature, the best of which is a handy little card marking the route from Ligonde to Santiago, seventy-five kilometers only, and for each kilometer, there is a verse from the Scriptures that can be read at the milestone. She and her friends are our *hospitaleros* for the night. We check in, have our *credenciales* stamped, and when it is time to pay the usual fee, we are told that their services are free. Free as well is a dinner for their pilgrim guests, which they will offer later in the evening. We promise to be present for it, then move in, find our beds in the very small dormitory at the top of a steep staircase, and begin getting to know our generous *hospitaleros*.

» *August 10: Ferreiros to Ligonde* «

I ask the American *hospitalera* what kind of group it is that sponsors this house and its good work on behalf of us pilgrims. I presume it must be some kind of Catholic youth group in Spain, but I am way off the mark. Instead, she informs me, she and her friends belong to the Spanish version of Campus Crusade for Christ, an American evangelical association that dedicates itself to bringing young people to the Christian faith in a very personal and committed way. This work of hospitality on the *camino* is their way of witnessing to Christ. They don't seem to have any devotion to the apostle James or any understanding of what it is to be a pilgrim; they are here because the *camino* is where the youth of Europe are. What better place to "evangelize" than on this road so chock-full of young people in search of something more in their lives? The logic of it makes perfect sense. I cannot help but feel sad that my own church does not seem to see it nearly so clearly.

I take a look at the prayer card; sure enough, it marks off exactly seventy-five kilometers between here and there. Three days of walking are left if we don't dawdle. Then we will be finished. This seems like a dream.

It isn't long before I discover the dark side of life in Ligonde: this place is a cow town if ever there was one. The lumbering animals roam the streets in a lackadaisical manner, and these streets are thus liberally covered with the cows' malodorous and watery excrement. What thrive in cow manure on a hot summer day, of course, are *moscas*, black flies. And though in most every other respect this town appears to be a pleasing place, there is no question that we will be dealing this entire afternoon with a plague of these foul little insects that are all the more irksome because no one has yet explained to my satisfaction why God bothered to add them to his list of created beings. These pests are everywhere and, most annoying of all, they are all too happy to pay an uninvited visit to the top of my sweaty forehead, the end of my nose, or the dusty back of my neck without so much as a please or a thank you. Uselessly swatting at them is clearly just part of life in Ligonde. With a moment's reflection, however, it strikes me that though it is not apparent to me *why*, God did in fact make these fat and dirty *moscas*, just as he made the fat and juicy *moras* I enjoyed earlier in the morning. Does the right of either to exist have to depend on whether we human beings enjoy them? Yet this is how we evaluate such things, which just goes to show how egocentric we actually are as a race — or, I should correct myself, how egocentric *I* am, for the flies don't seem to be distracting anyone else from enjoying their lives here and now.

Shortly after I have settled into the *refugio*, Rafa walks into town with a girlfriend who has joined him in the *camino* in the last day or two. He introduces her to me, and with the delight of discovery she says, "So *you* are the Kevin I've heard so much about along the *camino!* You're the priest from Belgium!" For the second time, I am surprised to realize that I have become something of a *camino* character. But what kind of character am I? Just yesterday a German girl informed me that I was the spitting image of Ernest Hemingway, the *old* Ernest Hemingway, and others agreed. I must admit that when I catch a look at myself in a mirror from time to time I now see a man I hardly recognize. Six kilos leaner, an unkempt gray beard covering my face, sunburned forehead, hair that has not been decently combed in weeks: such is my new look. "Grizzled" is the word that comes to mind. Even to myself, in a way, I have become a new character, or, better, a richer character: I am who I always have been, but now I am also that middle-aged pilgrim doggedly lumbering his way all the way to the Field of Stars.

After washing up, we are informed that the only place to buy a meal is in the next town over, a walk of about a kilometer or two. So we head down the well-manured road, eventually taking a shortcut through a field that leads us into a tangle of brambles and stinging nettles. Finally we make our way out of the field, back to the road, and into the lowly bar across the way. It is packed to the gills with pilgrims both inside and out; we have no choice but to wait for a table to open up, a wait which keeps us standing at the ready but which also has the advantage of allowing us to quaff a couple of nicely chilled beers and begin the process of restoring our energy. The plump young waitress, whom I presume to be the daughter of the bartender, becomes a source of comic relief in the midst of the heat and the noise and the jostling of the crowd; as she weaves her way through this sea of bodies to serve an order she issues a high-pitched warning of her approach to anyone who might be in her way. The sound is very much akin to that of the cartoon world's Road Runner: *Beep-Beep!* Despite her portly physique, she is an expert at twisting just so and dodging this way or that with her tray of beers held high and level; before each twist: *Beep-Beep!* With each dodge: *Beep-Beep!* At every fleshy obstacle:

» *August 10: Ferreiros to Ligonde* «

Beep-Beep! Her sound effect immediately becomes part of our own *camino* vocabulary; as one of us makes his way to the toilet, *Beep-Beep!* or moves up to the bar for another beer, *Beep-Beep!* or nudges another to get her attention, *Beep-Beep!*

We finally get our table, enjoy an ample salad and tender slice of pork, pay our bill, and walk back to our *Fuente del Peregrino* for a nap and an idle afternoon. Yet upon our return the *hospitalera* asks if any of us would be interested in seeing a movie about the life of Jesus. We amiably agree, and with the big door of the garage pulled down and a few adjustments to a bedsheet serving as a screen, the garage is turned into a makeshift cinema. The film, as it turns out, is very dated, and the dubbing into Spanish is out of sync with the characters' facial movements. Miracles are portrayed with cheap Hollywood tricks, and booming voices from the heavens abound. There are parts of the show that are not all that bad, but overall the depiction of the life and work of Jesus lacks profundity or depth. I stay for the duration but others wander out at discreet moments. Afterwards, the young *hospitaleros* earnestly ask if we have enjoyed it, and I must admit that in reporting that I indeed liked it I do not tell the full truth. In fact, I should tell them before I leave on the morrow that their own gestures of hospitality and witness to the kindness of Christ are far more evangelizing than the cheesy film.

Eventually dinner is made ready at the big table that dominates the main floor of the old house. Perhaps twenty of us gather round and are led in a prayer of blessing by a young man who then instructs us that all this meal is a gift but if we'd like to leave a donation to further their work and allow them to continue caring for pilgrims, they'd be more than happy to receive our support. His appeal for donations is about as eloquent as I have ever heard.

The dinner is humble but ample and the conversation around the table is animated. Seated across from me are two young *hospitaleras* who are engaged in a rather serious conversation between themselves about the merits of evangelical Protestantism over stodgy old Catholicism. I say nothing about my own vocation as a Catholic priest, preferring to listen to their points of view without them being varnished for my Catholic ears. But as part of some other conversation Rafa announces to everyone in the dining room that Kevin here is a priest. The girls look pained to realize that their critical comments about the Catholic Church have been made within my hearing. Even more than before, I do my best to affirm them in their faith and good works, for they are doing an arguably better job than my own Church in tending to the spirits of the pilgrims along the way. I hope that by being a good guest and a good pilgrim I might give them perhaps a little more positive view of the church that is the love of my life even with all her warts and wrinkles.

We all help clean up, do a little more visiting, and then go to our beds. Before crawling atop my sack, I whisper to José: "Imagine, only seventy-five more kilometers to go." He nods back sadly, "Imagine."

» *August 10: Ferreiros to Ligonde* «

So Close Yet So Far
Yet So Close

August 11: Ligonde to Melide

We are awakened this morning by the crowing of a rooster just outside our bedroom, but it is a crowing that is so feeble as to be almost as funny as the young waitress' *beep-beep! Cock-a-dooo-dul-duh!* goes the poor old man. And again: *Cock-a-dooo-dul-duuuh!* I thus begin the day chuckling to myself at the lackadaisical rooster who accomplishes the morning reveille with about as much energy as a worn-out pilgrim who has been on the road way too long.

Our morning routine is now immensely precious to us because we all know there are very few of these mornings left to us. This one and perhaps three more, and then we will no longer be stretching our tendons, filling our water bottles, stuffing our *mochilas*, anointing our feet, gulping our yogurts, and in the dark of six in the morning walking silently and solemnly out the door.

Mist covers the earth as we depart the *Fuente del Peregrino*; our procession is accompanied by wisps of heavy fog that wrap themselves around us as if they were clouds of diaphanous incense. I imagine that we are being led ever more profoundly into the interior of this great cathedral called *la Tierra*, the Earth. Silence reigns; it is a deep silence that is made all the more poignant by the soft tramping of our feet and the rhythmic pecking of our staffs on the roadway. There is yet another sound within this cathedral: that of heavy drops of dew from the leaves above us. They tumble from leaf to leaf and then land atop our heads or on the end of our noses or all the way to the ground and with each voyage earthward they make the slightest of drip sounds which when multiplied a thousand or a million times over forms a background of chanted praise in this holy place. Drip, drop, drip: this hymn seeps into me and fills me.

Even at the first milestone I come to, seventy-four kilometers to Santiago, I realize that the pretty little seventy-five-kilometer card will be useless to me; my fify-year-old eyes can't focus on the minuscule print of the Scripture verses and I'm not going to wear my glasses all day as I walk just to read it. Even if I could read it, I'm not sure I would; I have enough in my heart and mind as I walk along these final days of the *camino*. Yet it is not useless after all: I fold up the card and put it in my breast pocket, right next to my little snack pack of unsalted almonds, where it reminds me of some young people's faith and hospitality in Christ. It also serves as an advisory that seventy-five kilometers are still seventy-five kilometers, and that is at least three days more of step after step after step along a road that always has its twists and turns, its aches and pains, and certainly its unexpected adventures. There is still time for a new blister, a crabby tendon, or a bite of bad food to lay any one of us low and foil our plans for the coming days. There is still time as well for spectacular salads to be thrown together, spaghetti to be cooked just right (or not), and time for conversations about life and God and what any of us will soon enough be going back to. There will yet be churches to wander about, all cool and dark, images of Christ on his cross to take time with, and the bare feet of a Santiago to light a candle before. There is still time to untangle my rosary beads and fall into the rhythm of its successive Hail Marys and Our Fathers and Glory Be's. I'm in church out here so that is what I do now.

In many places our dirt path becomes remarkably soft. As the way meanders through forested areas, a canopy of green above our heads covers us with lovely shade while the earth under our feet is softened by the brown mulch that is the result of years of leaves letting go, falling, and ever so quietly disintegrating into a beautiful dust that muffles the sound of our footsteps. This is not just walking that I am doing now; I am traversing tender flesh, passing over the very womb of this mother of us all, and she allows me to do so and even encourages me along this most intimate of passages; and though no word be spoken between us, this earth and I have come to know each other and we now love each other. The blackberries and the oaks, the chestnuts and the fields of wheat, the intensely purple flowers and the just as brightly painted yellow ones, the snails and the columns of ants, the one-by-one pilgrims who pass me by, each with his or her own stories of love and loneliness, all this is hers, and beyond and beneath and through her, it is God's. There is such unity and coherence and glory in this universe in which I now find myself that for just a moment the deep awareness of it sends a shiver up my spine and makes the hair on the back of my neck stand on end. Here I am, walking across the very womb of God!

The canticle from this morning's prayer captures the moment better than any camera:

> Every shower and dew, bless the Lord.
> All you winds, bless the Lord.
> Fire and heat, bless the Lord.
> Cold and chill, bless the Lord.
> Dew and rain, bless the Lord.
> Frost and chill, bless the Lord.
> Ice and snow, bless the Lord.
> Nights and days, bless the Lord.
> Light and darkness, bless the Lord.
> Lightning and clouds, bless the Lord.
> Let the earth bless the Lord,
> Praise and exalt him above all forever.[1]

I am walking well today. My legs and feet are in good condition. I keep up with my companions. As the day opens up into light and warmth, the mysterious feelings of the first hour wane and we lose our solemnity, becoming more social, chatting and teasing and laughing about the simplest of things: *Beep-beep! Cock-a-dooo-dul-duh!*

We pass through the city of Palas de Rei, stopping long enough for the morning *café con leche* and *tortilla*. We no longer are even close to following the plan of attack we worked out in Calvor, but the basic scheme

---

1. Daniel 3:64-74.

remains the same: avoid the big cities and spend our afternoons and nights in the smaller places. After Palas de Rei, our path leads us through aromatic forests of towering eucalyptus trees; Toni tells me that though they are beautiful and their leaves provide a valuable ingredient to teas and cough drops, these trees imported from Australia are a plague in Galicia, doing terrible damage to the local ecology, for they are heavy drinkers and suck up precious groundwater into their trunks and high branches, leaving little behind for other vegetation. With my untrained eye it is hard to see them as an evil, but I guess they are, not through any fault of their own but because we human beings must always be tampering with nature's good order, to its detriment and ours.

We eventually come to our day's destination, Melide. It is a bigger city than I had imagined, with plazas and markets and restaurants and traffic. We are not that far from the sea now, and so as we walk down its busy sidewalks, the main topic of conversation among the pilgrims is of taking advantage of the specialty of Melide: *pulpo*, octopus. Toni knows the town and knows the best place to consume the fleshy meat of this sea creature, a small restaurant seemingly famous far and wide for the quality and quantity of the *pulpo* it serves. In fact, we pass by the very restaurant on our way to the *refugio*; there is a crowd already queued up along the sidewalk outside waiting for table space to open up both inside and out on the street. The place is a beehive of activity and does not attract me at all.

The *refugio* is large and it is almost a culture shock to be back in one of these big places after having gotten used to the more intimate ones of the past few nights. We settle in as always, and as soon as everyone is showered a group decision is made to return to the famous *pulpo* restaurant for our main meal of the day. I go along for the ride, steeling my will to taste something of the local culture even if I'd much rather be in a quiet bar with my friends enjoying pork or beefsteak. The beehive atmosphere continues to reign as we take our places in the loosely formed line out front. We finally get in and are led past the bar, where the poor octopuses are being boiled in big copper vats and then violently chopped into morsels for our dining pleasure. We seat ourselves at one of the long dining-hall tables, the top of which is sticky with the greasy detritus left behind by previous diners. The commotion all about us is extraordinary. We get our beers and some baskets of bread, which we consume with a vengeance; Toni then comes through the crowd, *beep-beep!*, with two large wooden boards piled high with boiled, fleshy chunks of the tentacled beast. While the others dive in, I am a bit more judicious. I pick at it. Savor it a bit. Wash it down with a gulp of beer. Then pick again. I discover that I rather enjoy the flavor, but the look of it on the table and the suction cup texture of the meat in my mouth make me feel just a bit queasy all the same.

Back at the *refugio* we take our naps, then wander out into town, where we buy ourselves ice cream and lounge about on the grass of a nearby plaza. We then get down to our daily business, passing through the streets and stopping here and there to shop for fruit, yogurt, and a few other essentials. We find a bar and enjoy afternoon beers. I take a look at my watch and announce to the others that I'm going to go to the seven o'clock Mass at the parish church just down the street from our *refugio*. José and Marisa go their own way to find an Internet bar, while Toni and Alessandra join me in the walk up to the church. This church was once the chapel of a medieval monastery that cared for pilgrims in the final days of their walk before arriving in Santiago. Since the other *camino* road from Oviedo in the north joined the *Camino Francés* at this spot, it must have been a very busy place in those former times, with pilgrims landing here from two directions at once.

Whatever tradition of hospitality and care of pilgrims that once animated this place, it now seems sadly gone. We arrive at the portal of the church a minute or two before the evening Mass is scheduled to begin; as I have found so often in the churches of Spain, before Mass a cadre of elderly women is deep into their common recitation of the rosary, a very different experience from my own private morning prayer each day. Their version is fast, loud, and follows hidden rules that are unknown in my own religious culture. The prayer nevertheless has a certain charm and even beauty as the rote recitation speeds along, attaining as it goes its own spiritual rhythm and depth. Other pilgrims take the odd place among the pews of the old church; one, a shaggy young fellow wearing a Che Guevara t-shirt, stands out from the others by the look of utter sadness in his visage. He slumps in his pew as if he were using his last ounce of physical and spiritual strength to settle there. On the hour the rosary finishes and out of the sacristy process three priests dressed in wrinkled albs and stoles. They begin the Mass without any reference to our presence in the nave of the church. Even the usual liturgical greetings of the opening rites are not extended to us, but are simply recited among themselves seemingly only because the ritual book requires that they be spoken aloud. The Scripture readings are rushed through without expression, and not followed by a reflection, homily, or even a moment of quiet to let us do the work of digesting them. The Prayers of the Faithful are abandoned. The Eucharistic prayer itself, including its most central segment, the commemoration of the Last Supper, is raced through without any obvious sense that this is in fact a prayer, a sublime prayer, *the prayer* above all prayers, to our Father in Heaven and Creator of the Universe. Communion is dispensed automatically. After a cold dismissal the whole thing is over, having taken less than twenty minutes. The old ladies' rosary probably took longer than this. The three priests disappear into the sacristy, never to be seen again.

I greet the fellow in the Che Guevara shirt with a nod. He stays in his pew praying, but I come out of the church furious. I have just had enough of this sacrilegious and inhuman manner of praying our great prayer. What possesses these men to presume that by lifelessly mouthing the words of our liturgy they are fulfilling their responsibility as *pastors*, "shepherds" to us, their pilgrim children? We kneel at their feet, hungry and hurting and *anxious* for even one word, one gesture, one moment of fleeting eye contact that will assure us that God is with us, that we are not alone, that all that we are doing out here has some importance, that our pilgrimage is part of something bigger than just us. But there is nothing. Like cold-hearted fathers who ignore their children, they walk in one door of the house as an obligation and just as quickly walk out the other, leaving in their wake absolutely nothing to sustain us beyond what we might scrounge up for ourselves. May I find a way out of my judgmentalism in regard to these men, for I do not know their life stories or what hurts and lacks in their own lives have led them to pray in this empty fashion, but what we have received from them is hardly recognizable as the beautiful liturgy that is the fount and summit of a Catholic's spiritual life. If that heap of a young man in the Che Guevara t-shirt came looking for the Lord in this church, I can't imagine that he found him, at least not in the version of the Catholic liturgy we have just been subjected to.

Toni, Alessandra, and I sit down on a park bench in the plaza outside the church doors. The early evening sun is bathing the court in lovely golden light. For a moment there is silence. They look at me and I suppose see something in my face they have not seen before: the deepest anger I am capable of. I begin excising that anger by expressing it in the best words I have available to me in my second tongue. They calmly and respectfully listen to me until my catena of protestations has run out of steam, then assure me that they understand, but in the end there is nothing to be done, for this is just the way things are most of the time. They are accustomed to this sort of Mass, and so the tragedy of it does not make much impression on them. Yet to me this, too, is a tragedy, even greater. Then José and Marisa come into the plaza from its far corner all smiles and laughter. Alessandra says to them, "Kevin is really mad." She then relates this newest *camino* tale of how Kevin found the Mass in Melide to be so miserable that . . .

Together we walk through the small streets around the church to look for a bar or restaurant so that we might enjoy an evening snack before returning to the *refugio* for the night. As we wander through one such street, a grandmother appears in the open window of her home with her infant grandchild cuddled in her arms, exposing the little one to the fresh air of the new evening. As she bounces the child against her breast, first Marisa, then Alessandra, then all of us gather around this little vision of heaven come to earth. We are allowed to tickle the baby's wrinkled pink feet, making her gurgle with delight. The grandmother beams with pride. My good spirits are restored by this moment of grace made flesh. This baby is the way out of my fruitless anger.

Such, in the end, is my old church: grace made flesh, but flesh it still is: soft and hard, young and old, new and worn, all at the same time. It is so close to God, yet so far from God, yet so close to God.

A Rest and Then the Rest

August 12: Melide to Ribadiso de Baixo

It is the twelfth of August and our walk from Melide to Ribadiso de Baixo is the shortest of my entire *camino*, only about twelve kilometers or so. We choose not to go into Arzua, just a bit further down the road, because the *refugio* there is reported to be very small, meaning that the likelihood of finding an open bed there will become increasingly slim as the morning wears on. The stream of pilgrims on the road — many of whom are the aggravating *sinmochilas* — has now become a flood.

The road this day, short as it is, leads us through more of the beautiful Galician countryside, much of it covered in those aromatic but thirsty eucalyptus trees. It is almost as if they know they are culpable of drinking too much, for though their skeletal fingers rise high above the earth, the bunches of leaves at branches' end droop downward as if ashamed of themselves and their skin peels off in long strips as if their nerves are getting the best of them. Poor things.

Other segments of the road wind through woods of pine and areas rich in ferns whose splayed and green hands reach praisefully toward the sky; they obviously do not suffer from eucalyptic shame. Several times we cross the highway that goes through to Santiago; to look at the maps of the road ahead, it seems that the remainder of our route will hug this same highway over the final days of our journey. We are losing the open country we have become so familiar with; already we can feel in our bones that the end is near. It is an increasingly sad feeling, a feeling that José picked up on several days before the rest of us. I admire his sensitivity to such things and I suspect that because of it the end of the *camino* may affect him more than the rest of us.

After only a few hours of walking, we enter Ribadiso, only fifty kilometers from Santiago. We are so early that there is no one even waiting at the gate of the *refugio* save one young man who is lying atop a stone wall reading a very hefty paperback novel. Our plan is to do a longer walk tomorrow, about twenty-five kilometers, to Arca; and then on Thursday complete the final twenty kilometers and land in Santiago before the noon Mass in the Cathedral. We justify our short day today by saying it is a rest day prior to our final assault on Compostela. We have plenty of time on our hands, so we follow some signs to a nearby river park; after a half-kilometer's walk we find the small resort still closed, but the lawns are spacious and there are pools where we can soak our feet in cold, refreshing water. After about an hour, the bar opens and we all take our turns ordering soda or beer, but before we can drink much a fellow pilgrim arrives, telling us that we'd better get back to the *refugio*, for the line outside is now becoming very long. He is incredulous that we did not leave our own *mochilas* lined up at the gate to mark our order of arrival. We abandon our drinks and hastily throw on our socks and boots and high-tail it back down the road to Ribadiso. The pilgrim's warning was no joke: there must surely be seventy or eighty *mochilas* already lined up in front of the main gate. We set our own packs in place to mark our order of arrival and join the other pilgrims dallying about until the gate finally opens and the queue of pilgrims for the day begins to be processed. We patiently wait our turn and then walk through the gate and into an astonishingly ample yard with a great field beyond. The field is bounded on one side by a light fence but on the other by the flowing waters of the river and a string of poplar trees the rustling leaves of which harmonize with the sound of river water flowing in and around and over the stones of its bed. Some of the pilgrims have already ditched most of their clothing and are splashing about in the cool river robed only in bras and skivvies, their laughter adding to the symphony being played by the flowing water and rustling poplar leaves.

Arrival in Ribadiso comes with some guilt feelings, at least for me.

» *A Rest and Then the Rest* «

Such a brief journey hardly seems like a journey at all. I am not used to so little work, and it seems strange to end the day with so much steam left in my engine. We reaffirm to ourselves that the rest will do us good, for the next two days will be much longer and we want to arrive in Santiago in good condition.

Outside of that guilt and the increasingly sad feelings that accompany the realization that the end is drawing nigh, the day is a pleasant one. After showering and doing my laundry, I find a quiet place out in the open field behind the *refugio* to write a bit, nap, and watch storm clouds build out to the east of us. Toni comes by and sits with me for a while. He asks me if after the *camino* I'd be interested in joining him and his family in their home village over the weekend for their parish fiesta. His father and his uncle, the bishop, will be there, as well as his aunts and uncles and cousins. I am pleased to accept his offer and look forward to being welcomed into his "real world." It will also give me a chance to decompress a bit before returning to my own "real world" in Belgium, hopefully making the transition less of a shock. A number of pilgrims talk of their plans to continue beyond Santiago, to walk all the way to the coast itself, to Finisterre, "the End of the World," as it has been known since Roman times, if not even before. I am not interested at all in that prospect; with Compostela I will be finished, physically, emotionally, and spiritually. Toni's invitation relieves me of even having to consider the possibility of going to the coast; I now have a program of my own for the end.

It is not long before the dormitories are full, all interior floor space is likewise full, and late-arriving pilgrims are setting up their makeshift camps in the open field. My teenage friends from Granada, Julio and Manuel, show up, which surprises me since I've seen neither hide nor hair of them for days. They spot me and yell to me, "KEVIN! KEVIN!" and come bounding through the field like young gazelles to greet me and tell me their stories. They report that they became terribly sick to their stomachs on bad food a few days before and had to sit out the infirmity; by walking a "double day" today, over forty kilometers, they have managed to make up the lost time and have caught up to their own wave of pilgrims. The two of them seem no worse for their troubles and are bursting with energy as always. The two Italian girls, Elena and Nicoletta, whom I first met at the *Cruz de Ferro*, roll in looking exhausted but are delighted to

» *August 12: Melide to Ribadiso de Baixo* «

find the five of us here ahead of them. They hug and kiss us all. Then Rafa and his girlfriend arrive as well. Several youth groups have set up camp, including a very large one from Italy whose leaders have erected their own field tent and are preparing to serve a major meal to their troop of hungry teens. This place is beginning to feel like the staging ground for a great battle. Others we have met even briefly along the way amble about and there are familiar greetings all around. It is an extraordinary atmosphere and excitement among all about their imminent assault on Santiago is like electricity in the air.

Both the rest we enjoy on this afternoon in Ribadiso and the conviviality among the pilgrims restore us. We are ready.

And the Stars Dance

August 13: Ribadiso de Baixo to Santiago de Compostela

If there is one thing that is true about the *camino* it is that it possesses a gravity all its own. This invisible force has been pulling us forward since the beginning, since even before the beginning, since we first heard of the *Camino de Santiago de Compostela*. But now, as we draw closer and closer to the Field of Stars, like a planet or a sun or a great galaxy it exerts a pull upon us that is each day more powerful and each day more irresistible. Santiago's gravity is now so fierce that all our carefully planned schedules are abandoned and, yes, we do something we would not have believed ourselves capable of accomplishing even on the very day we accomplish it.

When I awake at five A.M. in the *refugio* of Ribadiso de Baixo on this Wednesday morning, all of us in our little *camino* family fully expect that we still have two days of walking ahead of us. Our game plan has been well discussed, decided upon by all, and is now set. Tomorrow, not today, we shall arrive at the zero kilometer stone in front of the cathedral, just in time for the famous pilgrims' Mass at noon.

The five of us become the seven of us, for this morning Elena and Nicoletta join our company as we walk out of the *refugio*. We move through fields of vegetables, then are pulled again deep into another of Galicia's great oak groves. We cross from one side of the Compostela highway to the other several times more, then find ourselves on a dirt road passing through a string of sleepy Galician villages interspersed with yet more stands of pleasant-smelling eucalyptus trees and woods of pine as well. The heat of the morning makes the pitch in those pine trees give off a strong scent; this is the stuff of which incense is made. I inhale its aroma and remember as I did the day before that out here, too, I am in church.

Along the way, the limping Nicoletta and her constant companion, Elena, join me while the others move ahead at a much speedier clip. Elena understands neither Spanish nor English, so Nicoletta speaks for both of them in her simple Spanish. They have something on their minds and they beat around the bush for a while, putting together a puzzle from bits and pieces of information they have picked up along the way.

"Kevin, you are American, but you work in Belgium?"

"Yes, that's right."

"You are an American who lives in Belgium, but you speak Spanish?"

"Yes, clearly."

"And where did you learn Spanish?"

"I learned it among the Mexican people who work in the fields and orchards back home in Washington State in the U.S."

"And did you work in the fields too?"

"No, not really."

"And would you mind, Kevin, if we ask you something?"

"No, not at all."

"What is your work?"

"I am a Catholic priest," I answer.

With that they explode with excitement: "We KNEW it! We guessed right! We were right! We were right! We figured you must be a priest! You just seemed like you should be a priest!"

I then ask them about their work and am happy to learn that they both work for an agency dedicated to assisting troubled young people sort out their confused lives. They deal with kids on drugs or with alcohol problems or even those who are suicidal. They love their work, but it exhausts them. They are on the *camino* to refresh themselves and restore their spirits before returning to the service of their lost young sheep. In the end, we find we have much in common as we talk about the issues faced by today's youth and how difficult it can be to help them become healthy and whole adults. They are lovely ladies and we walk along together as if lifelong friends even though we only just recently have gotten around to knowing one another.

By noon we have arrived at our destination for the day: Arca, a decidedly unpretty place that looks as though it has developed along the highway as little more than a long series of truck stops and services for tourists. We have eighteen easy kilometers already under our belts for the day. This is where we shall stay put until tomorrow morning's final march into Compostela, now only twenty-some kilometers away. We find the Arca *refugio*, but are distressed to discover a very long queue of pilgrims already waiting at the front door, their *mochilas* lined up domino-style. We drop our own *mochilas* at the end of the line and before long there are many more even after ours. The place is advertised as having eighty beds, and, if floor space is included, probably a hundred pilgrims can find a place to sleep indoors. Toni begins counting the *mochilas* in the queue to see how far back in the line we are; the news is not good: we are right at the one hundred mark. The chances of getting a place to sleep here are slim unless some of the pilgrims ahead of us decide to move on, which doesn't seem likely.

I have already taken off my boots and socks and am cleaning my feet and examining a newly discovered problem: a fresh blister has developed at the base of my big toe. So I dig in my pack for the Betadine, my old sewing needle, and the last of my thread, and run a stitch through the top of the thing. I wince; I have hit raw flesh beneath, so I pull back and try again and succeed, then tie it off and complain aloud as if I were Job, "What have I done to deserve this? Even to the end, O God, you afflict me!" The complaint gets a laugh and then we get down to a serious discussion about our options. José is anxious to move on; "Let's go to Lavacolla, where we will have a better chance at finding beds. It will be only another seven or eight kilometers and the afternoon is not so hot. We can do it." Marisa buys into José's suggestion, as do Alessandra and Toni. Nicoletta is suffering from a very sore leg but both she and Elena are willing to give it a try. I agree as well, and so I prepare my feet with a new covering of Vaseline, slip on clean socks followed by my dusty boots, and cinch down my *mochila* one more time. We haul our stuff back up to the highway and a settle into the parking lot of a grocery store, where we buy ourselves sandwiches, yogurts, and whatever else we think we might need for the next two hours of unexpected walking. I lift my *mochila* up to my back, and we are off through town with a revised plan for the march on Compostela. It is almost as if we cannot stop ourselves from pushing on. Santiago is having his way with us. He is pulling us forward and we cannot resist him.

As the highway leads us beyond the outskirts of the city, Elena comes to the sudden and pained realization that she has left her purse behind either at the *refugio* or the grocery store. This is an extraordinary turn of bad luck, for it not only means that all her money, bank cards, *credencial*, and identification may be lost forever, but it also means turning back and thereby adding a half hour or more of walking time to get to the day's new destination. We huddle in the middle of the street and revise our plan. Elena and Nicoletta will go back to retrieve the wallet if it is still retrievable, while the rest of us will walk on at a leisurely pace and wait for them to catch up at the first decent rest area.

So off they go, back into Arca. There is nothing so painful as retracing steps on the *camino*, especially now when we are so close to the goal. The sadness at this reality is shared by all of us, but there is nothing to be done. As they go their way we go ours. The route beyond Arca has a fair amount of shade trees along it and the afternoon is not as blazing hot as the previous days, so we are doing pretty well; even my new blister seems to be behaving. I am still walking with energy and enjoying myself as we move along at a brisk clip. I walk with Toni while Marisa, Alessandra, and José trail a ways behind. A couple hours pass and then we happen upon the outer fence line of a substantial airport. "What is an airport like this doing way out here?" I ask Toni. But he is rather astonished at my question and answers me: "This is the Lavacolla Airport, the airport of SANTIAGO!" I am simply stunned to find myself so close to the holy city. "Don't get too excited, we still have more than fifteen kilometers to go before getting to Compostela," he warns me. But I just can't take in the fact that I am now passing the Santiago airport; for heaven's sake, I've been walking for thirty-four days and have traversed over seven hundred and fifty kilometers of mountain and plain on foot with a miserably burdensome *mochila* harnessed to my aching back and I have endured blisters and tendonitis and I have lost an unknown amount of weight and unknowable gallons of sweat and after all this, I am now at the *Santiago airport!* How can I not be excited? As an Iberia airliner takes off with a roar from the strip just a half-kilometer from where we are walking, I have to wonder how many of the passengers on that plane are pilgrims now on their way back home. Perhaps most. I will soon be among their company. It won't be long before the great goal of my heart for the past thirty-four days — a lifetime it seems — will slip from before my eyes to somewhere behind me. In just fifteen kilometers, the unachievable will become the achieved, the present challenge will become the memory, I the pilgrim will return to being a sedentary modern man. This will be a sort of ontological change both of the goal and of me, who has held the dream in my heart for all these long days. It is a sort of death. How will I mourn?

Toni and I cross a highway and wait for the others at a small park bench set to the side of the road. Marisa, José, and Alessandra are a long way behind us so there is nothing to do but idle away the time and talk about inconsequential things: airplane wings and chamomile plants and what the city of Compostela looks like. Finally our companions come into view and of course have to take their own rest, for they too are hot and tired. I am a little amazed that for the moment I am walking better than they. After taking their ten minutes, we pick up our *mochilas* and follow the path behind the airport runway. The highway is just off the right side of our gravel path. I spot an overhead highway sign that reads, "SANTIAGO: 15 KM" and this again leaves me incredulous and excited and sad all at the same time.

We come into a village called San Paio and here we find an upscale little bar, so we drop our equipment and have ourselves some beers and lemonades. As we sit at one of the outdoor tables, we suddenly spot Nicoletta and Elena trudging towards us, looking almost dead but smiling and waving. We greet them with enthusiastic hugs and are all delighted that Elena's purse was right where she had left it with not a euro missing: another Santiago miracle! Suddenly and joyfully, we are back together again, back to our family of seven!

With the afternoon getting warmer, we set out again for the town of Lavacolla, our destination for the day. It is not far, and we are grateful for this, for we have now completed almost thirty kilometers since leaving Ribadiso this morning. I am dog-tired and I can see that Nicoletta is limping badly as she walks along. The town is a pretty little place, but we arrive to the old Christmas story refrain: "No room at the inn!" The *refugio* is completely full, as are the local hostel and a nearby hotel. Another hotel still has rooms but the place is filthy and the ladies will have none of it. We continue on our way out of town because we are told that there is another hotel just down the highway a bit. As the rest of us wait at a crossroads, Toni and José go to check it out but bring back to us no good news. Our group dynamics begin to fall apart as tiredness settles deep into our bones. I am feeling a growing urge to just move down the road and get the whole thing over with. I am increasingly frustrated by our manner of stopping and going, stopping and going, and getting no-where in the process. We have killed almost an hour in this little town looking for lodging and that does not even count the happier hour we knocked off in San Paio with our beers and lemonades; we could have been four or five kilometers closer to Santiago had we been more disci-plined.

Somehow I am missing out on whatever decision-making process is at work here, for rather suddenly it is determined that we will walk on, but only a bit, then find a place to take yet more rest and lose even more time from the road. When I figure out what is happening, I find myself deeply annoyed and can hardly talk to these people. I go along with the plan but do so in a spirit of utter dejection.

We find an open field of deep green grass on a slight hillside over-looking Lavacolla and there *mochilas* are dropped, snacks are pulled out of bags, and leftover sandwiches are nibbled at, while I sit by myself in a pout. I love these people like my own family, but exhaustion from over thirty kilometers of hiking, frustration at plans turned upside down, a new blister on my big toe, and that growing urge to push on all the way to Santiago *now* have all conspired to make a big baby out of me in their presence. I punish them by not speaking to them. Toni comes over and asks me how I'm doing and I express to him as kindly as possible what is eating at me. By his understanding manner as much as by anything he says, he calms me down and helps me become my better self. I lean back into the sweet grass, close my eyes, and try to expel this awful crankiness from my soul.

When word comes that we are ready to push on, I actually have rested and feel much stronger; I throw the *mochila* over my back, grab my *bastones*, and move into my low-gear, automaton walking mode, climbing up the rather steep grade of the highway with mindless abandon, leaving the others a short ways behind. Eventually, Alessandra, beautiful Alessandra, overtakes me and begins talking to me, and little by little I regain consciousness and become a human being again and before long she and I are laughing over some small thing, perhaps the *beep-beep!* of the plump restaurant waitress two days behind us.

With more walking we come to a large picnic area and campground. Its green lawns and garden pavilions are very attractive. Once again there is talk in the group of taking a break, but I am now determined to push on even by myself if need be; according to my simple map we should be within spitting distance of the *Monte de Gozo*, the Mount of Joy, the last stop before Santiago, a hilltop that overlooks the city and from which pilgrims for over ten centuries have had their first tearful view of the city they have longed to see. "Let's just move on to the *Monte de Gozo* and we can stop there if we want. It can't be that much further," I opine. The Compostela gravity pulls at all of us; it cannot be resisted. This Santiago is a mighty jealous saint; he will not let us out of his grasp now. All agree with me, so water bottles are quickly refilled and we are back on the paved road; our spirits lift and we are filled with new energy and a new camaraderie that is deeper and richer even than before. I think we have just worked our way successfully through a test, or at least I have. I ask Toni to sing for us our favorite Galician folk song, the one with all the *ai-la-la-le-lo's*, "*Catro Vellos Mariñeros*." He happily begins and we all join in as we traipse down the hot pavement past massive television towers. Then Alessandra starts in with the Italian song, "*Volare*": "*Volare, oh-oh. Cantare, oh-oh-oh-oh* . . . We are flying now!" I suggest we sing an *American* folk song for a change, and begin with the opening words of "Singin' in the Rain," and before we know it all of us are locked arm in arm, stretched across the breadth of the roadway, dancing, really dancing, as we go up the road *singin', singin' in the rain*. I don't know if I have ever been happier in my whole life. An hour before, I was never more miserable. I much prefer this joy, this perfect joy. I must be going crazy, crazy with love and hope and complete trust in these sisters and brothers of mine. If this is crazy, I'm sorry for my lifetime of sanity. God: keep me crazy like this for a while longer! I only wish there was a lamppost I could swing on or a great puddle to splash in: we're singin', singin' in the RAIN!

We sing ourselves around a wide curve in the road and see over the top of a low hill the silhouette of a monumental cross towering above the horizon: it is the cross atop the *Monte de Gozo*. We are almost there! We walk down one street, then take a turn up another, and a few blocks farther on we find ourselves actually at the foot of that massive monument to Pope John Paul II's visit to Compostela. We drop our bags, rest, then climb the slight hill up to the sculpture and cross. From that height we take our first look down into the city of Santiago. We can't see much, for a haze softens the image of the city into a thin wisp of vague colors and shapes. Nevertheless, there it is: the Field of Stars, and I'm seeing it with my own eyes. These eyes don't cry, they just look and look and look.

Thank you, Lord. Thank you, Santiago. Thank you, Mom and Dad. Thank you, my poor feet.

We take a few minutes to size up the monument's four great bronze panels depicting the visits of St. Francis and John Paul II to the city below. Then we return to our possessions just in time to welcome Elena and a badly limping Nicoletta onto the *Monte de Gozo.*

One final decision needs to be made yet today: it is now almost six P.M.; do we stay the night up here in the massive *refugio* on this hilltop, or do we go all the way now, go into Compostela itself, to the zero kilometer stone, to the Cathedral of the Apostle? José says "Go!" Marisa says "Go!" Alessandra says "Go!" I say "Go!" And Toni says, "¡*Vámanos, pues!* Let's go, then!" Elena and Nicoletta decide to spend the night on the hilltop, for Nicoletta's leg is hurting her greatly. They walk with us as far as the entrance to the *refugio* and we embrace and kiss and promise to see each other at the pilgrims' Mass in the cathedral tomorrow. We get back on the dirt track beside the highway and continue on our way. Thirty seconds later, we hear a commotion from behind us and it is Nicoletta and Elena, our dear friends, joyfully yelling to us that they are coming too! We wait for them and once again, our family of seven heads down the path to Santiago, which is now so close I can almost spit and hit it.

We cross a bridge over a deep gully and at the far end is a small sign announcing the city limits of Santiago de Compostela; my eyes well up now, and as I step off the bridge, I fall to the ground, *mochila* and all, and kiss the earth under my feet, the dirt of Compostela. In getting up I strain a muscle in my upper leg but I don't care; I catch up to the others and we silently walk through a park towards the old city. In the park, I make a small detour across the green lawn and walk through the whirling sprinklers like a kid; it is my version of the ancient bath of purification required of filthy pilgrims before they entered the holy city. The jets of cool water across my legs and chest and the fresh mists settling on my face are a delight and I feel clean. Toni directs us through the *Puerta del Camino* and into the old city where our boots and *bastones* make a racket on the stone streets that reverberates off the stone walls of the houses and shops. I ask for a brief moment to stop and buy a disposable camera; I want pictures of our entry into the cathedral plaza and the others allow me this privilege. I deliberately chose not to bring a camera with me on the *camino* so as to rely on my journal and my memory as the record of this project in my life, but now I want pictures of these friends of mine, all of us together for a few precious moments before it is irretrievably done and gone; I want pictures of us gathered together right on top of this ancient Field of Stars that is only a street or two away.

We gawk as we pass by one side of the cathedral, then turn a corner and suddenly the street opens up into the stunning *Plaza del Obradoiro* itself into which our small troupe of sisters and brothers magnificently process spellbound and in silence. With the Baroque façade of the cathedral towering above our left shoulders and with Santiago himself perched in its uppermost niche looking down upon us, Toni leads the way to the stone inscribed simply, "0 Kilometer"; the image of the conch, our conch, is cut deep into its surface. We take turns bending down to touch it with our full hands and then to kiss it, and finally, as an afterthought, we throw off our *mochilas* right there in the center of things, drop our *bastones* and staffs, and begin laughing. I kiss the conch hung on the back of my *mochila* long ago in Saint-Jean-Pied-de-Port. It has accompanied me all seven hundred and eighty kilometers and I love it for its fidelity.

I have often imagined along the way that at this moment of which I have dreamed I would cry, but I don't, no one does, Toni and Marisa and Alessandra and José and Elena and Nicoletta don't shed a tear; we just laugh and embrace and kiss and laugh some more. I don't miss the absent tears. Our laughter is enough. It is wonder enough.

Finally, we unceremoniously sit ourselves down on the stone pavement, pull off our boots and socks, get back up, take snapshots of one another with our various cameras, and then we call home. I pull my own mobile phone from deep within my pack. While sitting on the stones in front of the Cathedral of Santiago, right atop this ancient Field of Stars, I dial America, to my elder sister's house, and into her answering machine I say, "Hi, Eileen, this is your brother, Kevin, and I've just arrived in the

» *August 13: Ribadiso de Baixo to Santiago de Compostela* «

heart of Santiago de Compostela after five hundred miles of walking and I'm fine and I want you to know that I love you. Let all the brothers and sisters know I am okay."

So do I see the stars dance at seven thirty this evening in the *Plaza del Obradoiro?* Let me tell you as clearly as I am able: I see José laugh. I see Toni laugh. I see Marisa laugh. I see Elena laugh. I see Nicoletta laugh. I see Alessandra laugh. And I laugh. Yes, I see the stars dance. I surely do.

"And the Pilgrim from America . . ."

August 14: Santiago de Compostela

After an hour or so of such joy expressed in the most simple pleasure at having done something important and wonderful, at having fulfilled a dream, at having arrived, we begin the final and most difficult *etapa*, or stage, of the pilgrimage: slowly letting go of one another. The force of Santiago's gravity changes direction now. We have crossed some kind of equator that reverses the flow of everything. Santiago begins to spin us away from its center, like stars on the far end of a galaxy's pinwheel arms being let go of, flung away into space in slow motion. Instead of pulling us in, it pushes us away.

For some days before I met Marisa, José, and Alessandra, they walked with a young couple from Santiago and their ten-year-old son. They made a promise to meet again once they had arrived in Santiago. From the plaza, Marisa gives the family a call and before long they join us at the zero kilometer stone. José gives to the ten-year-old boy, Carlos, his beloved yellow and green Brazil football shirt, which is a real gift from his heart. Little Carlos is energetic and active and in joy he is all over them with hugs and kisses and unstoppable chatter. These folks with their bright little boy are very good people but they are not *my* people, since we have not walked together. Though we take pleasure in seeing Alessandra, José, and Marisa reunited with them, Toni, Elena, Nicoletta, and I don't belong to their "family." Though we are happily introduced to one another, it is clear that our relations with them will never be what José, Alessandra, and Marisa feel. Already there is the slightest tug of separation in the air.

The cathedral is closed now and there is nothing more to do, so Toni calls a friend who offers us a flat for the night not far from the plaza. Elena and Nicoletta go off to spend their night in Compostela at a hotel. The rest of us limp along with our sore feet, aching ankles, and pulled muscles, slowly making our way down a few commercial streets to the apartment block of Toni's friend; we enter, and in a few minutes we are settled into the small space. Toni and I throw our mats and sleeping bags on the living room floor, José takes the worn-out sofa, and the ladies settle in the bedroom. We wash up, then go out to a nearby restaurant for an unremarkable dinner; we are too tired to enjoy the food. Upon returning to our flat, our last *refugio* of this pilgrimage, we count up the day's kilometers and our best guess is that we have done the impossible: we have walked at least forty-two kilometers since we left Ribadiso de Baixo this morning. We did not do it ourselves; we were pulled, compelled, urged on. The mysterious gravity of Compostela carried us here. We exhaustedly wish one another a good night, tuck ourselves in, and turn off the lights. This day is done.

It is not until nine the following morning that we begin to stir. We take turns washing up, walk down the street to a nearby bar, grab a quick *café con leche* and a croissant, and finally head together to the diocesan pilgrims' office next door to the cathedral. It is time to obtain our *Compostela,* the official certificate of completion that is awarded to pilgrims who can prove they have walked at least one hundred kilometers of the *camino;* that proof, of course, is supplied by the now colorfully stamped *camino* passport, the *credencial.* The line into the ancient building is long and moves slowly; it takes us an hour to arrive at the front desk and have our *Compostelas* signed, sealed, and delivered into our hands. We are as proud and pleased as kids at an eighth-grade graduation ceremony.

The five of us then rush over to the cathedral just in time for the noon pilgrims' Mass to begin. Toni, José, and I are somehow separated from Marisa and Alessandra, losing sight of them altogether in the huge crowd of pilgrims and tourists who are quickly filling every centimeter of available floor space. The three of us manage to shoulder our way into a spot

» *"And the Pilgrim from America . . ."* «

close to the altar and sit on the floor of the transept; we huddle there surrounded by the washed and unwashed, yesterday's arrivals and those who have arrived just moments ago. A young pilgrim stands at a microphone in the sanctuary; she tenderly intones a hymn. The organ blasts. The long procession of priests enters and so the pilgrims' Mass begins. The presiding priest welcomes and greets us all, then begins a long list of more specific greetings: "We welcome the five German pilgrims who began in Astorga. We welcome the fifteen young pilgrims from the parish of Santa María in Sevilla and their pastor who began in Burgos. We welcome the three Italian pilgrims who began their pilgrimage in Pamplona. We welcome the Dutch pilgrim who began his pilgrimage in Maastricht." Then I hear this: "We welcome the American pilgrim who began his pilgrimage in Saint-Jean-Pied-de-Port." I nod to José and Toni and we all smile, for that welcome is surely addressed to me.

The Mass is exuberant and beautiful. "Truly it is right and just that we give you thanks, O Lord." Truly it *is* right and just. We stand as a body and are invited to pray the Lord's Prayer, each pilgrim in his or her own language — and for a moment I can't decide after all these weeks of speaking mostly Spanish if "my own language" is Spanish or English; I choose English. The wave of languages filling that church with Jesus' own words makes my heart swell with thanksgiving and joy. We work our way up to one of the priests distributing communion and, as at few other times, those simple words that I myself say so often, make utter sense to me, they make me know I am home: "*Cuerpo de Cristo.* The Body of Christ." Amen. So be it. So it is. I believe. I know. I know this Christ. I have walked with him. He has walked with me. I have hurt with him and he has hurt with me. I have sat on the ground with him eating and drinking and telling tales. I have been alone with him and he with me. I have gazed into his face and kissed his feet. After all is said and done, I love him. *Cuerpo de Cristo.* Amen.

As Mass ends, there is a murmur of disappointment flowing through the crowd of pilgrims, for they have not seen one of the spectacles of the cathedral, the famous *botafumeiro*, fly through the air. This is a massive silver incense burner that is dramatically swung through the open space of the church's transept, reaching its zenith on either side almost to the height of the ceilings and at its nadir, sweeping across the tops of the pilgrims' heads with a tremendous whoosh and a sweet-smelling cloud of smoke trailing behind it. To have come all this way and not see this wonder of the medieval world is a great pity, but there is nothing to be done. I, at least, will be here another day, so there is a chance I might view the marvel tomorrow.

After Mass, we gather in the plaza and reunite with Elena and Nicoletta and the family we met last night, the friends of Marisa, José, and Alessandra. I am delighted when a boisterous group of young people breaks into a circle dance around the zero kilometer stone and I watch them as they hold hands, swing to the right and then to the left, singing and swaying and praising their God. I am even more delighted when an old priest crossing the plaza with a briefcase in one hand spontaneously jumps into the circle and with mouth open in laughter and eyes sparkling with life, joins the young people for a couple rounds of their joyful dance; he then lets go of them, saluting them as he does so and continues on his way. This priest who dances is a star; through him I forgive the other priests I have complained about along the way and hope that they might some day dance as this man dances. May I, too, dance as he dances.

I see the first Toni of my journey, the young man with infected blisters on his feet whom I left behind in Villadangos. He is just now arriving into the plaza; his feet are still bandaged and he is limping badly. I wave to him and call his name and he comes to me and we embrace and tell each other a few of our *camino* stories, then there seems nothing more to say and he moves on.

We walk to a nearby restaurant for a rich meal accompanied by plenty of wine and never-empty baskets of bread for all of us to enjoy. After lunch we go our separate ways, agreeing to reunite in the plaza at seven P.M. We instinctively know that we need our own time and space to absorb all this, savor it, reflect upon it, attempt to penetrate its meaning for us. I want most of all to accomplish the final act of my pilgrim journey: to give to the ancient image of Santiago above the main altar of the cathedral the traditional pilgrim *abrazo* or embrace and then pray at the small chapel deep under that same altar where his bones rest.

I enter the cathedral by myself and take my place at the end of the queue that will lead me up a stone stairway to the bust of Santiago. It is a long line and it takes me about an hour of slowly moving forward before I am at the foot of a steep stairwell. I slowly climb the stone steps that so many other pilgrims have climbed before me over the past millennium. I

» *"And the Pilgrim from America . . ."* «

264

stop on the final step to let the couple ahead of me have their moment, then they move on and it is my turn. With one final step up, I find myself behind Santiago, looking out over his shoulder at what seem like swarms of pilgrims and tourists milling about on the cathedral floor far below. He and I watch them together for a moment and we love them from this height, we love them all. I then reach my arms around his shoulders and lean full up against his back and I embrace dear brother Iago, and then I kiss him. I pause like this for a moment, then let him go and slowly and carefully descend the steps on the other side while other pilgrims behind me take my place at Iago's shoulders.

The stairwell drops down to the ground floor, then after a spiral turn a second small stairwell descends beneath the sanctuary, delivering me into a dark chapel equipped only with a kneeler situated before a silver sarcophagus set in a small alcove; the reliquary holds the bones of Santiago and his disciples, Theodore and Athanasius. I kneel and remarkably I find myself here. I make my request.

"Santiago: I thank you for carrying me here. Now I make bold to offer you my intention in coming to you. Send our seminary good men. Help us to make of them good 'fishers of men' as you were, men who serve our brother, Jesus, with faith and wisdom and love. Help me to be a good pastor to them. Let me carry them on my shoulders when they hurt. Make of them good pastors, too."

This is not enough, so I add: "And Santiago, I thank you for this road and these thirty-five days to walk it. Thank you for all that I have seen, felt, and come to love. Thank you for the earth. Thank you most of all for opening my eyes to stars that dance. Take care of my *camino* friends, all of them from Jean Luc on the first day to Toni, José, Elena, Nicoletta, Marisa, and Alessandra on this last day. Take care of my brothers and sisters and greet my mother and father already with you. Help me live a good life. Help me die a grateful death. *Gracias, Iago, por todo.*"

After some unknowable amount of time, I walk up the small stone staircase back to the ground floor of the cathedral, having finished my prayer and completed my pilgrimage to Iago, my brother.

I find a pew in the nave of the great church and just sit. I cannot keep my eyes open and each time I fall into a moment of sleep, the dream image that remains when I jerk back awake is of some moment on the camino: a field of yellow sunflowers facing the sun in morning praise, a road dappled in shade and light passing through a grove of chestnut trees, a crossroads with fields of wheat extending to the four corners of the horizon, small plane trees lining a long straight roadway like beads on a rosary. The disparate images and distinct moments of the journey are pulled into one through those momentary drops into sleep. A tear rolls down my cheek, my first since arriving. I later find the *Capilla del Santísimo* where it is very quiet and there are few tourists and say my final rosary of the *camino*. Hail Mary . . . Hail Mary . . . Hail Mary . . . Glory be . . . deliver us from all evil. Amen.

I return to the streets of Santiago and wander about looking for a few small *recuerdos*, or souvenirs, to bring home. I buy a Compostela t-shirt and a small gold lapel Santiago cross. As I walk about I keep my eye open for any of my former companions on the road, who, if all went well, should have arrived only a day ahead of me: Fermín, Alfredo, Catherine, Robert, and Josh. I see none of them. If they arrived at all perhaps they have already gone on to Finisterra or started home. I do see the Spanish gentleman who told me, "*Nada de sufrimientos*. No suffering!" He looks fit as a fiddle as he walks by, so he must have made his way here with no sufferings. He does not recognize me and we pass without greeting one another.

I locate an Internet shop and send a long e-mail to my family and friends, then over the Web buy a plane ticket from Madrid to Brussels for the following Tuesday. I find a quiet plaza to the side of the cathedral and write a few postcards, dropping them in a nearby postbox. I then take up a seat on the stone pavement of the *Plaza del Obradoiro*, leaning my back against the column of an archway opposite the cathedral façade. I take in that massive stone face in all its wideness and height but attend to the statue of Santiago the Pilgrim in his niche high above the great central doors. He looks at me.

"Thank you, Iago, for bringing me here."

"It is a very good thing you have done."

"It is, I know. The pilgrim to Jerusalem told me."

"In a month you will understand more, and in six months even more, and in a year more still. And when you die, then you will truly know how good it is that you have done this."

"Will I die grateful, Iago?"

» *"And the Pilgrim from America . . ."* «

"You will. You will dance with the stars."

"I hope. Iago?"

"Yes?"

"I have one more question for you."

"Yes?"

"By any chance did you have anything to do with that storm in Santa Catalina dividing in two and saving my ass from being fried?"

"Ah, *Peregrino*, I'll tell you when you get here."

"I'll wait. I've learned some patience out here."

"And one more thing, *Querido Gringo*: tell the tale."

"I will, Iago. I will do my best."

"*Gracias, Peregrinito.*"

"*Gracias a tí, Iaguito.*"

I watch the newly arriving pilgrims walk into the plaza as we did yesterday and it is both wonderful and sad to see them live what we have already lived. They laugh and embrace and weep and touch the stone. That was yesterday for us; it is already our past. Our little family will have one last supper tonight and then we will drift back to the four corners of the world, each one of us finding our way to our "real worlds," the families waiting for us in Brazil and the Basque Country and Galicia and Italy and Belgium. So it must be. If there be one truth in the *camino* that is only really understood at its end, it is that this pilgrimage is a moment in our lives, not our lives themselves. All these thirty-five days, and all these footsteps and all these encounters and all these friendships and all these families we form out here, they are all just moments and we have to let them go, let them become memories. But still and all, there is more to it than that: the life and the love within them remain. Remembering and giving thanks make real; that is the heart of the Eucharistic mystery I celebrate in the Mass every day. As I remember any of this and all of it and give thanks for it, especially with a cup of wine and a few pieces of broken bread before me, it is made as real as real can be. My pilgrimage, our *camino*, is consecrated in the remembering.

We gather a final time for dinner in Santiago de Compostela. We break bread, share good wine, and tell stories, and we are both sad and glad as we slowly let go of one another's hands.

» *August 14: Santiago de Compostela* «

267

The Field of Stars

And so I spend the weekend with Toni and his family and friends. I am invited to an endless *Galega* feast with all his cousins and aunts and uncles, including the bishop, in their home village and come to feel like one of the family at their table. The next night we join his scouting companions for yet another Fiesta de San Roque in another village where, under the Galician stars, I get my chance to dance. When Toni teases that Americans are not known for having been blessed with much in the way of bodily rhythm, I say, "Oh yeah?" and take the hand of his friend, Ana, and together we dance a reasonably rhythmic *cumbia* as the band plays enthusiastically from its grandstand. I look to the night sky above and realize I am dancing as much with these stars as with Ana. This is just beautiful.

The next day, Toni, his father, and I tour a bit of Galicia by car, then I make a final farewell to this great *amigo* and *caminante* and to his *papá* before catching an overnight bus to Madrid, where I pick up my flight to Brussels.

One of our young seminarians waits for me at the Brussels airport but doesn't recognize me as I amble through the arrivals area; the loss of seven or eight kilos and the addition of more than a month's worth of gray beard, as well as a very tan forehead and well-worn clothes, all contrive to disguise me as an old pilgrim (or maybe Ernest Hemingway after a hard week of *sanfermin*-ing in Pamplona) rather than a seminary rector.

I catch the train to Leuven on my own and with my cobalt blue *mochila*, my fat little brother, hefted onto my back one last time, I walk the reverse of the route I had followed when I began my pilgrimage so many weeks ago: down the Bondgenotenlaan, past the University Library, across Herbert Hooverplein, through the Sint-Donatus Park, over to the Naamsestraat, and down to Number One-Hundred. After digging my front key out of my backpack, I walk back in the door of my old world. I just walk back in. It is that easy. My room is just as I left it; even the abandoned box of Kellogg's granola is sitting on the bed, tossed there so long ago in a frenzied effort to reduce the weight of my pack before I had taken even one footstep toward Santiago. I drop my backpack to the floor, then untie my conch and hang it on my door. I pull off my old boots, and I lie down on my bed. I gaze at my ceiling. And I gaze. And I gaze through the ceiling and through the slate roof above that and through the blue of the daytime sky and straight into the grand universe of suns and constellations and galaxies pinwheeling, freewheeling, cartwheeling their way through ineffable space. The stars! The stars! Yes! They sing! They cry! They laugh! Ah! See them now! See them dance! This big-banged universe, this ozone-blued sky, this slate-gray roof, this plaster and lath ceiling, this room, this seminary, this flesh and blood, bone and spirit life of mine: all this, all this is my field of stars!

Afterword

Qui dicit se in ipso manere debet sicut ille ambulavit et ipse ambulare.

He who says he abides in him ought himself also to walk, even as he walked.

I JOHN 2:6

In telling this story I have depended on my memories and the notes in my pilgrim's journal, both of which are far from complete. I know that at times I have used my imagination to fill in gaps, make connections, and express the meaning of things; I can only hope that those imaginings, if not accurate depictions of the actual events as they happened, are faithful to the truth of what happened.

I have taken the liberty of changing some names and details for the narrative's sake or to protect others' privacy.

To all whose paths I crossed on the way to the Field of Stars, those mentioned in these pages and those unmentioned, I will never be able to express how profoundly grateful I am for having walked with you to Compostela, to the Field of Stars.

I am likewise grateful to those who have assisted me in telling this story by carefully reading the text and offering valuable suggestions and corrections, pilgrims with me in heart if not on foot: Wally Platt,

Denis Carlin, John Steffen, Gene and Caroline Foley, Jack Dick, Diane Codd.

I gratefully acknowledge my friend Rev. Willard Jabusch as the composer of two hymns mentioned in these pages: "Whatsoever you do to the least of my brothers" (p. 105) and "The King of glory comes, the nation rejoices" (p. 138).

Finally, to the seminarians of The American College in Louvain: I will hold you in my pilgrim heart until it beats its last.

» *Afterword* «